Praise for *The Death of Corporate Reputation*

"In his path-breaking new study, *The Death of Corporate Reputation*, Yale Law Professor Jonathan Macey offers a fresh, provocative, and insightful analysis of the intersection of reputation and regulation. In his characteristic manner, Professor Macey invokes close institutional and legal analysis with a commanding understanding of economics, finance, and politics to describe a set of profound changes to the system of American finance that regulators, market participants, and the public at large ignore at their peril. The book is an indispensable read for anyone who cares about the very survival of our system finance and those who are dependent on its functioning."

—**Ronald Daniels**, President of Johns Hopkins University who previously has served as Provost of the University of Pennsylvania and Dean of the University of Toronto Faculty of Law

"The book contains a frank and compelling account of some of the problems that plague our so-called corporate democracy. Drawing on the lessons in this book, we should craft stronger rules to require the corporate directors and the law firms, investment banks, and other businesses that are paid with shareholders' money to work on behalf of the shareholders and not on behalf of themselves. The topic of reputation is an important one that all companies in the financial world should be concerned about."

—**Carl Icahn**, one of the most successful financiers in U.S. history

"In *The Death of Corporate Reputation*, Jonathan Macey chronicles the demise of an era in which ethics and integrity mattered for both personal and economic reasons. Using brilliantly curated real-world examples, Macey describes a new era in which regulatory (and other) forces displace, but fail to replace, traditional incentives for upstanding individual and corporate behavior. Students of finance and participants in the markets will both benefit enormously from and enjoy Macey's provocative and thoroughly engaging book."

—**David Swensen**, Chief Investment Officer at Yale University

"*The Death of Corporate Reputation* is a brilliant, provocative, and persuasive exploration of a root cause of the failure of modern financial market regulation, engendered by lawmakers, regulators and prosecutors, and their legal and accounting acolytes. Systemic change in corporate behavior cannot be engineered solely by externally imposed fiat; it must come from within. In this seminal work, Professor Macey demonstrates, with unerring accuracy, unassailable logic, and wit, that modern financial regulation effectively nullifies and destroys the most potent antidote to corporate malfeasance—the innate drive to create, maintain, and enhance positive organizational reputations. A must-read for anyone concerned about the health and well-being of our capital and financial markets."

—**Harvey Pitt**, CEO of global business consultancy Kalorama Partners, formerly 26th Chairman of the U.S. Securities and Exchange Commission (2001–2003)

"*The Death of Corporate Reputation* is a revolutionary book. It blends incisive analysis and colorful narrative to track the demise of the traditional theory of reputation, with a focus on the decline of Wall Street banks and their dysfunctional support network of accounting firms, law firms, credit rating agencies, and regulators. In a skillful and refreshingly frank about-face from some of his previous writings, Yale Law School Professor Jonathan Macey, once a leading proponent of traditional theories of reputational capital, systemically hacks to pieces the assumptions that once supported those theories and argues for a far more skeptical approach to the complexities of modern financial markets and their regulatory apparatus. A new conversation about reputational theory has begun, and with this comprehensive and engaging book, Professor Macey has emerged as one the movement's leading and most compelling voices."

—**Professor Frank Partnoy**, George E. Barrett Professor of Law and Finance at the University of San Diego, author of *F.I.A.S.C.O.: Blood in the Water on Wall Street*, *Infectious Greed: How Deceit and Risk Corrupted the Financial Markets*, and *The Match King: Ivar Kreuger, the Financial Genius Behind a Century of Wall Street Scandals*

The Death of Corporate Reputation

How Integrity Has Been Destroyed on Wall Street

Jonathan R. Macey

Vice President, Publisher: Tim Moore
Associate Publisher and Director of Marketing: Amy Neidlinger
Executive Editor: Jeanne Glasser Levine
Editorial Assistant: Pamela Boland
Operations Specialist: Jodi Kemper
Marketing Manager: Lisa Loftus
Cover Designer: Chuti Prasertsith
Managing Editor: Kristy Hart
Project Editor: Betsy Harris
Copy Editor: Cheri Clark
Proofreader: Debbie Williams
Indexer: Erika Millen
Compositor: Nonie Ratcliff
Manufacturing Buyer: Dan Uhrig

© 2013 by Jonathan R. Macey
Published by Pearson Education, Inc.
Publishing as FT Press
Upper Saddle River, New Jersey 07458

FT Press offers excellent discounts on this book when ordered in quantity for bulk purchases or special sales. For more information, please contact U.S. Corporate and Government Sales, 1-800-382-3419, corpsales@pearsontechgroup.com.
For sales outside the U.S., please contact International Sales at international@pearsoned.com.

Printed in the United States of America

First Printing March 2013

ISBN-10: 0-13-303970-6
ISBN-13: 978-0-13-303970-2

Pearson Education LTD.
Pearson Education Australia PTY, Limited
Pearson Education Singapore, Pte. Ltd.
Pearson Education Asia, Ltd.
Pearson Education Canada, Ltd.
Pearson Educación de Mexico, S.A. de C.V.
Pearson Education—Japan
Pearson Education Malaysia, Pte. Ltd.

Library of Congress Cataloging-in-Publication Data is on file.

This book is for my family: Amy, Josh, Ally, and Zach,
individually and collectively, who are invaluable
and precious sources of moral, spiritual,
and intellectual inspiration for me.

Contents

Acknowledgments

I am extremely grateful for support from Dean Robert Post and many of my colleagues at Yale Law School. I presented several chapters of this book to the Hoover Institution's John and Jean De Nault Task Force on Property Rights, Freedom, and Prosperity at Stanford University. I am very grateful for the financial support and intellectual stimulation I received from this task force at Hoover. I also am deeply appreciative of the comments and conversations regarding the ideas in this book at the Yale Law School Faculty Workshop and from colleagues at Bocconi University, as well as from Bruce Ackerman, Ian Ayres, Richard Brooks, Luca Enriques, Henry Hansmann, John Langbein, Yair Listokin, Jerry Mashaw, Geoffrey Miller, Maureen O'Hara, Nicholas Parrillo, Roberta Romano, and Alan Schwartz.

I am very grateful to Logan Beirne, Yale Law School class of 2011; Douglas Cunningham, Yale Law School class of 2014; Arnaldur Hjartarson, Yale Law School class of 2013; Drew Macklin, Yale Law School class of 2015; Gillian Weaver, Colgate University class of 2013; and Michael Wyselmerski, Yale College class of 2012, for providing outstanding research assistance.

Portions of this book derive in various degrees from my previous teaching, including my seminar on "Reputation in Capital Markets" at Yale Law School and from my prior scholarship, including "The Value of Reputation in Corporate Finance and Investment Banking (and the Related Roles of Regulation and Market Efficiency)" 22 *Journal of Applied Corporate Finance* 18 (2010); "The Demise of the Reputational Model in Capital Markets: The Problem of the 'Last Period Parasites'" 60 *Syracuse Law Review* 427 (2010); "From Markets to Venues: Securities Regulation in an Evolving World," 58 *Stanford Law Review* 563 (2005) (with Maureen O'Hara); "Was Arthur Andersen Different? An Empirical Examination of Major Accounting Firm Audits of Large Clients," 1 *Journal of Empirical Legal Studies*, 263 (2004) (with Ted Eisenberg); "Efficient Capital Markets, Corporate Disclosure and Enron," 89 *Cornell Law Review* 394 (2004); "A Pox on Both Your Houses: Enron, Sarbanes-Oxley and the Debate Concerning the Relative Efficiency of Mandatory Versus Enabling Rules,

81 *Washington University Law Quarterly* 329 (2003); "Observations on the Role of Commodification, Independence, Governance, and the Demise of the Accounting Profession," 48 *Villanova Law Review* 1167 (2003) (with Hillary Sale); "The Economics of Stock Exchange Listing Fees and Listing Requirements" 11 *Journal of Financial Intermediation* 297 (2002) (with Maureen O'Hara).

About the Author

Jonathan R. Macey is Sam Harris Professor of Corporate Law, Corporate Finance, and Securities Law at Yale University and Professor in the Yale School of Management. He is a member of the Board of Directors of the Yale Law School Center for the Study of Corporate Governance, a member of the Faculty Advisory Group of Yale's Millstein Center for Corporate Governance and Performance, and Chairman of Yale's Advisory Committee on Investor Responsibility. He has served as an independent director of two public companies and is a member of FINRA's Economic Advisory Council and the Bipartisan Policy Center Task Force on Capital Markets. His many books include *Corporate Governance: Promises Kept, Promises Broken* and *Macey on Corporation Law*.

Introduction

My goal is to describe the role that reputation once played in fostering the high-trust environment that is critical to the successful operation of capital markets and corporate financing transactions generally and to try to explain what has caused so many firms in the financial industry to lose interest in cultivating and maintaining their reputations for integrity. Corporate finance and capital markets traditionally relied heavily on the ability of companies and other firms to develop what is known as reputational capital. For the industries on which I focus in this book, credit rating agencies, law firms, investment banks, stock exchanges, and accounting firms, reputational capital historically has been the primary mechanism by which businesses establish trust in markets and in contracting relationships.

I argue here that there has been a collapse in the market demand for reputation, at least in heavily regulated countries like the United States that increasingly rely on regulation rather than reputation to protect market participants from fraud and other forms of abuse. It used to be the case that for a diverse array of companies and industries involved in the capital markets, nurturing and maintaining the organizations' reputation was absolutely critical to their growth and continued success. I argue that this simply is no longer the case, at least in the U.S.

On Wall Street, company reputation matters far less than it used to matter, for three reasons. First, improvements in information technology have lowered the costs of discovering information about people. This, in turn, has made it worthwhile for individuals involved in the financial markets—lawyers, investment bankers, accountants, analysts, regulators—to focus far more on the development of their own individual reputation than on the reputation of the companies for which they work.

Second, law and regulation serve as a substitute for reputational capital, at least in the minds of regulators and market participants. In modern times, particularly since the promulgation of the modern securities laws, market participants have come to rely far more on the protections of the law, and far less on the comfort provided by reputation, when making investment decisions and in deciding whether to deal with a particular counterparty. The current financial crisis, in my view, demonstrates that, in reality, regulation is no substitute for reputation in ensuring contractual performance and respect for property rights.

Third, the world in general and the world of finance in particular have become so complex that rocket scientists who design complex financial instruments have replaced simple, high-reputation practitioners of "Old School Finance."

One empirical implication is that we should expect firms in the financial services industry to have weak reputations relative to firms in other, less regulated industries. A second empirical implication is that financial firms in countries like the United States, which have systematic and pervasive laws and regulations for the financial services industry, will have weak incentives to invest in developing and maintaining their reputations. The evidence discussed in this book is consistent with the hypothesis developed in the book.

In each of these contexts, my story involves important variations on a single theme. The single theme is the rise and subsequent fall of a simple economic model in which companies and firms in time period 0 find it rational (profitable) to make investments in reputational capital, and then, in time period 1 it turns out that it is no longer rational to do this, so they stop. The investments in human capital that occurred early on required companies and firms to make costly commitments to being honest and trustworthy in order to compete successfully in their businesses. Concomitantly, the later decline in investment in reputational capital by such companies and firms necessarily resulted in a dramatic decline in the amount of honesty and trust in the business sectors in which these companies operate. Corporate downfalls from Enron to Madoff can, in my view, best be explained by the theory of reputational decline that is the core of this book.

The traditional economic model of reputational model I use as a historical baseline is very straightforward. Companies and firms find it profitable, and therefore rational, to invest money immediately in developing a reputation for honesty, integrity, and probity, because doing so allows the company or firm to charge higher prices, and thus earn superior returns in later periods. The theory is that resources expended to develop a strong reputation enable the firms that have developed such reputations to make credible commitments to clients and counterparties that they are honest and reliable, and therefore are desirable contracting partners.

The reputational model posits that companies and firms start their corporate lives without any reputations. This lack of reputation is of far more importance and relevance in some businesses than in others. When the quality of the product or service being offered by a business can be evaluated accurately in a short period at zero cost, then reputation matters little. People are willing to buy name-brand wrapped candy or newspapers at any newsstand or kiosk because the proprietor's reputation (or lack thereof) is largely irrelevant to a rational purchaser. A Baby Ruth candy bar or *The Wall Street Journal* is the same price and the same quality at every newsstand.

In contrast, the industries in which I am interested—investment banking, capital markets, accounting, law, credit rating agencies, etc.—require enormous amounts of human capital to deliver their products or services. Indeed, in these sectors of the economy, human capital is the only significant asset that participating businesses actually have. The physical capital necessary to conduct such businesses is trivial. In these sorts of businesses, reputation plays a very important role. In such businesses, it takes a substantial amount of time for a customer to observe the quality of the businesses' human capital. In my view, however, analysis of this sort, though historically accurate, is completely out-of-date because it no longer describes today's world. Specifically, although it used to be the case that loss of reputation generally was fatal to accounting firms like Arthur Andersen, law firms like Vinson & Elkins, and credit rating agencies like Moody's (all of which appear to have failed flamboyantly in protecting their reputations in the Enron scandal), I argue here that this is no longer true. Whereas these sorts of firms once depended on their reputations to attract and retain business, such firms no longer depend on maintaining their reputations as a key to survival. Instead, regulations often, either directly or indirectly, require companies that issue securities to retain various Wall Street service providers such as outside auditors, credit rating agencies, investment banks, and law firms. Because the demand for the services of these firms is driven by regulation, the firms don't need to maintain their reputations in order to attract business. As such, reputation is no longer an asset in which it is rational to invest.

I am extremely grateful for support from Dean Robert Post and many of my colleagues at Yale Law School. I presented several chapters of this book to the Hoover Institution's John and Jean De Nault Task Force on Property Rights, Freedom, and Prosperity at Stanford University. I am very grateful for the financial support and intellectual stimulation I received from this Task Force at Hoover. I also am deeply appreciative of the comments and conversations regarding the ideas in this book at the Yale Law School Faculty Workshop and from colleagues at Bocconi University, as well as from Bruce Ackerman, Ian Ayres, Richard Brooks, Luca Enriques, Henry Hansmann, John Langbein, Yair Listokin, Jerry Mashaw, Geoffrey Miller, Maureen O'Hara, Nicholas Parrillo, Roberta Romano, and Alan Schwartz.

Portions of this book derive in various degrees from my previous teaching, including my seminar on "Reputation in Capital Markets" at Yale Law School, and from my prior scholarship, including "The Value of Reputation in Corporate Finance and Investment Banking (and the Related Roles of Regulation and Market Efficiency)," *Journal of Applied Corporate Finance* 22 (2010): 18; "The Demise of the Reputational Model in Capital Markets: The Problem of the 'Last Period Parasites,'" *Syracuse Law Review* 60 (2010): 427; "From Markets to Venues: Securities Regulation in an Evolving World," *Stanford Law Review* 58 (2005): 563 (with Maureen O'Hara); "Was Arthur Andersen Different? An Empirical Examination of Major Accounting Firm Audits of Large Clients," *Journal of Empirical Legal Studies* 1 (2004): 263 (with Ted Eisenberg); "Efficient Capital Markets, Corporate Disclosure and Enron," *Cornell Law Review* 89 (2004): 394; "A Pox on Both Your Houses: Enron, Sarbanes-Oxley and the Debate

Concerning the Relative Efficacy of Mandatory Versus Enabling Rules," *Washington University Law Quarterly* 81 (2003): 329; "Observations on the Role of Commodification, Independence, Governance, and the Demise of the Accounting Profession," *Villanova Law Review* 48 (2003): 1167 (with Hillary Sale); and "The Economics of Stock Exchange Listing Fees and Listing Requirements" *Journal of Financial Intermediation* 11 (2002): 297 (with Maureen O'Hara).

This book is for my family, Amy, Josh, Ally, and Zach, who both individually and collectively are invaluable and precious sources of moral, spiritual, and intellectual inspiration for me.

—New Haven, Connecticut, January 2013

1

The Way Things Used to Work: Reputational Theory and Its Demise

This chapter introduces the traditional theory of reputation in financial markets and gives a few examples of why that theory no longer seems to be accurate. First, it describes the old economic model of reputation, which argues that simple cost-benefit analysis ordinarily should discourage financial firms from acting fraudulently or dishonestly. This is especially relevant in financial markets: Rational individuals will not invest unless they trust that their money will be safeguarded, and this trust can be cultivated only by means of government regulation or a good reputation.

Second, this chapter shows how companies in the manufacturing and consumer goods sectors develop a good reputation by means of warranties and other guarantees of quality. Financial firms cannot offer customers these kinds of warranties because their products fail or decline in value in complex and opaque ways. This product difference is exemplified by the failure of the Facebook initial public offering (IPO). Morgan Stanley, Facebook's lead underwriter, has refuted claims of fraud by insisting that the devaluation of Facebook's stock was out of its control. Morgan Stanley's continued success in spite of its bungling of the Facebook initial public offering highlights the demise of the traditional theory of reputation.

In the world of business and particularly in the field of finance, developing a "good" reputation has been viewed as critical to success. Economists developed an elegant and highly useful grand theory of reputation to explain why having a good reputation is critical to success, particularly for companies in the financial sector, like insurance companies and banks. The point of this book is to explain why that theory has lost its explanatory power when it comes to understanding the way Wall Street works today.

The old theory was simple: Firms invest in reputation so that customers will do business with them. Rational customers prefer to do business with companies with good reputations because a strong reputation for honesty and integrity serves as a sort of bond, or credible promise to customers that the business will not act in a dishonest or immoral way. The theory works like this: Reputations are easy to destroy but difficult and expensive to build. As such, it is downright irrational for a company with a good reputation to treat even a single customer dishonestly or unethically because the short-term, one-shot profit gained from doing this inevitably will be less than the long-term cost that will result from the diminution or destruction of the company's reputation. In other words, according to the traditional economic theory of reputation, simple cost-benefit analysis predicts that companies will invest in reputation because doing so enables them to attract customers who will pay a premium to deal with the company with the good reputation.

Because trust is particularly important in financial transactions, the reputational model always was thought to apply with particular force in the world of investment banks, big corporate law firms, credit rating agencies, major accounting firms, and other firms that do business in the financial markets. This is because it is unusually easy for companies—particularly financial ones—to rip people off: Money is easy to steal and hide relative to other sorts of assets. Money is fungible, meaning that one dollar looks like every other dollar and money can be moved offshore electronically and instantaneously. After money, securities might be the next easiest thing to steal. They can be converted easily into cash and they can be moved electronically, and often even anonymously.

People pay premiums to insurance companies and put their money into banks and into accounts with broker-dealer firms, and they know that it is easy for the companies to which they entrust their money to steal this money. It is especially easy to avoid being caught if one steals only small amounts of money. Banks do this in a number of ways. They do it with hidden fees, late-payment penalties, rigged foreign exchange rates, and commissions on services and transactions.

The Bernie Madoff case and other famous Ponzi schemes prove that it is even possible for crooked bankers and dishonest professional investors to get away with massive theft and fraud for very long periods, although not forever. They do this by taking money from new victims, stealing "only" some of it, and using the rest to pay off the first group of victims in order to trick those first investors into thinking that their money is being invested. These schemes, called "Ponzi schemes," work as long as the people behind the fraud can keep attracting new investors and can manage to prevent enough of their old investors from demanding the return of their money. History shows that it is possible for fraudsters to keep their Ponzi schemes going for quite a while before the house of cards collapses.

The problem is that it is hard to tell the difference between the good guys and the bad guys in business. They dress the same. They look the same. They make the same claims about what they plan to do with your money and about how trustworthy they are. The difficulty of distinguishing the good guys from the bad guys, which economists have dubbed the "adverse selection" problem, is extremely serious. Businesses and government must figure out a way to solve this problem or else robust economic growth will become impossible. If people lack confidence that their money will be kept safe, they will refuse to invest.

Without investment, economic growth simply will not happen. Nobody wants to lose all of their money. Because there are a lot of crooks around, people will not part with their money unless they are confident that the people to whom they entrust their savings will safeguard it rather than steal it.

There are only two ways to instill confidence in people that they can invest safely, one of which is generated by the government in the form of regulation. Government regulation can work directly, which is what happens when laws are enacted—and enforced—that make stealing illegal. Government regulation also can work to support private contracts by instilling confidence in consumers that warranties for products and similar promises are enforced. Government regulation also facilitates the ability of companies and people to engage in private contracting to the extent that the government uses its state power to help people enforce the promises that were made to them when they bought financial assets like insurance or securities.

For many reasons, regulation, whether acting by itself or in tandem with private actors, does not work perfectly. In fact, often government regulation does not work very well, and sometimes it does not appear to work at all. This is why reputation plays a vital role in capital markets.

As is the case with regulation in the financial sector, the primary purpose of investment in reputation is to assure investors that they can invest with some degree of confidence that they will not be defrauded. And like regulation, which of course is very costly, developing and maintaining a reputation for honesty is very expensive. It is more expensive to be honest than it is to be dishonest; if it were not, then everybody always would be honest.

Reputations take years to build but can be destroyed in seconds. This adage is no less true for being used so often and by so many. For example, the website of the American Psychological Association advises newly minted psychologists, "It takes years to build a good professional reputation, but only seconds to destroy it....One major mistake can significantly damage your reputation, lead to missed opportunities and make it difficult to restore others' confidence in you."[1]

Still another common feature of regulation and reputation is that neither works perfectly. A major lesson to be learned from the economic history of the U.S. is that neither regulation nor reputation works quite as well in practice as it is supposed to in theory.

Regulation, of course, works by making fraud illegal and then enforcing the rules against those who break them. To the extent that financial fraudsters think they will be caught and punished severely, they will be less likely to engage in fraud. And to the extent that investors think that financial fraudsters will be caught, they will be more willing to invest.

In this sense, regulation helps all firms that are subject to the regulation. For example, tough regulation of the mutual fund industry helps all mutual funds because people will be more likely to invest in mutual funds to the extent that they are confident that they are protected by the applicable regulatory scheme.

Reputation works in a slightly different way because it does not work on an industrywide basis. Whereas regulation affects all companies in an industry, reputations are built (or used to be built) one company at a time.

The theory of reputation posits that reputations are like buildings. They are built slowly and expensively over time. The idea is that companies build a good reputation by engaging in such activities as offering guarantees and warranties that are expensive and then honoring these promises scrupulously. Companies give "no-questions-asked money-back guarantees." They honor manufacturers' warranties even when they are not obliged to do so. According to the traditional theory of reputation, businesses trying to build or maintain their reputations waive fees when customers complain, even if they are not legally required to do so.

Profit-maximizing businesses, however, can be trusted to make these sorts of costly investments in reputation only as long as the investments pay off. If the costs of investing in reputation are greater than the benefits, then even really honest people will be driven out of business if they persist in investing in reputation, because when this happens, businesses lose money by investing in reputation.

In other words, building a reputation is an investment. Reputation is a valuable investment because people want to do business with businesses that have strong reputations for being honest and trustworthy. From the business's point of view, a reputation is a "credible commitment" that sends a very strong message to customers and counter-parties that they can deal with the business with confidence.

Economists studying reputation have long recognized that even when a business has a good reputation, there is money to be made from tricking and deceiving customers. There are two ways to think about this problem. First and foremost, the theory of reputation posits that companies that have strong reputations are far less likely to engage in fraud, sharp business practices, and other shenanigans because they have more to lose from behaving badly. Firms with little or no (or bad) reputations have little or nothing to lose by cheating people. Firms with solid reputations will refrain from cheating as long as profits garnered from such cheating are lower than the losses from whatever reputational damage the fraud is likely to produce.

This is one way in which regulation and reputation work together. Government action against fraudsters has the potential to supplement and enhance the value of businesses' investments in reputation because when the government successfully sues (and when the government accuses) a firm of fraud, the firm's reputation is damaged. Government regulation supplements businesses' investment in reputation because the publicity that surrounds government action can increase dramatically the reputational cost to a business of engaging in fraud.

Second, the theory of reputation posits that firms will not invest in developing reputations for honesty and trustworthiness unless the benefits from making such investments are greater than the costs. Just as government regulation can increase the benefits of investing in reputation by noisily enforcing antifraud rules against fraudsters, so too can government regulation diminish the benefits of investing in reputation. For example, if businesses think that the government will undermine their reputations by charging them with fraud falsely or unfairly, they will be less likely to invest in developing their reputations in the first place. It is for this reason that financial regulators like the U.S. Securities and Exchange Commission (SEC) sometimes go to great lengths to keep their investigations secret until they think that they have sufficient proof of fraud to merit announcing that they are bringing a lawsuit to enforce the law against a financial firm. On its website, the SEC acknowledges the threat its own actions pose to the reputations of the companies they regulate:

> Securities and Exchange Commission (SEC) investigations are conducted confidentially to protect evidence and reputations....A confidential process...protects the reputations of companies and individuals where the SEC finds no wrongdoing by the firm or the individuals that were the subject of the investigation. As a result, the SEC generally will not confirm or deny the existence of an investigation unless and until it becomes a matter of public record.[2]

On the other hand, the SEC is not above garnering publicity for itself when it does file suit. The publicity comes whether the SEC actually tries a case or merely announces that a settlement agreement has been reached and that judicial approval for that settlement is being sought. As the SEC puts it, "An investigation becomes public when the SEC files an action in court or through an administrative proceeding. The SEC website contains information about public enforcement actions."[3]

Unfortunately, government regulators like the SEC sometimes have incentives to jump the gun and announce their lawsuits prematurely. Regulators sometimes do this in order to bolster their own reputations for toughness. Sometimes regulators and others think that a lot of businesses are engaging in bad behavior. They come under considerable pressure from the public and from their Congressional overseers to do something about the actual or perceived problems, so they announce lawsuits (called "enforcement actions") against innocent market participants in an effort to curb bad behavior by making "examples" of one or two businesses.

Another reason SEC officials often seem like publicity hounds is because they are. The SEC is largely evaluated on the basis of how well its Division of Enforcement performs. In the words of the SEC's own website, "First and foremost, the SEC is a law enforcement agency."[4] As the economic sociologist William Bealing has observed, the activities of the Enforcement Division of the SEC are what "legitimize the Commission's existence and its federal budget allocation to Congress."[5] Political scientists have observed that the SEC's enforcement agenda is designed to meet the interests of the relevant Congressional leaders responsible for the SEC's funding.[6]

The SEC satisfies its monitors in Congress, in academia, and in the press by focusing on factors that can be measured. In particular, the SEC focuses on two factors: (1) the raw number of cases that it brings, and (2) the sheer size of the fines that it collects. The more cases that are brought and the greater the amount of fines collected during a particular time frame, the better the enforcement staff at the SEC is thought to have performed. This has long been the case, but the problem got worse as a result of the political challenges that the SEC has faced from politically opportunistic state attorneys general, most notably Eliot Spitzer, the former Attorney General of New York who parlayed a campaign against Wall Street into an election as governor of the state, a position he held until he was forced to resign due to salacious public revelations about his involvement with a high-priced prostitute.[7]

Even worse, regulators sometimes pick on the weakest firms in an industry. They do this not only because the weakest companies are the least able to defend themselves against cadres of government lawyers, but also because their actions have the greatest impact on the weakest firms. It would be hard for the government to drive giant firms like Bank of America or Goldman Sachs out of business. These firms simply have too much political clout and too many resources to have to worry too much about the government. But it is easy for the government to drive smaller firms and new entrants out of business.

Perhaps the most important reason small firms get picked on is because of the so-called "revolving door." Small firms do not hire as many people as big firms. Many government lawyers want to move from their low-paying, low-prestige government jobs into the private sector with big firms like Deutsche Bank and Citibank (former government officials currently hold the top legal jobs in these big firms). Suing one's prospective employers is not considered a winning strategy for garnering a job in the future.

In other words, while reputation always has been important, there always have been a few market failures—this is what economists call major glitches in their theories—when it comes to the application of reputation in the real world.

One aspect of the traditional theory that still appears to have force is that the need for reputation is far greater in the world of finance than in the world of manufacturing or even in the world of technology. This is true for several reasons. For one thing, as mentioned at the outset of this chapter, it is generally far easier to rip off customers in financial transactions than in other sorts of transactions. In the financial world, buyers part with their money in exchange for highly ephemeral financial assets; sellers part with their financial assets in exchange for cash. They must trust financial intermediaries to carry out these transactions on their behalf. There are so many ways for unscrupulous financial institutions to defraud their customers that it is difficult to list them all. Here are some examples:

- It is common for customers to give their stockbrokers an order to purchase securities at the "market price." When this happens, the law requires that customers receive the best available price in the market and that the markups or commissions that the stockbrokers charge are reasonable. Unfortunately, it is very hard to monitor stockbrokers who are executing market orders for customers, especially, as often happens, when the stockbroker is filling the customer's order from its own inventory rather than going out and buying it in the market. And, of course, there is a conflict of interest when a stockbroker is buying from one customer in order to sell to another customer.

- Another problem is called "front-running." If a stockbroker receives an order to buy a substantial number of securities, the stockbroker can profit by entering its own buy order ahead of the customer's in order to profit when the price of the securities goes up in response to the large buy order. The problem here is that front-running drives up the price of the securities, which of course is bad for the customer who is buying.

- Front-running also happens when customers are selling securities. Unscrupulous stockbrokers can sell securities before they execute the customer's sell order, thereby getting out before the price drops. Of course, this hurts the customer because the stock generally drops when the stockbroker sells, which causes the customer to receive a lower price for her securities than she would have received if the stockbroker had not sold ahead of her.

- Problems also arise when customers ask their stockbrokers for advice. Stockbrokers can be tempted to advise their customers to buy securities that are already in their inventories, particularly when they have had a hard time selling these securities and are worried that they will drop in value.

- Stockbrokers work on a commission basis, so they have incentives to sell the securities that pay them the highest commissions rather than the securities that are best for their customers.

- Stockbrokers work as investment banks that are trying to get underwriting business from their corporate clients. The most common type of underwriting is when an investment bank like Morgan Stanley or Goldman Sachs buys securities from a company that is issuing securities and sells those securities to the public. Investment banks want to show their prospective corporate clients that they trade a lot of their securities at high prices in order to garner underwriting business from those clients. This creates a temptation for investment banks to give their stockbrokers incentives to tout stocks of favored or prospective customers rather than the investments that are best for the customers.

- Customers put money in accounts with stockbrokers. This money is supposed to be used to buy securities. It is not difficult for stockbrokers to steal some (or all) of this money and tell their clients that the money was lost on improvident investments.

- Stockbrokers can simultaneously buy and sell the same security. Then, if the security goes down in value, they can claim to have owned the security that they sold. If the security goes up in value, they can claim to have owned the security that they bought. The other security goes into the customer's account.

- One of the most prevalent ways that stockbrokers abuse their clients is by doing what is known in the securities industry as "churning" customers' accounts. Churning occurs when a stockbroker engages in many trades in a customer's account in a short period for the purposes of garnering trading commissions, rather than to benefit the customer. Although it is not difficult to notice that a stockbroker is churning if the frequency of trades is egregious, sometimes it is difficult to tell. Worse still, customers who are unsophisticated might not realize that this is happening to them until it is too late.

- Selling investments that are not suitable for a customer is another common problem. As one plaintiff's lawyer observed on his website, "A disturbingly prevalent form of abuse occurs when a broker either lies outright to the client or offers up half-truths in order to induce a client to purchase or sell [particular] securities....Common misrepresentations and material omissions include: (1) telling a client that a company is a "hot prospect" when it is virtually bankrupt; (2) implying that the broker has inside knowledge about a company's plans or prospects ("I know that the stock will double after the company announces its new contract," etc.); (3) describing an investment as safe, secure, guaranteed or government-backed when it is not; and (4) recommending a stock without telling the client that the broker or his firm is receiving "undisclosed" payments from the issuer or others."[8]

Another reason it is easy for financial firms to defraud or outright steal from their customers is that, unlike with regular products, when stocks and bonds and other securities decline in value, it often is difficult or impossible to tell whether fraud was involved. When a refrigerator or a car breaks, the problem often will be attributable to one of two sources: a defect in manufacturing or the customer not using the product properly. It generally is not difficult to distinguish between these two causes, particularly when experts like mechanics or repairmen become involved. On the other hand, securities can decline in value and even become completely worthless for many reasons.

For example, financial assets can decline in value for reasons that have nothing to do with a particular company or security. When the financial markets decline, by definition, individual financial assets like stocks and bonds decline with it. Even when a particular stock goes down while markets generally are going up, the reason for the loss might not be fraud. A company could have a glitch in its manufacturing process, or have a problem with a patent or some other sort of intellectual property. A new product might be introduced that outcompetes the products made by the company whose stock is falling precipitously, or consumers' preferences might simply have changed.

Another important reason it is easier to defraud people in the securities markets than in other markets is the complete absence of warranties for securities. Companies that sell stocks and bonds, and investment banks that underwrite these securities for the companies that issue them, do not have the same ability to make credible, binding contractual promises that their products are of high quality. Take the case of a manufacturer of new cars or refrigerators. Of course it is difficult for most people to figure out the value of these manufactured goods until they actually start to use them. It also is true that manufacturers have financial incentives to cut manufacturing costs and quality control expenditures if they can get away with it. But there are ways in which high-quality manufacturers that lack reputations can distinguish themselves in the marketplace.

For example, in 2009 the Korean automaker Kia announced that every new Kia sold in Europe offered a seven-year, 150,000km bumper-to-bumper, parts-and-labor warranty for all vehicles sold and registered starting January 1, 2010. As Gizmag, a popular and influential European website observed, "This is far-and-away the longest fleetwide warranty ever offered by a car manufacturer anywhere at any time and the move could have far reaching consequences."[9]

Gizmag fully understood the relationship between the new Kia warranty offer and Kia's efforts to enter the European car market against existing manufacturers with established reputations. These established brands charge much more than Kia, yet are clearly unwilling to financially back their quality in the same way. So, perhaps "the public finally understands that new price does not reflect quality, that quality is measurable, and that reputations for quality are distinctly at odds with reality."[10]

In other words, Kia used its warranty as a way to substitute for its lack of reputation in the marketplace. It did this by offering a long warranty that was extremely generous. The warranty had few exceptions or exclusions, and it was transferable to subsequent owners. As the Kia Press Release noted, "The comprehensive new 7-Year Kia Warranty is a 'bumper-to-bumper' full manufacturer's warranty and covers each vehicle for up to seven years (whole car)."[11]

As Gizmag observed, "We expect the new warranty to become a disruptive force in the auto market as it will add significant pressure to other car manufacturers to stand behind their production quality and offer similar guarantees of workmanship."[12]

Other car companies have tried to offer generous warranties. Fifty years ago Chrysler "upset the industry" and offered a five-year, 50,000-mile warranty. But Chrysler cars were not worthy of the warranty and Chrysler lost significant amounts of money honoring these warranties for older models that were breaking down at unexpectedly high rates. Rivals were forced to match the Chrysler warranty, but all of them, including Chrysler, "quickly reverted to the tried and true 12 month/12,000 mile warranty which more accurately reflected the quality of the products of the period."[13]

Warranties work like reputations to signal product quality. If the quality of a product does not live up to the promise implied by the product warranty or the company's reputation, the company offering the reputation and the warranty will suffer exactly where it hurts companies the most: in their wallets. As product quality improves, companies can offer better warranties at low cost because, by definition, higher-quality products do not break down as often as lower-quality products.

Firms in the securities industry, however, cannot offer warranties in the way that automobile manufacturers can. Warranties, like other forms of insurance, work only because of the law of probabilities. Manufacturers calculate that a certain percentage of their products will stop working properly at some point over their lives and need to be repaired. Manufacturers, of course, have much better information about the reliability and longevity of their products than consumers do. If manufacturers consistently offer reliable and long-lasting products over long periods, they will develop a reputation for quality. Alternatively, through research and development manufacturers can improve the quality of their products over time, and through product testing, the same manufacturers can measure improvements in the quality and reliability of their products. As product quality and reliability improve, manufacturers can make credible, binding, costly promises to consumers that they really are making better products by offering more generous warranties, just as Kia did. This, in turn, puts pressure on other companies in the industry, which have to offer similarly strong warranties, or explain why they can't or won't.

Thus while warranties can supplement and reinforce the work that reputation does in assuring customers of product quality, the same process does not work for financial products such as stocks, bonds, and financial derivatives because these products are fundamentally different in one important way: Concerns about defects in products such as cars and refrigerators can be alleviated by manufacturers' warranties, but concerns about fraud or other problems with financial products like stocks and bonds cannot be alleviated by warranties from the issuer.

Manufacturers like Kia can make hundreds of thousands of products and then estimate statistically what percentage of these products will fail. They can work to reduce the number of failures as a percentage of the total number of products manufactured in order to increase sales by improving their reputations and offering better, less costly warranties than their competitors. This dynamic does not work for financial products. When an issuer hires an investment bank to sell securities, the securities are not differentiated the way that manufactured products are. Specifically, one refrigerator can break while dozens of others work perfectly. In sharp contrast, securities do not fail one by one. An issuer cannot default on just one security. If the issuer goes bankrupt, all of that company's outstanding securities simultaneously decline in value. All the equity is wiped out and creditors such as bondholders usually get pennies on the dollar.

In recent years, however, the quality of automotive products has improved dramatically, and Kia and its parent company, Hyundai, seem intent on bringing this to the attention of the consumer in the most logical way possible: by offering a warranty on their vehicles that other companies will be very reluctant to match.

In other words, the securities markets have significant problems. It is easy to rip people off. It is sometimes difficult for people to figure out when they have been ripped off. The IPO of stock by the social media giant Facebook in the spring of 2012 provides a good example of the difficulty of distinguishing between honest mistakes and fraud in the financial markets, as well as a good example of the uselessness of warranties in the world of finance.

Facebook

Facebook stock was priced at $38 per share. This was the price at which Morgan Stanley, the lead underwriter, and the 32 other underwriters involved in the deal were able to buy the $16 billion worth of stock that Facebook was selling in its IPO. The lucky selected few (favored institutions and big clients) that were able to get stock in the IPO bought in at this price. Immediately after the underwriting, Facebook's shares started trading at $42.05.

Just four days after the IPO, Facebook and its investment bank underwriters were sued for fraud. This was only the first of dozens and dozens of lawsuits that were filed in the month following the Facebook IPO. The plaintiffs in these cases typically allege that Facebook, and many of its officers and directors, lied on the official documents that they had to file with the SEC and distribute to investors. The forms used in IPOs like Facebook's are SEC Form S-1/A Registration Statement (the "Statement"); the Prospectus, which provides crucial information about the company's financial results; and the so-called

"MD&A," or Management's Discussion and Analysis of the company's current business and future prospects.

The complaints filed in the various lawsuits further charge that the Registration Statement and Prospectus issued in connection with the Facebook IPO were false and misleading because the Company and its employees and underwriters did not tell investors that Facebook was experiencing a pronounced reduction in revenue growth at the time of the IPO due to an increase of users of its Facebook app or Facebook website through mobile devices rather than traditional PCs. In addition, the complaints allege that the Company gave this important negative information to some of its biggest underwriters and told them that they should lower their predictions and estimates about how well Facebook would perform in 2012, but that this information was not passed along to the general public until much later, after all the shares in the IPO had been sold at a profit by the initial investors. Some of the lawsuits allege that Facebook made downward adjustments to its own internal earnings estimates, and that this negative information was passed along to certain of the underwriters by a Facebook financial officer and that these underwriters then sold their own allotments of Facebook stock to unsuspecting clients and members of the general public.

Needless to say, there was a lot for investors to be unhappy about. The Facebook IPO was such a disaster that it even got its own Wikipedia page! The page informs readers that after the IPO, Facebook stock "lost over a quarter of its value in less than a month and went on to less than half its IPO value in three months."[14] A quick look at what happened to the unlucky investors who wound up with Facebook shares after the dust settled at the end of the IPO, as charted in Figure 1.1, tells the story.

Private investors were not the only people mad at Facebook after the IPO. The Facebook IPO was a big black mark for regulators as well. As one of the biggest, and certainly the most highly publicized, securities deals in history, the Facebook IPO did not make regulators look very good either. Regulators were considerably embarrassed. Because many large sophisticated investors stayed away from the Facebook IPO, unsophisticated public investors of relatively modest financial means bought a far bigger percentage of Facebook's shares in the period immediately following the IPO than they generally are able to. Usually, shares in IPOs by "hot companies" like Facebook are accessible only to a select group of big customers and insiders. This is why most sophisticated observers consider the whole IPO process to be a "sucker's game."

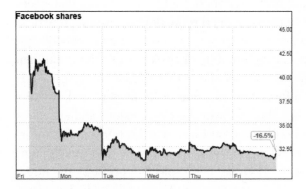

Figure 1.1 Facebook IPO.

As one blogger observed in a post on the VentureBeat website, "If there was any doubt that Wall Street is a sucker's game designed to take money from stupid people and put it into the hands of bankers and powerful corporations, Facebook's initial public offering should clear that up."[15] Another person posting on a blog observed, "Most IPOs are a sucker's game. For every Google (up 8 times since its IPO) there are dogs like Facebook and Groupon."[16] This post, which was on "a personal finance blog aimed at regular folks," followed an article whose author observed:

> [IPOs] are best for the underwriting companies who make millions by underwriting the initial public offering of the stock. They are also usually very good for founders, early stage investors, and venture capital firms that own a share of the company that is going public. Coming in dead last is the individual investor that buys into the company at a price dictated by the underwriting firm in hopes of the shares either skyrocketing immediately or over time.[17]

The intuitions that these angry bloggers are expressing have a sound basis in economic theory. Over 25 years ago, in what has come to be one of the most famous and important papers in finance,

University of Chicago professor Kevin Rock explained that the IPO market in the U.S. is plagued by what is known as a "Winner's Curse," which means that the so-called "winners"—the investors who wind up owning the stock that is sold in an IPO—are really losers, because the securities they succeed in buying so often decline in value.[18] This is due to the fact that big, influence-wielding investors who have access to privileged information about stock offerings are able not only to avoid IPOs that are "losers" but also to gain privileged access to the IPOs that are likely to be winners. This means that the only securities to which the real investing public is able to gain access are the losers. Therefore, according to Professor Rock, new issues must be priced cheaply in order to be sold, and, on average, they are. This pricing strategy produces some big winners, but also some big losers in IPOs; and the big winners overwhelmingly tend to be insiders while the big losers tend to be "outsiders," which is to say that the losers are ordinary investors without fortunes large enough to generate millions of dollars in fees for their bankers and advisors.

Not surprisingly in light of all of this, regulators have piled on the litigation bandwagon. The SEC and the Financial Industry Regulatory Authority (FINRA) and state officials like Massachusetts Secretary of State William Galvin are investigating the claims that Morgan Stanley and other Facebook underwriters leaked information to select clients and did not share it with the general public.

A big question, which will be dealt with at length in Chapter 3, "The Way Things Used to Be: When Reputation Was Critical to Survival," is what impact (if any) all of these lawsuits by class action attorneys and regulators have on the behavior of the companies in the financial industry. The short answer is that people are no longer embarrassed to be sued the way they used to be. It is just a cost of doing business. Moreover, there are so many nonmeritorious lawsuits mixed in with the meritorious lawsuits that getting sued does not send a strong negative signal in the financial industry about the cost of being sued. Everybody is sued all the time. In addition, virtually all lawsuits settle; and they settle without the bank or investment bank admitting or denying any guilt or responsibility, so the public never even finds out whether a judge or jury would have decided that they are guilty. In sum, litigation, whether it is brought by private plaintiffs or by government agencies like the SEC, no longer provides a reliable indication about whether the companies or individuals being sued actually have done anything wrong.

Interestingly, one of the most troubling characteristics about IPOs is that the underwriters make tons of money regardless of what happens to the stock price of the company (or indeed to the company itself) after the underwriting. If the company goes broke, the under-writer still keeps the millions in fees it makes on the underwriting. Stranger still, investment banks serving as underwriters in IPOs make money in the period immediately following an IPO regardless of whether the value of the stock being underwritten goes up or down. In fact, the underwriters can make even more money when the stock goes up than when the stock goes down. This is because underwrit-ers routinely sell even more shares in the underwriting than they buy initially from the company. As for the excess shares that they sell, the underwriters usually make an agreement with the issuer granting them the option (that is, the right but not the obligation) to buy the additional shares needed to fill customers' orders directly from the issuer. If the share price goes up immediately after the underwriting, the underwriters buy the shares from the issuer at a discount and sell them to their customers at a healthy, risk-free profit.

Even if the share price of the stock in the IPO goes down imme-diately after the underwriting, the underwriters can still make a lot of money. When the stock price goes down, underwriters can decline to exercise their option to buy the additional stock they need to fill customers' orders directly from the issuer. Instead, they can take advantage of the drop in market price after the offering and buy the low-priced shares in the open market. If the shares have fallen by enough, the underwriters will make even more money buying cheap shares in the open market and using those shares to fill their custom-ers' preexisting orders. This is exactly what happened in the Facebook IPO. The underwriters, led by Morgan Stanley, made significant prof-its by buying up shares of Facebook at depressed prices and using those shares to fill their customers' orders.

But what about the reputation of Morgan Stanley, the lead underwriter of the Facebook IPO—was it in any way injured by the debacle at Facebook? It would seem to be inevitable that a company like Morgan Stanley would be hurt significantly by the reputational fallout from the Facebook IPO. Claims that Facebook's problems were leaked selectively and that individual investors were sold stock at prices that the underwriters knew were inflated would be particularly damaging.

Under the traditional economic model of reputation, this sort of thing simply could not happen. There would be no way that a company like Morgan Stanley could survive this sort of reputational fallout. But it seems there is something very wrong with the traditional theory because this sort of thing now happens all the time.

First, there is no question that Morgan Stanley's reputation was damaged by the way it ran the Facebook IPO. Although it is difficult, if not impossible, to measure empirically the rise and fall of companies' reputations, it is not hard to tell when a company's reputation has been tarnished because people notice. With regard to the reputational fallout from Morgan Stanley's handling of the Facebook IPO, the best source of information about the public reaction is the immensely popular website Wikipedia, which attracts billions of readers a year (470 million during February 2012 alone).[19] Although Wikipedia is not written by professionals, it is written, edited, and read by masses of people, so Wikipedia often provides good information about what the public is thinking about a particular issue.

According to Wikipedia, "The reputation of both Morgan Stanley, the primary IPO underwriter, and NASDAQ were damaged in the fallout from the botched offering."[20] Wikipedia noted that Morgan's reputation in technology IPOs was "in trouble" after the Facebook offering. And Morgan Stanley clearly had plenty of reputation to protect: The underwriting of equity offerings like Facebook is an important part of Morgan's business after the financial crisis, generating $1.2 billion in fees since 2010. According to Wikipedia, however, "By signing off on an offering price that was too high, or attempting to sell too many shares to the market," Morgan damaged its own reputation.[21] And it would appear that the mishandling of the Facebook IPO clearly would be "something that other banks will be able to use against them when competing for deals" in the future.[22]

Sure, Morgan Stanley made a lot of money on the Facebook IPO. Morgan Stanley made hundreds of millions of dollars in underwriting fees and in secondary market trading in Facebook shares immediately after the IPO. One industry insider at one of Facebook's other underwriters asserted to CNN Money, "We think Morgan has done pretty well on the deal....Reputation of the bank aside, Facebook hasn't been a bad trade for Morgan." This is because even as the share prices dropped, Morgan "racked up big profits" trading the shares.[23] For several years running, they were the number one investment bank for the tech industry. In light of these facts, the traditional reputational model in finance would predict that Morgan Stanley would suffer losses in the value of its reputation that would dwarf the one-shot gains that Morgan Stanley made on its Facebook deal.

But the traditional reputational model almost certainly is broken, and has been for some time. Brad Hintz, a financial analyst at Sanford Bernstein who follows Morgan Stanley and recommends Morgan's shares, acknowledged that "the fact that Morgan Stanley is a powerhouse in equity underwriting is not going [to] change."[24] Morgan Stanley appears to be able to ignore the reputational consequences of its very high-profile, exploitative bungling of the Facebook underwriting without suffering the reputational damage that traditional reputational theory would associate with this debacle.

Morgan Stanley is certainly not the only firm to have taken a reputational hit in recent years. Many other firms, perhaps most notably the venerable and infamous investment bank Goldman Sachs, have taken even more serious blows to their reputations.

This chapter introduced the traditional theory of reputation and demonstrated why that theory is no longer correct. Under the old model, the economic cost of a bad reputation exceeded any financial gains a company might achieve through fraud or dishonesty. Moreover, a good reputation is essential for financial firms to gain customers' trust and investments: It is expensive to build but easy to destroy. So rational economic actors in the financial industry should always choose to preserve a good reputation at the expense of short-term profit.

In the manufacturing and consumer goods sectors, companies highlight their good reputations by offering warranties and other money-back guarantees. These are not available for financial firms, because their products decline in value for complex and opaque reasons, and it is not always clear whether the failure is the result of dishonesty or of unavoidable factors. The failure of the Facebook initial public offering is a perfect example of this: Morgan Stanley refutes claims of fraud by insisting that Facebook's stock lost value for reasons out of its control. Morgan Stanley's consistent success in the financial markets since the Facebook debacle emphasizes that the traditional reputational theory is no longer relevant.

Endnotes

1. www.apa.org/gradpsych/2007/03/matters.aspx, accessed November 11, 2012.

2. www.sec.gov/answers/investg.htm, accessed November 11, 2012.

3. Ibid.

4. http://sec.gov/about/whatwedo.shtml, accessed December 21, 2012.

5. William E. Bealing, Jr., "Actions Speak Louder Than Words: An Institutional Perspective on the Securities and Exchange Commission," *Accounting, Organizations and Society*, vol. 19, issue 7, October 1994, 555-567.

6. Jonathan Macey, "The SEC's Publicity Hounds," *Defining Ideas*, July 7, 2011, www.hoover.org/publications/defining-ideas/article/84831.

7. Ibid.

8. http://stockbrokerripoff.com/investor-tookit/stock-broker-fraud/, accessed November 5, 2012.

9. www.gizmag.com/kia-offers-7-year150000-km-warranty-on-all-cars-sold-in-europe/13826/, accessed December 21, 2012.

10. Ibid.

11. www.kia-press.com/press/products/7-year_warranty_01_10.aspx, last accessed December 21, 2012.

12. www.gizmag.com/kia-offers-7-year150000-km-warranty-on-all-cars-sold-in-europe/13826/.

13. Ibid.

14. http://en.wikipedia.org/wiki/Facebook_IPO.

15. http://venturebeat.com/2012/05/29/dylans-desk-facebooks-ipo-proves-the-playing-field-is-permanently-tilted/#GB5ofLL1Dd1yxq05.99, accessed November 5, 2012.

16. http://freefrombroke.com/what-is-an-ipo-and-should-i-care/.

17. Ibid.

18. K. Rock, "Why New Issues Are Underpriced," *Journal of Financial Economics* 15 (1986): 187-212.

19. http://en.wikipedia.org/wiki/Wikipedia:About, accessed November 5, 2012.

20. http://en.wikipedia.org/wiki/Facebook_IPO, accessed November 5, 2012.

21. Ibid.

22. Stephen Gandel, Senior Editor, CNN, "Morgan Stanley Made Big Money on Facebook Share Drop," *CNN Money*, May 24, 2012, http://finance.fortune.cnn.com/2012/05/24/morgan-stanley-facebook-ipo-drop/, accessed November 5, 2012.

23. Ibid.

24. Stephen Gandel, "Facebook IPO Blunder Adds to Morgan Stanley Woes," *CNN Money*, May 23, 2012, http://finance.fortune.cnn.com/2012/05/23/facebook-ipo-blunder-morgan-stanley/.

2

Thriving the New Way: With Little or No Reputation—The Goldman Sachs Story

"Our reputation is one of our most important assets."
—Goldman Sachs Annual Report, 2007

This chapter describes three recent events involving the investment bank Goldman Sachs that serve as further proof that the traditional theory of reputation is dead. First, it notes the publication of an Op-Ed by Greg Smith, a Goldman employee who quit in order to publicize his insider's perspective of Goldman's blatant disrespect for its customers. Next, it presents Goldman's involvement in a merger between El Paso, Inc., and Kinder Morgan, Inc. The case stemming out of this merger, In re El Paso Corporation, *presents a sordid tale of Goldman's obvious conflict of interest in the transaction: Although a significant Kinder Morgan shareholder, the bank served as a merger advisor to El Paso. Nevertheless, market uncertainties prevented the court from blocking the merger.*

Finally, this chapter explores a complaint filed against Goldman by the SEC that relates to its participation in a credit-default swap (CDS) transaction immediately preceding the 2008 financial crisis. The complaint alleged that Goldman made material misrepresentations to two counterparties while arranging a CDS for its client, hedge fund Paulson & Co. These misrepresentations obscured the fact that Paulson had an active hand in selecting the reference securities underlying the CDS. These three events have combined to sully Goldman's public reputation, but the bank continues to be among the most profitable American financial institutions.

Like Morgan Stanley and every other firm on Wall Street, Goldman Sachs claims that it cares about its reputation. One of the company's key business principles is "Our assets are our people, capital and reputation, and if any of these is ever diminished, the last is the most difficult to restore."[1]

This ode to reputation remains on the Goldman Sachs web page even after Greg Smith, a Goldman Sachs executive director and head of the firm's United States equity derivatives business in Europe, the Middle East and Africa, published a blistering editorial in *The New York Times* on the day he resigned from the firm. In his Op-Ed, Mr. Smith wrote that Goldman Sachs's loud, frequent, and very public proclamations about its concerns for its reputation described the golden age of the company but not the current reality. Mr. Smith has a particular view of the way that reputation works in the world of finance. He believes that trust and reputation are important. Mr. Smith professes to be astounded by "how little senior management gets a basic truth: If clients don't trust you they will eventually stop doing business with you. It doesn't matter how smart you are."[2]

One of the major claims in this book is that it might be Mr. Smith, and not the senior management at firms like Goldman Sachs, that has it wrong. Mr. Smith appears to be embracing the traditional economic model of reputation, whose core tenet is that the costs of losing customers' trust generally are greater than the benefits. It might well be the case that, as indicated by the Facebook example, financial giants like Goldman Sachs and Morgan Stanley can cheat their clients without suffering the devastating consequences that our existing reputational theory predicts.

In his Op-Ed, Mr. Smith notes that Goldman historically was known for teamwork, integrity, humility, and doing right by its clients. This culture helped turn the 143-year-old bank into one of the titans of the financial industry. However, Mr. Smith explains that he departed Goldman because that culture had turned "toxic and destructive...the interests of the client continue to be sidelined in the way the firm operates and thinks about making money."[3] Rather than encouraging investments that produce value for its customers, Goldman's culture rewards employees who promote trades that maximize the firm's own profit, champion opaque derivative instruments, and use clients as counterparties. Within Goldman's offices, employees refer to clients as "muppets" and brag about "ripping eyeballs out" and "getting paid." According to Mr. Smith, this cultural shift gestures toward Goldman's impending downfall: No client will continue to pay a bank that does not respect its interests.[4]

But is Mr. Smith's prediction really true? If Mr. Smith were right, then Goldman Sachs should be in big, big trouble. In fact, according to Goldman Sachs itself, Goldman Sachs should be in big trouble. After all, the company itself lists its reputation as one of its principal assets, and acknowledges that a lost reputation is very difficult to restore. But Mr. Smith certainly appears to be wrong. He does not appear to be wrong about Goldman Sachs's behavior, nor does he appear to be wrong about Goldman's reputation. But he is very likely wrong in his prediction that Goldman's callous actions will bring the firm to its knees. By all objective measures, the firm is doing great, particularly in light of current economic conditions.

One possible response is that Goldman still has a sterling reputation for integrity. In other words, perhaps Mr. Smith is just a misguided, disgruntled employee and Goldman Sachs's reputation is just fine, thank you very much. But this clearly is not the case. A good example of this is that in the wake of the financial crisis of 2007 and 2008 (which continues in Europe to this day), the *Financial Times* published a high-profile article called "Goldman Sachs' Reputation Tarnished."[5]

The article pointed out that Goldman Sachs has faced a deluge of negative publicity as a variety of lawmakers, corporate governance experts, and magazines blamed the bank for the financial crisis, "vilified its plans to pay bonuses on a par with those handed out in the frothy days of 2006 and 2007,...and claimed Goldman was relying on its alumni network in Washington to insulate it from the consequences of the failure of AIT."[6]

According to the *Financial Times,* the criticism originated with the failure of Lehman Brothers and the government rescue of AIG in September 2008 and continued to build over the following months as the U.S. fell into the worst recession in decades. It "reached a crescendo...after Goldman paid back its taxpayer rescue funds and posted record profits, thus positioning the firm to ladle out bonuses" at levels rivaling those before the financial crisis.[7]

Not long ago, Goldman was famously described in a *Rolling Stone* article as a "great vampire squid wrapped around the face of humanity."[8] The headline on the cover of *New York* magazine recently asked: "Is Goldman Sachs evil? Or just too good?"[9] The article itself clearly favored the hypothesis that Goldman Sachs is evil rather than good.

Goldman's behavior is interesting precisely because it appears to be so self-destructive under the traditional economic theory of reputation. Big prestigious companies are not supposed to act the way Goldman Sachs has been acting.

Judges as well as journalists have been outraged by Goldman Sachs. But, tellingly, judges like journalists do not seem to have the power to do anything about Goldman other than write about it (and a judge's readership is considerably smaller than a journalist's).

In 2012, in one of the most widely distributed legal opinions in the history of corporate law, Goldman Sachs was publicly rebuked by one of the nation's most famous judges for ethical lapses in a massive business deal in which it had major conflicts of interest. The judge, Leo Strine, is aptly described as "greatly respected."[10] He also has been called "Delaware's leading jurist," "Delaware's most talked-about jurist," and "an incredibly impressive jurist."[11]

His opinion in the case, called *In re El Paso Corporation,*[12] involved Goldman Sachs's conduct in a transaction involving the sale of El Paso, a large publicly held corporation involved in oil and gas exploration, production, and transportation (through pipelines), to another large corporation, Kinder Morgan, Inc. The opinion provides great insight into just how little reputation seems to matter to big financial institutions like Goldman.

The issues in the case could not be simpler. When one company is trying to sell itself to another, the job of the company and its board of directors, CEO, and financial advisors is straightforward. They are supposed to maximize the sale price because their moral, legal, and fiduciary obligations are to the shareholders on whose behalf they are working. On the other hand, as in any sales transaction, the buyer's goal is to get the deal done on its best terms, that is, at the lowest price it can negotiate. These basic rules are not complicated, obscure, or controversial. But they do not seem to have applied to Goldman Sachs in the El Paso case, and it appears that there was nothing the law could do about it.

Amazingly, in the Kinder Morgan–El Paso deal, Goldman Sachs was allowed by the seller, El Paso, to provide financial and tactical advice on the transaction even though Goldman Sachs had a massive investment in the buyer. Goldman owned 19% of Kinder Morgan, which translated into a $4 billion investment. Goldman Sachs also controlled two Kinder Morgan board seats. In other words, Goldman had been hired by El Paso to help it to get the best possible price, and to sell to the highest bidder. But Goldman had very strong incentives to sell to Kinder Morgan, even if (especially if) Kinder Morgan was not the highest bidder, and it had strong incentives to sell to Kinder Morgan at a low price in order to maximize the value of its massive stake in that company.

In fairness to Goldman, the company's conflict was disclosed fully to its client El Paso. The story of how El Paso dealt with the conflict is epic. They did not eliminate Goldman Sachs. Another investment bank, Morgan Stanley, was brought in to give advice. The theory for bringing in Morgan Stanley, of course, was that because Morgan Stanley did not have the same conflicts of interest as Goldman, they would be able to provide objective independent advice.

But Morgan Stanley was not objective, because it was hired on a contingency basis and would receive a fee if and only if El Paso was sold to Kinder Morgan.

In other words:

> Goldman continued to intervene and advise El Paso on strategic alternatives, and with its friends in El Paso management, was able to achieve a remarkable feat: giving the new investment bank (Morgan Stanley) an incentive to favor the Merger (with El Paso) by making sure that this bank only got paid if El Paso adopted the strategic option of selling to Kinder Morgan. In other words, the conflict-cleansing bank only got paid if the option Goldman's financial incentives gave it a reason to prefer was the one chosen.[13]

Goldman's investment in Kinder Morgan was not the only conflict faced by the firm. Steve Daniel, the lead Goldman banker advising El Paso, personally owned approximately $340,000 of stock in Kinder Morgan, a fact that he neglected to disclose to his client, El Paso.

In light of all of these conflicts among El Paso's advisors, it is not surprising that the Company adopted what Chancellor Strine described as a "less than aggressive negotiating strategy."[14] Among other things, when Kinder Morgan made a bid for El Paso, the target company did not make any overtures to other bidders who might have offered a higher price.

Kinder Morgan's interest in acquiring El Paso arose after El Paso announced that it wanted to sell the energy and production (E&P) segments of its business, leaving it better able to concentrate on its remaining pipeline business. Kinder Morgan made contact with El Paso on a confidential basis to acquire the whole company, both the E&P and the pipeline business. Kinder Morgan was particularly interested in the pipeline portion of El Paso's business and did not want to face a bidding war for this business segment as a stand-alone proposition after the E&P segment had been sold.

Kinder Morgan, of course, as is consistent with business practice in mergers and acquisitions, wanted to avoid getting into an expensive public bidding war for El Paso. As is sometimes the case, it appears that El Paso wanted to avoid this too. Sometimes it is reasonable and prudent for target companies like El Paso to agree to a privately negotiated sale rather than to an auction. This occurs when a bidder makes a particularly strong bid, but makes the bid conditional on a privately negotiated sale rather than an auction. If the target thinks that it will get a higher price in a negotiated sale, it will agree to forego an auction. After all, the world is an uncertain place. There is no guarantee that an auction will generate a higher price than the negotiated offer that the seller has in hand. Sometimes auctions fail to generate any bids at all, because it is very risky and expensive for bidders to participate in the auction process for a big company.

However, under the circumstances of Kinder Morgan's offer for El Paso, the arguments for an auction were strong. An auction would have legitimized what was clearly a tainted sales process. The negotiating process also suggests that an auction should have taken place.

The negotiating between Kinder Morgan and El Paso began on September 16, 2011, when El Paso approached Kinder Morgan and offered to sell itself in exchange for a combination of cash and Kinder Morgan stock that was worth a total of $28 per share for El Paso. After negotiations, Kinder Morgan drove the price down to $27.55 per share, and El Paso's CEO, Douglas Foshee, who had been designated as the company's sole negotiator for this deal, reached an agreement in principle with Kinder Morgan's lead negotiator, Rich Kinder. This was memorialized in writing by means of documents known in the industry as "term sheets" (because they memorialize the terms of a business deal). But this was not the end of the story. Within a day or two of the agreement between Foshee and Kinder, the buyer decided that the price it had agreed to days before was too high.

Chancellor Strine elegantly describes this part of the story: "Kinder said, 'Oops, we made a mistake. We relied on a bullish set of analyst projections in order to make our bid. Our bad....[W]e just can't stand by our bid.'" Ultimately, El Paso's CEO "backed down." In what Strine described as a "downward spiral," El Paso accepted a bid that was worth $26.87 as of signing on October 16, 2011, composed of $25.91 in cash and stock, and a sort of option that is known in the financial world as a "warrant." This warrant gave El Paso shareholders the right to buy Kinder Morgan stock at a price of $40 per share, which was more than $13 higher than Kinder Morgan's then-current stock price of $26.89 per share. Thus, Kinder Morgan's stock price would have to go from their current price of $26.89 per share to a price above the $40 "strike price" (that is, the price at which the options could be exercised) before they could be exercised at a profit, because until Kinder Morgan's stock price rose above $40 shareholders would lose money by exercising an option to buy the shares for $40. Until Kinder Morgan's stock price rose above $40, any El Paso shareholder interested in becoming a Kinder Morgan shareholder would simply go in the market and buy shares at the market price.

In other words, the only value of the warrants that El Paso shareholders were to receive under the renegotiated terms of the deal related to the probability that Kinder Morgan's stock would increase by almost 50%, from $26.89 per share to $40.00 per share, in the future. Despite the low odds of such a price increase, the overall dollar value of Kinder Morgan's bid was estimated to be $26.87 per share at the time of the signing of the Merger Agreement between the two companies. Because a portion of the price that El Paso's shareholders were receiving was in the form of Kinder Morgan stock, the value of the merger consideration moved up and down as Kinder Morgan's share price fluctuated. This price translated into a substantial premium for El Paso's stock. It should be noted, however, that estimating the value of the out-of-the-money warrants, which were "out-of-the-money" because they could not be used until Kinder Morgan's share price jumped to $40 per share from $26.89, involved a lot of imprecise guesswork about the probability of Kinder Morgan's stock going above $40 (not to mention estimates about when, if at all, this happy event might occur). Moreover, the company performing this analysis was Morgan Stanley, the bank that would not be paid anything unless the deal went through. This arrangement, of course, gave Morgan Stanley a strong incentive to give these speculative out-of-the-money warrants a high value so that the deal would look good to El Paso shareholders and board members and be more likely to go through.

On October 14, 2011, just before the Merger Agreement between the two companies was signed and the bid became public, El Paso's stock was estimated to be worth $19.59 per share.[15] This represents a substantial premium of 37% for El Paso's shareholders (assuming, of course, that the warrants were worth what Morgan Stanley said they were worth).

What we will never know is how much more El Paso's shareholders would have received if their company had been sold in an arms-length transaction, in which the seller had independent advisors whose principal interests were in maximizing the sales price rather than minimizing it. To fend off lawsuits, the Merger Agreement between the two companies gave the El Paso board of directors what is known as a "fiduciary out." A fiduciary out permits the board of directors of a company that has agreed to sell itself to accept a subsequent higher bid in order to fulfill its legal and fiduciary duties to maximize the value of the enterprise.

In this particular deal, the fiduciary out was somewhat limited. To abandon the Kinder Morgan deal, El Paso would have to receive what the Merger Agreement called a "superior proposal." However, superior proposals could not be for just the E&P assets, which were the particular assets that Kinder Morgan wanted. El Paso could sell the whole company or the pipeline business, which was the part of the business that Kinder Morgan did not want, but it could not just sell the E&P business that Kinder Morgan wanted.[16] And, in the event El Paso managed to find a superior proposal, it would have to be greatly superior, because if El Paso accepted a superior proposal it would have to pay Kinder Morgan a fee of $650 million for terminating the deal. Despite its conflicts of interest, Goldman Sachs played an important role in advising the El Paso Board by suggesting that the Board should avoid causing Kinder Morgan to end negotiations and try to acquire the company in a hostile tender offer. In addition, Goldman advised El Paso that it should not try to spin off the pipeline segment but should sell the whole company to Kinder Morgan instead.

Morgan Stanley, which would earn $35 million if the sale of El Paso to Kinder Morgan went through—and earn nothing if it did not go through—met twice with the El Paso Board of Directors and on each occasion advised that, in their opinion, the final merger consideration offered by Kinder Morgan was "fair."

Chancellor Strine also notes in his opinion that, though Goldman Sachs claimed that it did not advise El Paso on the deal, it requested a $20 million fee for its advice. Yes, that is correct, Goldman asked for $20 million for advice that it claims that it did not give. And even though Goldman claimed in court that it had not advised El Paso on this transaction, Goldman issued a press release claiming credit as an advisor in the merger between El Paso and Kinder Morgan, "a move at self-promotion its rival Morgan Stanley called Goldman 'at its most shameless.'"[17]

Unsurprisingly, in his opinion, Chancellor Strine observes that Goldman's claim that it did not give advice to El Paso is "a claim that the record does not bear out in large measure."[18]

Wrapping up his opinion, Chancellor Strine observed, "The court is not swayed by Goldman's assertions that it was not influenced by its own economic incentives to maximize its $4 billion investment in Kinder Morgan by steering El Paso towards a deal with Kinder Morgan at a suboptimal price."

Other ugly news about Goldman's role in the deal that came out in the trial was that earlier in the deal process, "Goldman had Lloyd Blankfein, its CEO and Chairman, give Foshee a personal, obsequious phone call to thank him for El Paso's retention of Goldman over the years and to try to secure a continuing role in working for El Paso during the pendency of the Kinder Morgan bid despite what Goldman deemed an 'appearance of conflict.'"[19] The transcript of that phone call from Lloyd Blankfein to Mr. Foshee makes for interesting reading:

> Doug—it's been a long time since we have had the chance to visit/[I] wanted to reach out and say thank you for everything from [Goldman]....You have been very good to [Goldman] in having us help on all kinds of transactions over the years..../And of course I was very pleased you reached out to us on this most recent matter [the Kinder Morgan proposal]—which I understand is very serious..../I know you are aware of [Goldman's] investment [in Kinder Morgan] and that we are very sensitive to the appearance of conflict./We have asked our board members to recuse themselves and I know you have taken on a second advisor..../Really just wanted to reach out and say thank you..../Please call me any time./I'll be watching this situation very closely....[20]

The purpose of the lawsuit against Goldman and Kinder Morgan and the other defendants was to block the merger before it occurred. The relief sought was what lawyers call an injunction. If the lawyers representing the El Paso shareholders won the case, the merger would be enjoined. Not surprisingly in light of the egregious facts of this case, Justice Strine concluded that he thought that "the plaintiffs have a probability of showing that more faithful, unconflicted parties could have secured a better price from Kinder Morgan." But the plaintiffs lost anyway. Kinder Morgan won really big because they were able to buy El Paso at their price without an auction. And, of course, since Goldman had a multibillion-dollar investment in Kinder Morgan, when Kinder Morgan won, Goldman also won big.

In the end, Chancellor Strine could not see a clear way to put a stop to this sordid deal because in the end the El Paso shareholders got an above-market price for their shares. As a frustrated Chancellor Strine observed in the opinion, "nobody," not even he, could claim to

know "what would have happened had unconflicted parties negotiated the Merger" because "that is beyond the capacity of humans."[21]
In the absence of another bid on the table for El Paso, Chancellor
Strine had no choice other than to let the merger go through; otherwise, he risked costing the innocent El Paso shareholders billions of
dollars. In other words, an injunction might do the El Paso shareholders "more harm than good."

The news about Goldman's role in the transaction did not end
with Judge Strine's opinion. Stunningly, on March 6, 2012, shortly
after the El Paso opinion was issued, *The Wall Street Journal* reported
that El Paso's counsel, the well-known New York law firm Wachtell,
Lipton, Rosen & Katz, which advises many companies on transactions
like the Kinder Morgan–El Paso deal, had advised the El Paso Board
of Directors not to use Goldman in *any capacity* in connection with
the proposed sale of the company to Kinder Morgan.

After the plaintiffs' lawyers failed in their attempt to get an injunction, the deal went through and Kinder Morgan now owns El Paso.
Kinder Morgan ended the litigation by paying $110 million to settle
the case.[22] In the wake of the settlement, Kinder Morgan and Goldman Sachs officials denied any wrongdoing as part of the settlement
and said they agreed to the accord "solely to avoid the substantial burden, expense, inconvenience and distraction of continued litigation,"
according to the filing.[23]

Goldman Sachs also agreed to abandon its claim for a $20 million
advisory fee in the deal. But it is hard to feel too sorry for Goldman.
As the plaintiffs' lawyers pointed out in court, based on Goldman
Sachs's interest in Kinder Morgan, which was in excess of $4 billion,
for every dollar that Kinder Morgan saved on the price it paid for El
Paso, Goldman saved $150 million.

The final analysis of Goldman's role in the Kinder Morgan acquisition of El Paso makes Goldman look pretty darn smart. On the cost
side of the equation, Goldman lost only a $20 million advisory fee that
it never should have received anyway, along with a few million dollars
in legal fees. On the plus side of the equation, Goldman was able to
increase the value of its multibillion-dollar investment in Kinder Morgan to the extent that it was able to give advice to El Paso that helped
Kinder Morgan acquire El Paso at a bargain price. Seen from this

perspective, if we do not subtract any costs associated with Goldman's reputation from the equation, Goldman clearly won big as a result of its actions on the Kinder Morgan–El Paso deal.

Turning to the issue of Goldman's loss of reputation, it looks pretty clear that Goldman's reputation has suffered. It probably did not suffer much from its conflicted involvement with Kinder Morgan and El Paso simply because its reputation was pretty well shot before that transaction (and the ensuing litigation) took place.

Notably, about a year before the Kinder Morgan–El Paso fiasco, Goldman paid the largest fine in SEC history—$500 million—to settle charges that it misled investors in a subprime mortgage product just as the U.S. housing market was starting to collapse.[24] Ironically, the claims in this litigation also involved conflicts of interest that had a major Goldman client on both sides of a deal in precisely the same way that Goldman itself was on both sides of the deal in the Kinder Morgan case. Also ironic in its settlement with the SEC, even though it paid half a billion dollars to settle the case, Goldman was allowed to settle without admitting or denying guilt. Still more ironic in the wake of the El Paso case: In its settlement agreement with the SEC, "Goldman acknowledged that it is presently conducting a comprehensive, firm-wide review of its business standards, which the SEC has taken into account in connection with the settlement of this matter."[25]

Perhaps most ironic of all is that in the settlement Goldman Sachs was "permanently restrained and enjoined from engaging in any transaction, practice, or course of business which operates or would operate as a fraud or deceit upon the purchaser."[26]

One thing we know for sure is that neither Goldman's "comprehensive, firm-wide review of business standards" nor the "permanent injunction" prevented Goldman Sachs from working both sides of the Kinder Morgan–El Paso deal the very next year.

This case was different from the El Paso case because the people harmed by the shady dealings in El Paso were El Paso's shareholders, a large, diffuse, and disorganized group of people and companies with relatively small investors. In the SEC enforcement action against Goldman and its employee Fabrice Tourre, Goldman was sued for the conflicts of interest and lack of full disclosure to two mid-sized, moderately important institutional clients, a Dusseldorf bank called

Deutsche Industriebank AG, and Edinburgh, Scotland–based Royal Bank of Scotland N.V. (which had acquired the bank formerly known as ABN AMRO Bank N.V.).

In the litigation, the SEC won settlements of $150 million for Industriebank and $100 million for the Royal Bank of Scotland. The fact that the SEC felt compelled to use taxpayer dollars to sue Goldman on behalf of two financial institutions that clearly had the resources to underwrite their own legal battles tells us a little bit about where the SEC's priorities are these days. Putting empty rhetoric aside, protecting small investors does not appear to be high on the SEC's list of priorities.

The SEC's lawsuit against Goldman Sachs involved the somewhat complex derivative securities tied to real estate prices and the performance of the U.S. home mortgage market that were the focal point of the near-total collapse of the financial system that occurred in the financial crisis that began around 2007. As the SEC observed in its complaint, securities like those involved in this case "contributed to the recent financial crisis by magnifying losses associated with the downturn in the United States housing market."[27] Goldman Sachs had a very big hedge fund client called Paulson & Company that sagely predicted the collapse of the mortgage market. Unsurprisingly, Paulson & Co. wanted to profit from the impending collapse. But figuring out how to bet against the U.S. housing market is not quite as easy as it sounds, and Paulson needed a lot of help from Goldman Sachs in order to be in a position to place its bet.

As is well known, investment banks like Merrill Lynch and Goldman Sachs made a lot of money in the years leading up to the financial crisis by dealing in various ways in the markets for home mortgages. This market began in the 1970s when investment banks and other financial companies began buying up home mortgages from the banks that issued these mortgages to people borrowing money to buy houses. The banks made money by creating and selling bonds tied to people's mortgage payments. The principal and interest that people paid on their mortgages was used to pay the principal and interest on the bonds that the investment banks sold to investors. Home mortgages were considered to be reliable investments because most people did not default on their mortgages, and when they did the bank responsible for servicing the mortgage could foreclose, sell the property and use the proceeds to pay the bondholders. Since U.S. real estate prices had been incredibly stable over the entire post–World War II period, the bonds based on people's mortgage payments were considered safe.

The process of taking a pool of assets like home mortgages, bundling them together, and selling bonds that are repaid with the principal and interest from the homeowners' monthly payments of principal and interest is called securitization. Later, investment bankers started taking pools of mortgage payments (and the payments on other obligations like credit card debt and car loans) and spreading it around over several securities issues. For example, investment bankers would take a pool of, say, 1,000 mortgages and promise that the first payments would go to buyers of a certain set (or "tranche") of securities and the next payments would go to another tranche. These investments are called collateralized debt obligations, or "CDOs" for short. The tranches at the end of the queue were very risky. The tranches at the head of the queue were considered very safe, although it turned out that many of them weren't so safe when the economy in general and the real estate market in particular came tumbling down in 2007.

The next major "innovation" in the world of finance after CDOs were invented was credit-default swaps, popularly known as CDSs. A CDS is just like an insurance policy: The seller of the CDS gets regular payments from the buyer of the CDS that are just like the insurance premiums that people pay periodically on their insurance policies. In return for these payments, the issuer of the CDS agrees to pay money if and when another financial asset, such as a CDO or a plain vanilla mortgage-backed security, defaults.

Credit-default swaps allow investors in risky tranches of CDOs to protect themselves against default. Credit-default swaps differ from regular insurance such as car insurance or life insurance in one very important way: Anybody with enough money can buy a CDS, but not everybody can buy regular insurance on somebody's life or property. In particular, it is illegal for a person to buy life or property insurance on someone else's life or property unless the person buying the insurance has some reason why she would suffer some harm if the insured-against event actually occurred. For example, a person can buy life insurance for her husband, because the spouse buying the insurance presumably (hopefully) benefits from the continued existence of her husband. The stake that somebody is supposed to have in the person or property being insured is called an insurable interest. If I loan you money and you put up an asset as collateral for my loan, I have a legitimate insurable interest in that property so I am legally entitled to buy insurance to protect my interest.

Laws restricting the purchase and sale of insurance contracts to those with insurable interests have been around since 1774. They were enacted to solve a problem that economists call "moral hazard," which is the problem that somebody will try to collect on insurance policies by actually causing the event that they have insured against. For example, I would not want someone I did not even know to buy a fire insurance contract on my house, and I certainly would not want a stranger buying a life insurance policy on one of my children. One of the first laws requiring that people have an insurable interest in order to buy insurance was a law enacted in 18th-century England to keep people (think, pirates) from buying insurance that would pay off if a ship sank.

Another justification for limiting the availability of insurance to people with insurable interests is because it limits the exposure of insurance companies, thereby reducing the repercussions of the insured event occurring. If insurance contracts were not limited to those with insurable interests, then there would be no limit whatsoever on the amount of insurance that could be sold against the occurrence of a certain event.

A remarkable feature of CDSs is that there is no limitation on who can buy these financial contracts, despite the undeniable fact that, for all practical purposes, they are insurance products. There is no particular reason for creating an exception to the insurable interest rule for CDSs other than the fact that banks do not want the rule to apply to their trading in CDSs because it would dramatically shrink a market that is highly profitable for them. The banks have so far been successful in their lobbying efforts to block CDSs from being classified as insurance. For example, in May 2010, *The New York Times* noted, "Wall Street won one this week when the Senate voted down a proposal to bar the so-called naked buying of credit-default swaps"; this proposal would have prohibited the "use [of] swaps to bet a company would fail" unless you had an insurable interest such as an investment in the company. The article also pointedly observed that if regulators had done their jobs, credit-default swaps would have been classified as insurance years ago.[28]

The ability of hedge funds and other investors to buy credit-default swaps, which are designed to pay off when a financial asset like a mortgage bond or a CDO fails, without actually owning the mortgage bond or the CDO had major implications during the financial crisis. Because there was no limit to the number of CDSs that could be sold, the market became gigantic. Savvy investors who saw the writing on the wall shortly before the mortgage market collapsed bought massive numbers of CDSs that would pay off if CDOs and other financial assets linked to the tottering mortgage market collapsed. One insurance company, AIG, sold the vast majority of these CDSs, and that company was wiped out when the housing market collapsed, saved only by massive infusions of cash from the U.S. government. Much of this cash infusion was funneled right to Goldman Sachs since AIG used the bailout money to pay 100 cents on the dollar on the credit-default swaps on CDOs and other exotic derivative securities it had sold to Goldman over the years.

It was trading in CDSs and CDOs that got Goldman into such trouble with the SEC that it had to pay a $500 million fine to extricate itself from the clutches of the regulators. A major Goldman client, hedge fund giant Paulson & Co., wanted to place a big bet that the mortgage market would collapse. Goldman arranged for Paulson & Co. to do this by convincing certain clients, Deutsche Industriebank and ABN AMRO (now known as Royal Bank of Scotland), to sell Paulson credit-default swaps. Part of Goldman's job was participating in the process of picking the exact securities (CDOs and mortgage-backed securities) that would be used as the so-called reference securities for the CDSs. Reference securities are simply the specific securities that the parties are betting on. When one or more of these reference securities defaults, then the seller of the CDS whose payoffs are linked to these securities has to pay off the buyer of the CDS. Paulson & Co. was the buyer of these CDSs. They were betting that the reference securities would default. Deutsche Industriebank and ABN AMRO were the sellers of these securities.

So far there does not seem to be much of a problem. We have three sophisticated parties: (1) Paulson & Co., which is buying insurance; (2) Deutsche Industriebank and ABN AMRO, which are selling the insurance/CDSs; and (3) Goldman, which is in the middle, and, for a large fee, is putting the buyer and the sellers together and figuring out which assets the buyer and sellers will be betting on. The crummier (more speculative) the CDOs and mortgage-backed securities that go in the reference portfolio are, the better for the CDS buyer, Paulson & Co. The safer (more creditworthy) the securities in the reference portfolio are, the better for the banks that are selling the CDSs to Paulson. The CDO reference portfolio that Paulson and the banks were using as the basis for their credit-default swaps is known as a "synthetic" CDO portfolio because there were no real CDOs in the portfolio. Particular CDOs and other financial assets simply are selected and agreed to by the parties. The parties then observe the price fluctuations of these assets, and when there has been a default the CDS seller must pay the CDS buyer.

If you are either the seller or the buyer, you would like to be able to pick the reference securities that are going into the synthetic CDO portfolio. The seller of the CDSs would of course pick the safest possible security. Similarly, the buyer of the CDSs would pick the riskiest possible securities. And, of course, if you were the seller you would be very interested in knowing whether the buyer of the CDSs was picking the securities in the reference portfolio. This would be like an insurance company selling life insurance to somebody and then letting that person choose whose life was being insured. The buyer of the life insurance would find some fellow in the nearest Hospice and have the insurance contract apply to that poor soul's life.

Clearly, the selling banks, Deutsche Industriebank and ABN AMRO, would be pretty interested in knowing whether their counterparty, Paulson & Co., was picking the CDOs that they were insuring through the sale of the CDSs. And this is where reputation enters the picture. As the intermediary between the buyer and the seller in this transaction, Goldman either had to be trusted to be fair and objective when picking the securities for the portfolio, or had to find somebody who was thought by the parties to be fair and objective to pick the securities for the reference portfolio. Otherwise, the parties would be foolish to engage in the transaction.

Goldman Sachs's marketing materials for this deal, which included a term sheet, a deck of overhead slides, and a detailed offering memorandum, all represented to prospective buyers and sellers of the CDS that the synthetic CDO reference portfolio "was selected by ACA Management LLC (ACA), a third-party with experience analyzing credit risk in RMBS (residential mortgage-backed securities)."[29] It appears that Goldman Sachs's marketing materials failed to disclose that Paulson & Co., which planned to buy CDS insurance protection on the securities in the portfolio, "played a significant role in the portfolio selection process."[30] Next, after participating in the selection of the reference portfolio, Paulson took a big bet against the portfolio by entering into credit-default swaps to buy protection on specific portions of the portfolio it had selected.[31] Of course, as the SEC pointed out in its Complaint against Goldman Sachs, Goldman's favored client, Paulson, had an economic incentive to choose RMBS that it expected to experience "credit events" (credit events are SEC-speak for things like defaults, rating downgrades) in the near future.[32] The SEC also alleged that Goldman failed to disclose Paulson's adverse economic interests or its role in the portfolio selection process to investors.

In its lawsuit, the SEC alleged that Goldman arranged a transaction at Paulson & Co.'s request in which Paulson heavily influenced the selection of the portfolio to suit its economic interests, but failed to disclose Paulson & Co.'s role in the portfolio selection process or its adverse economic interests to investors as part of the description of the portfolio selection process contained in the marketing materials used to promote the transaction. The SEC and some of the other investors who lost money also claimed that they knew that Paulson & Co. was involved in picking the securities in the portfolio, but that they were led to believe that Paulson & Co. was *selling* CDS insurance along with them, when in fact Paulson & Co. actually was *buying* CDS insurance in the deal.

According to the SEC, Paulson & Co. performed an analysis of recently issued mortgage-backed securities and other financial assets that it expected to go into default, and it identified more than 100 securities it thought would experience default.[33] Paulson & Co. asked Goldman to arrange for it to buy CDS insurance against the default of the assets it had identified. It is quite interesting that the parties selling the CDS protection did not trust Goldman to select the portfolio to be insured. The SEC noted that Goldman appears to have been fully aware that "the identification of an experienced and independent third-party collateral manager" to select the portfolio "would facilitate the placement of the CDO liabilities in a market that was beginning to show signs of distress."[34] In addition, Goldman apparently specifically knew that at least Deutsche Industriebank AG was reluctant to invest in the liabilities of a CDO that did not utilize an independent firm to analyze and select the reference portfolio.[35] As Fabrice Tourre, the Goldman official in charge of the deal, observed in an email: "One thing that we need to make sure ACA [the independent portfolio selection company] understands is that we want their name on this transaction. This is a transaction for which they are acting as portfolio selection agent[;] this will be important that we can use ACA's branding to help distribute the bonds."[36]

In other words, it appears that the parties did not fully trust Goldman and tried and failed to protect themselves from Goldman's shenanigans. And they had good reason not to trust Goldman. Like its favored client Paulson & Co., Goldman appears to have been well aware that the whole mortgage-backed securities market was about to collapse, an event that would, of course, be disastrous for its clients who were selling CDS insurance contracts on these securities. As Goldman's Fabrice Tourre observed in an email: "More and more leverage in the system, the whole building is about to collapse anytime now....Only potential survivor, the fabulous Fab[rice Tourre]... standing in the middle of all these complex, highly leveraged, exotic trades he created without necessarily understanding all of the implications of those monstruosities [sic]!!!"[37]

The full magnitude of the ethical implosion at Goldman Sachs is reflected in a U.S. District Court judge's reaction to a lawsuit filed against Goldman Sachs claiming that Goldman committed fraud against its own shareholders in connection with its failure to disclose that it was allowing Paulson to pick the securities that he planned to short. Goldman's fraud, according to the plaintiff, was that it made false and misleading disclosures to shareholders. The fraud was that Goldman claimed to behave ethically when it did not. Specifically, Goldman was charged in the Complaint with making these fraudulent claims:

"Our reputation is one of our most important assets."[38]

"Integrity and honesty are at the heart of our business."[39]

"[W]e increasingly have to address potential conflicts of interest, including situations where our services to a particular client or our own proprietary investments or other interests conflict, or are perceived to conflict, with the interest of another client...."[40]

"We have extensive procedures and controls that are designed to...address conflicts of interest."[41]

"Our clients' interests always come first. Our experience shows that if we serve our clients well, our own success will follow."[42]

"We are dedicated to complying fully with the letter and spirit of the laws, rules and ethical principles that govern us. Our continued success depends upon unswerving adherence to this standard."[43]

"Most importantly, and the basic reason for our success, is our extraordinary focus on our clients."[44]

It should come as no surprise that the judge's endorsement of this lawsuit did not go unnoticed. *The New York Times* called this the "lawsuit that haunts Goldman Sachs."[45] This seems right. After all, it is pretty unusual—and disturbing—for a major company to be sued for fraud because it lied when it claimed that it tried not to lie and worked to avoid cheating its customers.

When the suit was filed, Goldman filed a motion to dismiss the case before any discovery occurred, but this motion was denied. A *New York Times* article on the story pointed out that the statements made by Goldman (quoted previously) "are fairly generic, the typical niceties issued by public companies about how much they value complying with the law," such as "our reputation is one of our most important assets," and "integrity and honesty are at the heart of our business."[46]

Even in defending against this lawsuit, Goldman's arguments in favor of dismissal seem to support the plaintiffs' argument that Goldman Sachs thinks that its own reputation is particularly important to investors. For example, in its Reply Brief Goldman claimed that nobody should take its claims of honesty and integrity seriously. Goldman claimed that these statements were what are known in the law as puffery. Puffery consists of subjective opinions contained in the promotional statements used in sales and advertising that no reasonable person would interpret literally. In response to this defense, the court made an observation that is at the heart of what this book is about. The judge took the view that Goldman's argument that its words were not meant to be believed by any reasonable person was not credible. He described Goldman's argument as "Orwellian," adding presciently that "if Goldman's claim of 'honesty' and 'integrity' are simply puffery, the world of finance may be in more trouble than we recognize." Well, the world of finance *is* in more trouble than most people realize.

A second argument asserted by Goldman was that the statements were not "material," that is, important enough to matter because reasonable investors would not consider them important. Just as it was odd for Goldman to claim that nobody should have believed it when it claimed to be honest, it is also strange for Goldman to argue that its claims that it conducts its business honestly would not be important to the ordinary investor. In documents posted on the Internet, sent to its shareholders and filed with the SEC, Goldman claimed that its reputation was "one of its most important assets." Then in court filings Goldman argued that its claims about being honest were immaterial, meaning that investors would not consider them relevant or important.

Goldman's reputation has been tarnished seriously by this series of very public body blows to its reputation. In light of all of this bad publicity, the question of how Goldman remains the world's leading, most profitable, and successful bank in spite of its reputation for predatory behavior is both interesting and difficult. Goldman's continued dominance in the world of finance is strong evidence that the traditional model of reputation, that predicts that investment banks like Goldman will put their customers' interest ahead of their own and avoid conflicts of interest, no longer has much, if any, explanatory force. In the next chapter, I argue that the model used to work pretty well. In fact, the complete demise of major investment banks including Bankers Trust Company and Salomon Brothers is wholly attributable to actions that eviscerated these firms' reputations and led customers and counterparties to stop doing deals with them. And even though this world no longer exists, it is well worth remembering.

Interestingly, one of the reasons the old reputational model no longer has much explanatory power is that when companies like Arthur Andersen and Salomon Brothers disappeared, no new financial giants emerged to take their places. Goldman Sachs and Morgan Stanley are among the very few investment banks still standing. This power and dominance in the market gives them considerable leeway to maneuver that did not exist when the financial world was more competitive. Goldman Sachs and Morgan Stanley do a lot of deals because there are not many options left. In fact, these two firms actually were the last investment banks in existence in the U.S. when they recently converted from investment banks into bank holding companies in order to get easier access to government loans, particularly from the Board of Governors of the Federal Reserve, which regulates bank holding companies and has the power to loan money to them at highly favorable rates.

Another reason Goldman marches on from scandal to scandal apparently unscathed and unapologetic is because it has a proven track record of getting deals done. Clients like El Paso might logically conclude that it is better to get a deal done at a suboptimal price using Goldman Sachs than not to get a deal done at all. And, in the end, one cannot dispute the fact that the El Paso shareholders were better off selling to Kinder Morgan than not selling at all. The bankers in that deal are protected by the harsh reality that there is no way of knowing how much more money, if any, the El Paso shareholders would have gotten for their shares had they not agreed to Kinder Morgan's terms and to Goldman Sachs's preferred structuring of the deal.

As the next chapter explains, another reason reputation no longer matters on Wall Street is that technological advances in computer trading models have led investment bankers to believe that they do not need customers in the old-fashioned sense of the word "customer." All they need are counterparties, meaning people willing to trade with them on an arms-length basis who do not ask for or receive advice and do not claim to trust the banks to do anything more than buy or sell at the price agreed on in the (recorded) telephone calls and documented electronic communications between the banks and their so-called "customers."

This chapter discussed a few recent events involving Goldman Sachs that demonstrate the failure of the traditional theory of reputation. First, this chapter covered how a disgruntled former Goldman employee published an Op-Ed in The New York Times *describing how Goldman's partners and managers consistently put the firm's profitability ahead of its customers' financial interests. Next, this chapter examined* In re El Paso Corporation, *a recent case in Delaware's state court that highlights Goldman's profit-seeking activities. The case concerns a merger between El Paso, Inc., and Kinder Morgan, Inc. Goldman served as an advisor to El Paso despite being a significant Kinder Morgan shareholder, raising concerns that it did not adequately assist El Paso's Board of Directors in obtaining a fair sale price.*

This chapter also discussed Goldman's controversial role in a credit-default swap transaction preceding the 2008 financial crisis. Goldman's promotional materials failed to disclose to two counterparties that its hedge fund client, Paulson & Co., helped select the reference securities underlying the CDS. Finally, the chapter discussed a recent lawsuit filed against Goldman for committing fraud by lying when they make claims about themselves like "Integrity and honesty are at the heart of our business." Despite the reputational fallout from these events, Goldman continues to enjoy remarkable profitability, making it clear that the traditional reputational model is no longer accurate.

Endnotes

1. www.goldmansachs.com/who-we-are/business-standards/business-principles/index.html, accessed December 21, 2012.

2. Greg Smith, "Why I Am Leaving Goldman Sachs," *The New York Times*, March 14, 2012.

3. Ibid.

4. Ibid.

5. Greg Farrell, *Financial Times*, August 2, 2009, www.ft.com/cms/s/0/ae3d459a-7f8e-11de-85dc-00144feabdc0.html#axzz2BO0lwTT2, accessed November 5, 2012.

6. Ibid.

7. Ibid.

8. Matt Taibbi, "The Great American Bubble Machine," *Rolling Stone Magazine,* July 9, 2009, www.rollingstone.com/politics/news/the-great-american-bubble-machine-20100405, accessed November 5, 2012.

9. Joe Hagan, "Tenacious G: Inside Goldman Sachs, America's Most Successful, Cynical, Envied, Despised, and (in its view, anyway) Misunderstood Engine of Capitalism," July 26, 2009, http://nymag.com/news/business/58094/, accessed November 5, 2012.

10. Alison Frankel, "Tortured Opinion Is Strine's Surrender in El Paso Case," *ThomsonReuters News and Insight,* March 1, 2012, http://newsandinsight.thomsonreuters.com/Legal/News/2012/03_-_March/Tortured_opinion_is_Strine_s_surrender_in_El_Paso_case/.

11. David Marcus, "Leo Strine's Marvelous Adventures," The Deal.com, www.thedeal.com/magazine/ID/020000/features/leo-strine's-marvelous-adventures.php#ixzz2BSMJo9aT; Barry Reiter, "US Decision Sheds Light on Directors' Duties," *Lexpert Magazine,* July/August 2007, www.bennettjones.com/BennettJones/images/Guides/update2871.pdf; Susan Beck, "Tell Us How You Really Feel, Leo," *The American Lawyer,* March 1, 2012, www.americanlawyer.com/PubArticleTAL.jsp?id=1202542160897&thepage=3&slreturn=20121006102701. These quotations about Chancellor Strine were collected by Stephen Bambridge; see "Leo Strine: Minor Prophet?" ProfessorBainbridge.com, March 1, 2012, www.professorbainbridge.com/professorbainbridgecom/2012/03/leo-strine-minor-prophet.html.

12. See In re El Paso Corporation, February 29, 2012, Delaware Chancery Court, http://newsandinsight.thomsonreuters.com/uploadedFiles/Reuters_Content/2012/03_-_March/El_paso_opinion1.pdf.

13. Ibid., 1-2.

14. Ibid., 2.

15. See Yahoo Finance, El Paso Corp. Historical Stock Prices, http://finance.yahoo.com/q/hp?s=EP+Historical+Prices, last accessed February 29, 2012.

16. Specifically, the Merger Agreement forbade the El Paso board from accepting any superior bid that was for less than 50% of the company's assets. The E&P assets made up less than 50% of the company, so those assets could not be sold alone under the Merger

Agreement. The pipeline business was more than 50% of the company, so that business segment could be sold.

17. Quoting an e-mail exchange between Morgan Stanley's Jonathan Cox and Morgan Stanley's Morgan Munger.

18. See In re El Paso Corporation, 16.

19. Ibid., 22.

20. Footnote 43 of the El Paso decision, quoting an e-mail from Goldman CEO Blankfein containing a script for a call to El Paso CEO Foshee.

21. Ibid., 24.

22. Jeff Feeley, "Kinder Morgan to Pay $110 Million to Settle El Paso Suits," Bloomberg, www.bloomberg.com/news/2012-09-07/ kinder-morgan-to-pay-110-million-to-settle-el-paso-suits.html, accessed November 6, 2012.

23. Ibid.

24. U.S. Securities and Exchange Commission, "Goldman Sachs to Pay Record $550 Million to Settle SEC Charges Related to Subprime Mortgage CDO: Firm Acknowledges CDO Marketing Materials Were Incomplete and Should Have Revealed Paulson's Role," www.sec.gov/news/press/2010/2010-123.htm.

25. Ibid.

26. SEC v. Goldman Sachs and Fabrice Tourre, Final Judgment as to Defendant Goldman Sachs & Co., Case No. 10-CV-3229.

27. SEC v. Goldman Sachs & Co., and Fabrice Tourre, Complaint, Case No. 10-CV-3229.

28. Floyd Norris, "Naked Truth on Default Swaps," *The New York Times,* May 20, 2010, www.nytimes.com/2010/05/21/business/ economy/21norris.html?_r=0.

29. SEC Complaint, 1-5.

30. Ibid.

31. Ibid.

32. Ibid.

33. Ibid.

34. Ibid., 7.

35. Ibid., 8.

36. Ibid. (quoting February 7, 2007, Goldman internal communication).

37. Ibid.

38. Complaint in class action lawsuit, Ilene Richman v. Goldman Sachs Group, 10 Civ. 3461 (PAC), Complaint paragraph 154 (taken from 2007 Goldman Annual Report).

39. Richman v. Goldman Sachs Complaint paragraph 289 taken from 2007 Goldman Annual Report.

40. Ibid., paragraph 134.

41. Ibid.

42. Ibid., paragraph 154.

43. Ibid.

44. Ibid., taken from recording of Goldman Sachs Conference Call.

45. Peter Henning, "The Lawsuit That Haunts Goldman Sachs," June 25, 2012, http://professional.wsj.com/article/ TPNYTB000020120625e86p003bi.html, accessed November 8, 2012.

46. Ibid.

3

The Way Things Used to Be: When Reputation Was Critical to Survival

This chapter presents the rise and fall of Bankers Trust Company as an example of how traditional reputation theory used to work. Founded in New York in the early 20th century, Bankers Trust grew quickly by acquiring smaller banks around the country, and suing to expand into markets from which it was barred. Eventually, under the leadership of CEO Charles Sanford, Bankers Trust moved out of retail banking and began to focus on merchant banking. It developed cutting edge risk-assessment techniques, pioneered derivative instruments known as swaps, and quickly became one of the most successful banks in the industry. In the 1990s, Bankers Trust entered into complex swap agreements with two large corporate clients that quickly turned sour. Although the bank emerged from the subsequent litigation as the nominal victor, Bankers Trust's reputation was seriously tarnished. It lost nearly all of its corporate clients and was sold soon after.

It is impossible to understand how reputation works in capital markets without understanding the dramatic fall of Bankers Trust from one of the most innovative and successful financial institutions in history to a shunned pariah whose damaged reputation led inexorably to its destruction.

Founded in 1903, Bankers Trust New York Corporation rose to become a multibillion-dollar bank holding company, and one of the largest commercial banks in the United States. Bankers Trust's transformation into a giant of the financial sector occurred right along with—and was largely attributable to—the growth of its reputation as a highly trustworthy institution that could be counted on both to safeguard the funds entrusted to it by high-net-worth individuals and by other financial institutions and to refrain from competing with its many clients in the banking industry all over the U.S.

In the late 19th and early 20th centuries, banking law forbade national banks from establishing any out-of-state branches or conducting trust powers, but required them to meet stringent capital and reserve requirements. These rules put big New York banks at a disadvantage to rival trust companies, which could make loans at more competitive rates and more profitably because they were subject to much less stringent regulations. In 1903, a group of powerful New York banks led by iconic financier J. P. Morgan formed their own trust company, which they called Bankers Trust, to provide a legal structure that would allow them to compete on a more level playing field with the trust companies. Initially, Bankers Trust limited itself to the provision of trust services, which basically involved acting as trustee and managing investments held by clients in trust. This business turned out to be very successful. Because Bankers Trust did not compete with other state and national commercial banks for loan customers or for customers in search of interest-bearing deposit accounts, banks all over the country turned to Bankers Trust to handle their trust business.

Bankers Trust had deposits totaling $5.75 million; within four months it had outgrown its original premises and moved to Wall Street.[1] Like any trust company that managed other people's money at the time, Bankers Trust Company's reputation was critical to its survival. Bankers Trust's staunch backing by the New York banking elite, and particularly by J. P. Morgan, allowed it to quickly earn the trust of its clients, which were almost exclusively other banks. The bank's strong performance during the October 1907 money panic was said to have "bolstered the company's reputation."[2]

Bankers Trust grew quickly, establishing international operations and introducing traveler's checks on behalf of the powerful industry trade group the American Bankers Association. Bankers Trust began an acquisition spree in 1911, acquiring other trust companies, including the Mercantile Trust Company and the Manhattan Trust Company.

When laws were changed to allow banks to engage in the trust business directly, Bankers Trust had to change its business model in order to survive. By 1917, Bankers Trust had become a full-fledged commercial bank and a member of the Federal Reserve System. By 1928, Bankers Trust had grown into an institution with $25 million in assets, which is over $330 million in capital in today's dollars. This was before the passage of the Glass-Steagall Act in 1933, which prohibited commercial banks from engaging directly or through affiliates in such investment banking activities as underwriting or buying and selling securities. Bankers Trust had created a subsidiary called the Bankers Company, which developed a very large national sales operation to underwrite and sell corporate bonds. This business had to be eliminated when the Glass-Steagall Act passed in 1933, and affiliations between banks like Bankers Trust and investment banks like the Bankers Company were no longer permitted. But this did not stop Bankers Trust from expanding. As a natural outgrowth of its trust business, Bankers Trust was one of the most important pioneers in the burgeoning business of managing corporate pension plans.

Despite the overall retrenchment, the trust department was allowed to continue growing. Bankers Trust's reputation was grounded in its traditional fiduciary business, which was the bank's core business. As it grew, the trust department had departments that specialized in managing all the asset classes that were held in trust, including mortgage finance, real estate, and, of course, corporate and government bond and equity investments.

These departments performed very well in the Depression, and, unlike thousands of other banks, Bankers Trust emerged intact and even financially strong. Although the bank did not grow fast during this period, by 1935, the bank's assets exceeded the $1 billion mark. The bank also survived World War II, closing its branches in Paris and Berlin, but continuing its London branch. The London branch was struck by bombs during the war, but never closed for more than a day despite the heavy German bombardments of the British capital.

After the war, Bankers Trust began lending to individual and smaller corporate borrowers, often on favorable terms and without requiring collateral. Throughout the 1950s, Bankers Trust grew and expanded the scope of its operations by merging with or simply buying a number of other banks. In 1950, Bankers Trust acquired Lawyers Trust Company, Title Guarantee & Trust Company, and Flushing

National Bank. In the early to mid-1950s Bankers Trust went on to acquire Commercial National Bank & Trust Company, Bayside National Bank, Fidelity Trust Company, and Public National Bank, which had a major network of branch banks throughout New York City.

By the end of the decade, the company's growth efforts were noticed by regulators in both New York and Washington. In 1959, the company announced that it planned to merge with another huge bank, Manufacturers Trust Company, but the merger plan was abandoned when the New York State Banking Commission and the Federal Reserve began to consider trying to block the megamerger. In 1960, the New York State Banking Commission actually blocked Bankers Trust's planned acquisition of the largest retail bank in Westchester County, New York, the Westchester County Trust Company. Westchester Trust at the time had 39 branches and over $380 million in assets.

In 1965, Bankers Trust Company was still in a high-growth mode. The bank incorporated a bank holding company, BT New York Corporation (later Bankers Trust New York Corporation) as the first step in a planned expansion into a number of business areas that could not legally be conducted by the bank itself. Over the next decade Bankers Trust expanded from a "bankers' bank" that focused on doing business with corporations and very high-net-worth individuals into a diversified financial institution with a significant retail banking presence in the U.S., a very successful international banking operation, and a large presence in middle market lending, construction lending, real estate and mortgage lending, credit cards, equipment leasing (particularly airplane leasing), and factoring (buying up the accounts receivable of companies at a discount and collecting the debts as efficiently as possible, earning a profit on the difference between the amount it collected on the money loaned by these other companies and what it paid to acquire the right to receive these obligations).

Interestingly, Bankers Trust Company became the most aggressive bank in the U.S. when it came to filing legal disputes challenging state laws that prohibited banks from expansion. For example, in 1973, Bankers Trust filed a suit in federal court challenging the constitutional validity of Florida laws that prevented out-of-state banks and bank holding companies, such as Bankers Trust and its holding company, from acquiring or controlling Florida trust and investment companies. In the same year, Bankers Trust sued again in Florida, this time to overturn a state law restricting out-of-state banks from providing trust services to Florida banks. Bankers Trust ultimately won both these cases on the grounds that the laws impermissibly restricted interstate commerce in violation of Article I, Clause 8, Section 3 of the U.S. Constitution, which contains a provision known as "the Commerce Clause," designed to protect companies like Bankers Trust from being frozen out of state markets by state laws that prohibit out-of-state competition. States often do this to protect locally powerful in-state businesses from competition by strong out-of-state rivals.[3]

Bankers Trust consistently did very well. Its expansion plans enabled the bank to take advantage of the fact that its reputation was no longer limited to the banking industry and the local New York banking market. Customers in Florida, California, and the Midwest also wanted to do business with such a well-regarded bank.

The beginning of the end came in the mid-1970s. A new management team that included future chairman Charles S. Sanford as vice chairman took over in 1974. By 1976, the bank's reputation took a major hit when the bank was accused by regulators of being in financial difficulty. The accusation arose when the Board of Governors of the U.S. Federal Reserve System surprisingly denied Bankers Trust's proposed acquisition of tiny First National Bank of Mexico, New York, on the grounds that Bankers Trust was experiencing financial difficulties. As observed in a historical account of Bankers Trust, "Although the [Federal Reserve] Board later issued another statement saying that the company was sound, the damage was done—public confidence in Bankers Trust was not fully restored until the mid-1980s. By the end of 1978 Bankers Trust was the least profitable major U.S. bank."[4]

At this point, the basic groundwork for the future was laid. First, Bankers Trust needed the support of federal regulators in order to continue to thrive and to grow. Second, Bankers Trust came to view litigation as a major weapon in its strategic arsenal. Finally, Bankers Trust began to specialize.

Bankers Trust decided to exit the retail banking business, a business segment that was growing increasingly crowded and competitive, and return to its traditional wholesale banking model of doing business with large commercial institutions and focusing on its four core businesses of commercial banking, money and securities markets, corporate financial services, and trust department services. It began selling off its retail banking networks in the late 1970s, largely freeing itself of its branch networks by 1981. By 1984, with the sale of its branches in Binghamton, New York, Bankers Trust was completely out of the retail banking business.

Charles Sanford, the new CEO, was promoted directly from the trading floor. Under Sanford, Bankers Trust returned to profitability with a vengeance. But the bank did far more than just make money during the Sanford era. The bank played a major role in the financial history of the United States by changing the way we think about risk. In particular, the bank was the first to put into operation the basic, but crucial, concept that different investors' returns on assets cannot be evaluated merely by looking at the returns garnered on those assets. Instead, the risks that were associated with those investments must be taken into account as well. For example, suppose that an investor has stock in two companies, and the companies perform identically during the course of a particular year, such that the investor has garnered the exact same 10% return on both assets. We cannot automatically conclude that the assets performed equally well because it is likely that each of the assets faced different risks. Suppose that one asset was highly risky and had a 90% chance of declining in value during the year under study. Suppose that the other asset was very safe, and had a 90% chance of not declining in value during the year. Because it is better (and harder) to find assets that produce good returns at low risk, we have to conclude that the safer investment performed better. After all, it is better to earn a 10% return while taking on only a little risk than to earn the same return while assuming heavy risk.

Bankers Trust's innovations in developing tools for more accurately measuring risk enabled Bankers Trust to evaluate its own performance—as well as the performance of the companies in which it was thinking of making investments—more accurately than any other financial institution. This helped Bankers Trust to improve its returns under Charles Sanford. Equally, if not more important, Bankers

Trust's innovations in measuring risk enabled the bank to determine how risky its own banking operations were, and to make sure that they always had a capital buffer large enough (but not too large) to protect it against the precise risk posed by the assets it owned.

The company's system of assigning risk factors to its assets became the world standard for evaluating, controlling, and measuring risk. This system, called risk-adjusted returns on capital (RAROC), not only improved Bankers Trust's financial performance substantially, but also improved the bank's reputation in the financial world and solidified the company's reputation as an industry leader.

The RAROC analytical framework was used to evaluate transactions and reallocate capital from low-return to high-return business.[5] Under Sanford, Bankers Trust "transformed itself from a second rate, ill-focused, near insolvent commercial bank into a dynamic, well-capitalized, highly profitable merchant bank."[6]

Bankers Trust Company's revolutionary approach seems disarmingly simple at first glance. As one historian of the period observed, "Sanford hit upon three principles well established in modern finance but never integrated and applied to managing a firm." These were the principles:

1. By taking a position—that is, by buying bonds—the trader brought risk into the bank and used the bank's expensive capital.

2. The only reason to take risk is to earn a return; therefore, in taking a position, the trader had the expectation of earning a return. Furthermore, the higher the risk, the higher the return the trader should expect.

3. To justify the use of shareholders' capital, the trader's expectation for a return must be consistent with the minimum return for similar risks required by shareholders.[7]

Bankers Trust came to dominate the world of merchant banking, which involves making big bets with one's own capital, because with its better measures for measuring risk it could outcompete its competition. Better techniques for measuring risk give a competitor a crucial advantage in the marketplace because "rivals who continue the age-old practice of doing business based on 'gut feel' or 'what was done in the past' may win business in the short term because they are not charging the full premium for risk. But they will lose out over time as unexpected losses take their revenge and customers migrate to more stable institutions."[8] Bankers Trust's specialty was the buying and selling—for its own account and for the accounts of customers—of complicated financial derivatives, particularly swaps. As the name implies, a swap is simply a financial transaction in which one party swaps a stream of payments or a single (usually large) payment for a single large payment (or series of payments) with another party. For example, suppose that a German manufacturing company sells a large number of subway trains to a company in another part of the world, like China. For tax reasons or regulatory reasons, or perhaps simply because the buyer insists on it, the sales price is denominated in China's domestic currency, the yuan. Suppose that the trains will be purchased as they are manufactured in a German factory over the next several years. In exchange for millions of euros' worth of subway trains, the German manufacturing company basically has agreed to accept payment in Chinese yuan that it will receive over the next several years. As a German company that is manufacturing its products in Europe, the company of course reports its earnings and its profits and losses in euros. The company also pays its employees in euros, and it pays dividends to its shareholders in euros. The 500,000,000 euros that the German company is scheduled to receive over the next decade or so might never materialize due to exchange rate fluctuations. As of mid-November 2012, the €500 million is worth ¥3,692,960,000. But if the yuan gets weaker against the euro in the future, this amount could decline considerably. Often companies in this position will go to a financial institution and "put on a swap," as these trades are known in the industry. The German company can pay a fee and "swap" its expected stream of yuan payments for a single payment in euros, relieving itself of the exchange rate risk associated with the transaction and allowing it to determine, with accuracy, the present value of this future stream of payments in its own currency. Similarly, a firm that has borrowed money at a variable rate of interest might decide that it wants to swap this obligation for an obligation to repay its loan at a fixed rate of interest. These two types of swaps, foreign exchange swaps and interest-rate swaps, are the most common types of swap transactions.

Bankers Trust also pioneered the concept of what is now known as the "naked swap." A naked swap simply is a swap with only one side. People also can engage in swaps even if they are not trying to hedge risk by making a unilateral promise to make a payment to another customer. For example, if a bank simply promised a client that it would pay it a certain amount of euros every month in exchange for receiving a certain amount of yuan every month, that bank would have entered into a naked swap. A company can simply make a promise to exchange a single future payment or a stream of such payments for a promise by their counterparties to pay them a stream of payments calculated in a different way as a way of making money on currency fluctuations or interest rate fluctuations or changes in the relative values of future assets like commodities. Sometimes swaps are done to hedge existing risk, and sometimes they are purely gambles on the direction the financial markets or commodities markets are heading.

There wasn't much demand for swaps, or for sophisticated risk management methods, until the 1970s. In the immediate aftermath of World War II, economists, financiers, corporate titans, and diplomats took the plausible view that the two world wars were largely attributable to economic uncertainty and instability. To mitigate these problems, and to solidify the U.S.'s post-war position as the leader of the free world, the U.S. hosted a conference of world leaders at the Mount Washington Hotel in Bretton Woods, New Hampshire, during the first three weeks of July 1944 as World War II continued to rage in Europe. This conference created the Bretton Woods Agreement, which immediately became the blueprint for world finance for the next quarter century. The two main features of the new financial order created by Bretton Woods were the establishment of major new institutions, the International Monetary Fund (IMF) and the International Bank for Reconstruction and Development, and the establishment of a system of stable, fixed exchange rates based on and tied to the U.S. dollar.

The Bretton Woods system remained in place until 1971, when the U.S. went off of the gold standard. Although some currencies continued to be linked informally to the U.S. dollar, many others were unlinked from the dollar. Some of these currencies were controlled by their issuing countries, and others became completely free-floating. This change, along with changes in U.S. banking regulations that allowed banks to offer competitive interest rates on checking accounts, savings accounts, and certificates of deposit, and the increased globalization of finance, led to much more competition, as well as much more risk, in the financial services industry. U.S. companies increasingly had to compete with both foreign rivals and domestic investment banks, all of which were less stringently regulated than U.S. commercial banks like Bankers Trust Company.

During this period the most important product offered by Bankers Trust and other large commercial banks was the commercial loan. Most of these banks' resources were deployed by making substantial commercial loans to their large corporate clients, such as railroads, manufacturing companies, airlines, and other big businesses. However, banks experienced a very large decline in the market for their loans. Increasingly, banks' best, most creditworthy customers would eschew commercial loans and instead obtain the funds they needed to run their businesses by selling short-term (90 days or less) promissory notes, a product known simply as "commercial paper."

A Depression-era law known as the Glass-Steagall Act prohibited banks from selling commercial paper to clients directly. So as the commercial paper market came to displace the commercial lending market as the primary source of credit for the largest and most important customers of the big banks, commercial banks like Bankers Trust began to suffer. Banks tried to make up this lost business by increasing their real estate lending and commodity-based lending and by making more loans overseas, particularly to less developed countries. These markets, however, turned out to be much more volatile and cyclical than traditional corporate lending, and banks like Bankers Trust simultaneously became less profitable and more risky. Bankers Trust was in an even worse position than many other big banks because it had exited the retail, consumer banking market. This market segment allowed many of Bankers Trust's large commercial bank rivals, such as Chemical Bank and Citibank, to continue to grow into the 1990s despite the many new challenges that had emerged.

Bankers Trust's salvation came from the ability of its management to transform advances in technology and financial theory into new ways to make money in an environment where the risks of its business could be measured, analyzed, and managed better than ever before. Although Bankers Trust's risk management applications did not have all the fancy bells and whistles of later permutations, "Sanford and his colleagues soon realized that it didn't take a highly developed, highly calibrated RAROC model to identify significant opportunities for improving performance."[9]

The naked swap previously described was used in conjunction with Bankers Trust's RAROC model to create the modern swaps industry. The extent to which Bankers Trust was a pioneer in both finance and technology is a critical, but largely unrecognized, chapter in U.S. history. As one industry participant cogently observed:

> In the early days of interest rate swaps, it could take several months to put together and execute a trade. Once a client with a particular interest was found, a counterparty with identically opposite needs had to be identified so the parties could be paired together in "back-to-back" transactions. Only at that point did the long and tortuous process of negotiating and agreeing on terms of the transaction and its price actually begin. The difficulty in finding both parties and negotiating the documentation for the transactions limited both the number and complexity of the trades.
>
> Since Bankers Trust had a trading culture and the ability to quantify risks explicitly with its RAROC methodology, in 1982-83 it began accepting one side of a trade on its own books before the other side was found (or maybe was never found). The bank then used market instruments to offset this risk and retained only the residual market risk resulting from imperfect hedges and counterparty credit risk. This innovation enabled its volume of trading activity to surge without requiring that the bank accumulate a significant amount of risk. It also enabled derivatives to be tailored to a customer's specific needs.[10]

Bankers Trust not only pioneered naked swaps, but also pioneered what now are called total return swaps, which are swaps in which the market risk of exchange rate or interest rate fluctuations as well as the credit risk of default are transferred. For example, in a traditional swap, a German company that sells trains in China can reduce or eliminate its foreign exchange risk by buying a swap that exchanges its expected stream of payments in yuan for the right to receive payments in, say, euros. In a total return swap the German company could buy a swap that would give it the right to receive payments even if the Chinese company defaulted on its own payments. In such swaps, the financial institution taking the other side of the swap became not only a counterparty to a contract in which streams of payments were promised, but also the guarantor of the performance of the German company's counterparty.

This performance guarantee makes the financial institution writing the swap contract into a guarantor, or insurer, of the payments to the German company by the Chinese company under the contract. Another kind of swap, the credit default swap, which is simply a promise to pay when a default or other "credit event" occurs, is a swap that involves only the credit guarantee and not the risk of interest rate or exchange rate fluctuations. As noted in Chapter 2, "Thriving the New Way: With Little or No Reputation—The Goldman Sachs Story," these Credit Default Swaps are like pure insurance contracts.

Bankers Trust's innovative RAROC models were used to analyze interest rate risk, foreign exchange risk (particularly important in the wake of the collapse of the Bretton Woods Agreement on fixed exchange rates), credit risk, management risk, operational risk, and liquidity risk.[11]

On the technology side, Bankers Trust deserves credit as the first major financial institution to develop and make available an early version of e-mail, a computer-based global communication system used within the bank, particularly among the bank's traders around the globe. By 1983, the system was in use by Bankers Trust worldwide: "Traders could alert one another to market events and developments so that 'real time' cross-market trading opportunities were created. Over time, these capabilities were developed to enable decision-making to be kept at the local level, where traders could respond quickly to client needs, while oversight was consolidated in a central location. With central oversight of a globally consolidated book, local traders were given discretion within risk parameters monitored by management."[12]

With its new technology, Bankers Trust was positioned to dominate any trading business in which it legally could compete, and

Bankers Trust sued to enter businesses from which it was barred, such as trading in commercial paper and underwriting and selling corporate equity and debt.

When mergers and acquisitions, particularly the risky variety known as leveraged buyouts (or LBOs), became popular in the 1980s, Bankers Trust was the market leader. LBOs are financings in which a group, often led by some of the company's own top managers, takes over a public company by buying up a majority of the company's stock. The buyout group in an LBO uses large amounts of debt (known as "leverage") to finance the purchase of a controlling interest in the business. The collateral needed to secure the loan is the assets of the business they are buying. Successfully participating as a lender in the LBO market requires a keen ability to measure risk.

Bankers Trust also became the world leader in the business of selling off commercial loans. Bankers Trust turned the commercial loan business into a business that earned profits in fees and by buying loans cheaply and selling them for a profit, rather than by making loans and sitting back and collecting the interest.

Bankers Trust's importance and prestige in the world financial sector became clear during New York City's financial crisis in 1975. Bankers Trust was a major underwriter of the City's municipal debt, particularly a form of short-term debt known as tax anticipation notes (TANs), which, as the name implies, are issued to provide short-term financing to municipalities in advance of their receipt of taxes from taxpayers. Bankers Trust refused to underwrite new securities being offered by New York City because the City was not able to certify conclusively what its cash position was at the time of the underwriting. The City's information was about a month old. In the past this sort of stale information was deemed acceptable by lenders, including Bankers Trust, but this was considered a risky practice because old TANs matured almost every month and almost every month new TANs with one-month maturities were being sold.

Here is one account:

> If the city could not make the representations required for the underwriting, [Sanford] was not prepared to put the bank at risk. He offered the lead position to any other bank in the syndicate that wished to take it. No institution stepped forward.

When the city published its financial reports several weeks later, it became evident that it did not have sufficient funds to redeem the notes, and the fabled New York City financial crisis unfolded.[13]

Bankers Trust's ability to use its own state-of-the art management tools to avoid the financial peril associated with the New York City financial crisis was a tremendous boon to the Bank's reputation. Bankers Trust's efforts to sell its risk tools beyond its own narrow customer base became highly successful. People wanted to do business with Bankers Trust. In 1977, Bankers Trust earned $20.1 million in revenues; by 1980, this number had more than quadrupled to $83.6 million.[14] As *Business Week* observed, "Bankers Trust's stunning success in the securities and investment area won it consulting work and provided solid bottom line profit."[15] With Bankers Trust Company's success, compensation levels within the company rose significantly. Bankers Trust abandoned the traditional, seniority-based compensation policies of the commercial banking industry and began paying on the investment banking model. Under this compensation model, the largest portion of many executives' compensation came in the form of bonuses, which, in the case of significant contributions to profitability, could be huge. Each department got money to put into its "bonus pool" and then distribute to employees based almost exclusively on the profitability of the department. In areas like bond trading, very successful employees could (and did) receive total compensation that exceeded that of the Chairman of the Board of the Bank.[16]

Bankers Trust's reputation for brilliant management in general and for brilliant management of risk exposure in particular also influenced regulators. In 1997, Bankers Trust became the first U.S. financial institution allowed by bank regulators to adjust its own capital levels on the basis of asset risk exposures calculated by its own models. This meant that, beginning in January 1998, when Banker's Trust Company determined that one of its assets was less risky than previously thought, the bank could reduce its capital by making dividend payments to shareholders or it could grow in size by making more loans or entering into more derivatives trades without the need to raise new capital to back those new ventures. This, of course, was a historic achievement.

At some point during this process, Bankers Trust began to think differently about its customers, and this was the beginning of the end for the company. For one thing, reputation risk was notably absent from the panoply of risks that Bankers Trust's RAROC models tried to measure. Reputational risk was a concept that does not appear to have factored into Bankers Trust's otherwise sophisticated analysis. This shortcoming led to the bank's complete downfall.

As *The Economist* pointed out,

> America's Bankers Trust liked to think of itself as...a modern investment bank. It boasted about its innovative trading strategies....And it boasted about its results: the bank made a net profit of over $1 billion in 1993.
>
> Such pride, however, came before an embarrassing fall. In April 1994 two...customers claimed that the bank had sold them high-risk, leveraged derivatives...without giving them an adequate warning of the potential pitfalls. Bankers Trust countered that the firms were trying to escape loss-making contracts by crying foul....The aggrieved customers sued the bank.[17]

The two clients that Bankers Trust was alleged to have cheated were among the most respected and iconic U.S. companies imaginable. The first, consumer goods firm Procter & Gamble (P&G), lost $195 million on two complex interest rate swap contracts. The second to be duped was the greeting card company Gibson Greetings. Both cases are worth studying.

Gibson Greeting Cards Versus Bankers Trust

Bankers Trust entered into a swap with the venerable greeting card company Gibson Greeting Cards that entitled Gibson to receive a then-above-market fixed rate of 5.5% and obligated Gibson to pay Bankers Trust a floating interest rate based on a benchmark interest rate called LIBOR. LIBOR is the "London Interbank Offered Rate," and it changes daily. At the time these loans were made, LIBOR reflected an average of the interest rates that the world's largest and most creditworthy banks charged one another for the short-term loans they made to each other on a daily basis. Although what Gibson owed Bankers Trust was based on LIBOR, the calculation of what was owed had a big twist on straight LIBOR. The contract called for Gibson to pay Bankers Trust an interest rate equal to LIBOR-squared, divided by 6%.

In this transaction, net payments remain in favor of Gibson for LIBOR up to almost 5.75%. In other words, if LIBOR is 5.5% on the day the relevant calculation is made, under the terms of the swap agreement Gibson Greetings must pay Bankers Trust only 5.05% interest on the nominal amount of the swap,[18] while receiving the better fixed rate of 5.5% provided for in the swap agreement. Under these interest rate conditions, Gibson Greetings made the difference between the 5.5% it received from Bankers Trust Company and the 5.05% that it paid to Bankers Trust Company, which translates into a profit of 45 basis points on the trade.[19] As LIBOR rose much above about 5.75%, however, the tables began to turn dramatically against Gibson Greetings.

Suppose, for example, that on the day of the swap, LIBOR was at 5.75%. At that juncture, Gibson would receive the 5.5% fixed rate called for in the swap agreement with Bankers Trust, and would be obligated to pay Bankers Trust 5.51%, or about the same amount. Suppose, though, that interest rates moved up just 1%, from 5.75% to 6.75%. Now Gibson is required to pay Bankers Trust at an interest rate of 7.59%, instead of 5.51%, a jump of over 200 basis points, or over two percentage points. On the other hand, if interest rates moved down 1% from 5.75% to 4.75%, Gibson would have to pay an interest rate of 3.76%, which is only 1.75% or 175 basis points lower than the 5.51% rate that Gibson had to pay when LIBOR was at 5.75%.

Moreover, when interest rate levels rise, Gibson's losses mount rapidly "since increases in LIBOR soon cause the floating-leg payments to rise more than twice as fast as the increase in payments on a simple LIBOR leg." For example, if interest rates go down by 300 basis points, from 5.75% to 2.75%, then Gibson would only have to pay Bankers Trust 1.26%,[20] for a savings of 425 basis points, or 4.25%. But a 300-basis-point increase in rates cost Gibson Greeting Cards an increase in interest payments of a whopping 725 basis points, or 7.25%, because Gibson's payment rate would go up from 5.51% to 12.76%.

So the structure was asymmetrical. As one risk expert described the Bankers Trust swap with Gibson Greeting Cards, "The question that must be asked of such a structure is what rationale does it have other than to hide the risk, which justifies a higher fixed rate, behind a haze of complexity."[21] Bankers Trust ultimately settled the case brought by Gibson Greeting Cards in January 1995, but only after Bankers Trust disclosed that it had found tape recordings that documented the fact that a managing director of the bank fraudulently claimed to Gibson that it risked losing less on the transaction than it actually did.

In retrospect, it is clear that Bankers Trust Company badly mishandled what turned out to be an existential threat to the company's survival. *The Economist* summed up the situation facing the bank during this period by noting that Mr. Sanford was "fighting hard to salvage the bank's reputation. As...the architect of the strategy that transformed Bankers Trust...into an aggressive financial powerhouse, his own reputation is also at stake."[22]

Stunningly, although *The Economist* clearly recognized the reputational risk that Bankers Trust Company was facing, the bank itself did not. Instead of worrying about its reputation, the big Wall Street bank's major concern was forcing its venerable middle-America customers to hold up their end of the swap contracts, regardless of how little they understood about these commitments and regardless of the extent to which Bankers Trust had induced these clients to enter into these trades by misleadingly or fraudulently representing the real risks associated with these transactions. According to Mr. Sanford, the market for swaps and other complex derivative instruments was growing. The only problem, according to Sanford, "is that people were using leveraged instruments to speculate. They won't do that again."[23] I believe that this is the most important quotation in this book and one well worth analyzing. Notice that Mr. Sanford does not say that "we" won't do that again. He is saying that they, the customers, won't do that again. If Mr. Sanford meant "no, they won't do business with Bankers Trust again and instead they will sue us and ruin our reputation so that virtually no other company will do business with us either," then he was correct. But this is not what he meant when he said, "They won't do that again." What Mr. Sanford meant, of course, was that these customers will not in the future trade in leveraged instruments like swaps that they do not fully understand.

In this colloquy, Mr. Sanford blames the customers for "speculating." There are a number of problems with this characterization. One problem is that Bankers Trust was speculating too. The only difference was that Bankers Trust knew what it was doing and neither Procter & Gamble nor Gibson Greetings did. So what Mr. Sanford apparently meant was this: "Stupid people like these counterparties should not speculate in derivatives, but we can because we are the smartest guys in the room." Not surprisingly, most objective observers and regulators viewed the clients as sheep and Bankers Trust Company as the big bad wolf.

An even more interesting feature about Mr. Sanford's comment is that he appears either not to know or not to care about certain important details of the transactions that his bank was doing. These details are highly relevant today, because they continue to characterize the way in which complex derivative transactions actually are done:

- Bankers Trust invented these swap products.
- There was no market price for these swaps.
- There was no market at all for these products.
- Bankers Trust explained the products to the customers.
- Bankers Trust sold these products by approaching these customers and convincing them that these products would be of some benefit to them.
- These products were sold for a price (payment was in the interest rate that Gibson received from Bankers Trust); calculating the price of these instruments was an extremely complicated endeavor that involved complex computer algorithms. The computer programs containing these algorithms were the property of Bankers Trust. Bankers Trust considered the programs highly proprietary and secret. They refused to disclose their valuation formulas or the computer programs themselves to their clients. In other words, the customers depended on Bankers Trust both to tell them what the financial products they had bought were worth *and* to tell them periodically precisely how much they had to pay Bankers Trust as a result of the agreements they had entered into with Bankers Trust.

It is difficult to imagine a contract in which trust is more important. Gibson Greeting Cards and Procter & Gamble, along with the rest of Bankers Trust Company's derivatives clients, bought extremely complex financial assets from Bankers Trust on the basis of Bankers Trust's own proprietary valuations of those assets. These financial instruments called on Bankers Trust to make periodic payments of money to the client and for the client to make periodic payments to Bankers Trust. Determining the amount of each payment required complex calculations that only Bankers Trust could make and that required the use of proprietary computer programs that Bankers Trust refused to share with the client. In other words, every month or every quarter when it came time for a client like Gibson Greeting Cards to make a payment to Bankers Trust under these financial contracts, Gibson relied on Bankers Trust to tell them how much they owed.

This sort of contract requires a great deal of trust between the contracting parties. And Bankers Trust was not trustworthy. As was observed in *The Economist,* "No other bank was more closely associated either with the derivatives business or with a profit-driven culture in which clients' interests often appeared to come second to the Bank's."[24]

Any doubt that Sanford really did mean to blame his bank's customers when he remarked that "the only problem is that people were using leveraged instruments to speculate" was removed emphatically when Bankers Trust allowed these disputes to go to litigation (other financial institutions quickly settled and tried to repair their relationships with their customers). And in the lawsuits, Bankers Trust argued that a strict rule of buyer beware (what lawyers refer to as "caveat emptor") should apply to its actions and that it was entitled to the billions of dollars its computer models said that it was owed under its various agreements with these customers.

Bankers Trust could not survive the loss of reputation associated with these deals, and it collapsed. At this particular time and in this particular case, the traditional reputational model worked exactly as the theory predicts: Bankers Trust needed its reputation to survive. It quickly lost its reputation in just a couple of deals by taking advantage of its customers. The fact that Bankers Trust had legal arguments to deploy in defense of its position was of no help. The legal niceties ultimately were not relevant. Bankers Trust never lost a case brought against it by its clients. Some of these clients actually ended up paying Bankers Trust on these contracts. Bankers Trust's problems had nothing to do with the legality of these contracts; it had everything to do with the message that these contracts communicated to the market about Bankers Trust's business practices.

As customers fled, Bankers Trust Company's profit tumbled and the company was forced to sell itself to Deutsche Bank, which ultimately jettisoned the now-tattered Bankers Trust name. In the financial quarter before selling itself to Deutsche Bank, Bankers Trust's earnings fell by 37%, to $140 million, attributable to lower revenues from its corporate finance unit, although the bank continued to do well in those sectors of its business, such as trading, that do not require much trust.

In anticipation of its sale to Deutsche Bank, Bankers Trust terminated its private client services group, and reshuffled its departments; brokerage, portfolio management, and traditional banking services for private clients were moved to a miscellaneous corporate unit. After the merger, Deutsche Bank moved several of Bankers Trust's high-trust activities, including global cash management, custody, investor services, and corporate trust and agency services, into a division of Deutsche Bank.

Procter & Gamble Versus Bankers Trust

Like Tolstoy's unhappy families, unhappy clients all seem to have their own distinct reasons for being unhappy.[25] Following this line, the trades between Bankers Trust and Procter & Gamble were different in certain noteworthy ways from the trades between Bankers Trust and Gibson Greeting Cards. In the midst of the ensuing litigation, Edwin Artzt, P&G's then-chairman, summed up his company's position very succinctly, making it clear that "the issue here is Bankers Trust's selling practices. There is a notion that end users of derivatives must be held accountable for what they buy. We agree completely, but only if the terms and risks are fully and accurately disclosed."[26]

Unlike Gibson Greeting Cards, which made no claim to great sophistication or experience in trading complex financial instruments like derivatives, the money management operation at Procter & Gamble, which operated under the direction of the Company's Chief Financial Officer, tried aggressively to manage the Company's currency and interest rate risk. They even tried on occasion to make money by trading just like the Wall Street investment banks did. In its trade with Bankers Trust, Procter & Gamble predicted that interest rates would fall. Unlike Gibson Greetings, it was P&G that sought out Bankers Trust asking that it manufacture interest rate swaps for it to buy.

After a great deal of back and forth in which P&G's finance team rejected Bankers Trust's proposed swap contracts, P&G and Bankers Trust reached an agreement in November 1993. The terms of the deal doubled, from $100 million to $200 million, the notional amount of the swap contracts. The deal was to last for five years.

Procter & Gamble's Obligations Under the Swap[27]

Here is a summary of the key terms of the financial contract between P&G and Bankers Trust:

- For the first six months of the deal, P&G agreed to pay a floating rate 75 basis points below commercial paper rates.
- For the 4 1/2 years after that, the floating rate was to be dictated by a "brain-twisting formula" whose components would include 5-year and 30-year Treasury rates as of May 4, 1994, the six-month anniversary of the deal. Under the best case for P&G, the floating rate would continue at 75 basis points below commercial paper rates for the full term of the swap.

Bankers Trust Company's Obligations Under the Swap

For all the deal's complexity, the gist of it can be stated quite simply: The swap had a "notional," or principal, value of $200 million. Assume that interest rates were as favorable to P&G as they possibly could be for the entire five-year periods. P&G would have saved 75 basis points for five years: On $200 million, that would be an interest rate savings of $1.5 million a year, for a total of $7.5 million. The annual savings would have cut P&G's interest bill, which runs around $500 million, by less than 1%.

And what risk did P&G accept in return for the hope of getting, at most, $1.5 million a year for five years from Bankers Trust Company? Bankers Trust agreed to pay nothing, but rather to "act as an insurer covering the risk of interest rate earthquakes."[28] In the beginning, these earthquakes actually occurred: Five-year Treasury rates rose from 5% in early November 1993 to 6.7% on May 4, 1994, a dramatic increase. P&G's other benchmark, 30-year Treasury rates, went from about 6% to 7.3%.

Things went so well for P&G in the beginning that the company entered into more swaps with Bankers Trust, essentially doing what gamblers call "doubling up." These swaps were all a bit different from one another, but all of them were based on a bet by P&G that interest rates would not go up significantly. For example, in one subsequent swap, P&G got a favorable floating interest rate for the first year of the swap and, "over its full term, offered the promise of about $940,000 in total savings if everything went right with a certain German interest rate. Procter & Gamble would save money if and only if the relevant German interest rate, which was 5.35% at the time, did not fall below 4.05% or rise above 6.10% at any point before April 14, 1995."[29]

The swap was called a "ring" because if the interest rate did fall below 4.05% or go above 6.10% at any point during this period, even for a day, the formulas to determine who owed what to whom changed dramatically (although the calculations remained complex). In other words, if the interest rate jumped outside of the ring, a whole new formula would be used to calculate how much P&G owed to Bankers Trust for the last 3 3/4 years of the five-year duration of the swap. If the interest rate jumped outside the "ring" between 4.05% and 6.10%, then another magic (and seemingly arbitrary) number came into play. This new magic number was 4.50%. If interest rates were outside the ring and above 4.50%, P&G was obligated to pay Bankers Trust the base rate of 5.35% for the first year plus a "spread." The spread was set at ten times the difference between 4.50% and the swap rate.

In early March 1994, the swap rate increased dramatically. It went outside of the ring and above 4.5%. P&G decided to renegotiate with

Bankers Trust and negotiate for a "lock-in interest rate" that would establish set rates that P&G would pay Bankers Trust for the duration of the swaps, thereby freeing itself from the risk that interest rates would go up still further.

P&G asserted in litigation that Bankers had repeatedly promised that it would offer P&G lock-ins at acceptable prices. P&G claimed, however, that when it tried to negotiate lock-ins with Bankers Trust, the bank claimed that it could not do so. In response to P&G's allegations that it could renegotiate, Bankers Trust responded that it "did not and could not represent in advance the cost to end these transactions prematurely. That [cost] necessarily would have to be based on the market when such a request is made."[30]

Bankers Trust also claimed that P&G's trades were so enormous that it had put on $3 billion in hedges to protect itself and that it could not unwind these hedges without disrupting the U.S. economy. P&G acceded to new terms dictated by Bankers Trust whereby P&G agreed to pay interest rates set at a staggering 1,412 basis points (14.12%) above the commercial paper rate for a certain period, and then to pay even more, at 1,640 basis points (16.40%) above the base rate specified by the swap.

In the ensuing litigation, Bankers Trust took the position that Procter & Gamble was a sophisticated counterparty that knew precisely the risks it was assuming. Procter & Gamble took the position that it trusted Bankers Trust and was fleeced. Perhaps both sides were right. The critical insight is that even if Bankers Trust was right, its caveat emptor business model did not work at the time. However, as the previous two chapters indicate, it might be working now.

The litigation was quite interesting, particularly because of the mountains of evidence that emerged in the discovery phase of the lawsuit. About 6,500 tapes and 300,000 pages of documents were presented in the litigation. Among the more widely reported and more salacious nuggets in this mountain of evidence were these:

- A conversation between two Bankers Trust employees in which one remarks that Procter & Gamble will "never be able to know how much money [in profits] was taken out of that [swap by Bankers Trust]." Her colleague replies, "That's the beauty of Bankers Trust."

- A videotaped *training session* for new Bankers Trust employees at which the instructor describes a hypothetical derivative transaction among Sony, IBM, and Bankers Trust and tells the students, "What Bankers Trust can do for Sony and IBM is get in the middle and rip them off—take a little money." This later was dismissed by the bank as "a very poor attempt at humor, but nothing more." One wonders whether Sony or IBM would have found this class as amusing as Bankers Trust did.

- An internal Bankers Trust document about a proposed derivative product for a client claims that Bankers Trust would make $1.6 million on the deal, including a "7 [basis point] rip-off factor."

- Two Bankers Trust employees are found on tape discussing a client's loss on a trade. One then tells the other, "Pad the number a little bit."

- In its lawsuit P&G quotes another precious nugget from the discovery process in which a Bankers Trust employee tells a colleague that they are in a "funny business, you know? Lure people into that calm and then just totally f—— 'em."

- In perhaps the most famous colloquy to emerge from discovery, one Bankers Trust employee is found asking another, "Do they [P&G] understand that? What they did?" His colleague responds, "No. They understand what they did but they don't understand the leverage, no."

- The admissions in the tapes include statements indicating that Bankers Trust, which controlled the calculations of how the payouts from the contract would be distributed, paid P&G only half of what its option was worth at one point. The employee making this observation observed that, at least for Bankers Trust, "this could be a massive huge future gravy train."

- The same employee calls one of the swaps with P&G "a wet dream."

- Another Bankers Trust salesman explains that P&G entered into a swap agreement with the bank because "we set 'em up."

- The tapes reveal that Bankers Trust employees had coined their own term, "ROF," which was an abbreviation for "Rip Off Factor."[31]

Even after these tapes were released, Bankers Trust took a very hard line in its litigation with Procter & Gamble, responding that

"P&G has...manufacture[d] a distorted view of transactions, markets, individuals, and the corporation...to serve its own objectives and to obscure P&G's own accountability."[32] But few agreed with Bankers Trust's perspective on the case. Other clients sued the bank with allegations similar to those of Gibson Greeting Cards and Procter & Gamble. The Securities and Exchange Commission, the Commodity Futures Trading Commission, and the Federal Reserve Bank of New York all investigated Bankers Trust's derivatives sales practices and fined, reprimanded, or censured the bank. Then, after the damning discovery, P&G filed a motion with the U.S. District Court in the Western Division of the Southern District of Ohio to add RICO (racketeer-influenced and corrupt organization) charges to its list of allegations against the bank. Bankers Trust continued to hold firm.

Hans Stoll, a well-regarded derivatives expert and finance professor at Vanderbilt University, observed that the swaps were simply "not something that a corporation that manufactures things should be involved in."[33] One could argue that Bankers Trust actually won the case because the case settled with Procter & Gamble agreeing to pay Bankers Trust $35 million, and Bankers Trust was never convicted of fraud or racketeering. It also settled its various cases with the SEC and the CFTC and other government entities.

Needless to say, Procter & Gamble, Gibson Greeting Cards, and other companies were not happy with Bankers Trust Company. But the ultimate reality is that while these horrific trades hurt the clients, they did not kill them. The clients survived. It was Bankers Trust that failed because it lost the trust of its customers. The key question is why Bankers Trust could not survive its loss of reputation when a mere 10 to 15 years later the companies that took its place at the epicenter of finance routinely survived scandals at least as serious as the ones that brought Bankers Trust to its knees.

This chapter discussed the rise and fall of Bankers Trust Company, a bank that became formidable in the 1980s before it swiftly collapsed as a result of an incurably tarnished reputation. Under the leadership of CEO Charles Sanford, Bankers Trust developed cutting edge risk-assessment techniques and pioneered complex derivative transactions known as swaps. However, Sanford also oversaw a shift in the bank's culture that emphasized profit over ongoing relationships with clients.

In the 1990s, Bankers Trust entered into swaps transactions with two prominent corporate clients, Gibson Greeting Cards and Procter & Gamble, serving as counterparties. These transactions dumped huge losses on the two clients, so they brought suit against Bankers Trust alleging that the bank had failed to warn them about the true risks of the transactions in which they were participating. Although the bank emerged from the litigation as the nominal victor, its reputation for client service had been destroyed, and it was sold to Deutsche Bank soon after.

Endnotes

1. Tina Gant, *International Directory of Company Histories*, vol. 2. (St. James Press, 2000); Bankers Trust Company, *Twenty-Five Years of Bankers Trust Company, 1902-1928* (New York: Bankers Trust Company, 1928); Fritz Redlich, *The Molding of American Banking* (New York: Johnson Reprint Corporation, 1968).

2. Funding Universe, "Bankers Trust New York Corporation: History," www.fundinguniverse.com/company-histories/bankers-trust-new-york-corporation-history/, accessed November 9, 2012.

3. The Commerce clause provides simply that Congress has the power "to regulate Commerce with foreign Nations, and among the several States, and with the Indian tribes." The Commerce Clause was considered an important part of the Constitution ever since the founding of the Republic. The Framers of the Constitution wanted to fix a major practical problem that exists in the absence of federal power to regulate commerce: the ability of states to pass anticompetitive, protectionist legislation that benefits local constituencies at the expense of out-of-state competitors like Bankers Trust Company. See the Federalist Papers No. 7, 39-41 (Hamilton); No. 11, 65-73 (Hamilton); No. 22, 135-137 (Hamilton); No. 42, 283-284 (Madison); No. 53, 362-364 (Madison). See also H. P. Hood & Sons, Inc. v. Du Mond, 336 U.S. 525, 533 (1949).

4. This quote, and much of the history of Bankers Trust Company, is taken from *International Directory of Company Histories*, vol. 2. (St. James Press, 1990).

5. Gene Guill, "Bankers Trust and the Birth of Modern Risk Management," Wharton School, the University of Pennsylvania, Financial Institutions Center Working Paper, March 2009, available from the Wharton School.

6. Peter Lee, "BT Looks to Sanford's Sorcery," *Euromoney,* January 1991, 24.

7. Guill, "Bankers Trust and the Birth of Modern Risk Management."

8. Ibid.

9. Ibid., 20.

10. Ibid., 31.

11. Ibid., 20.

12. Ibid., 21.

13. Ibid., 19.

14. Bankers Trust Annual Reports.

15. Wholesale Banking's Hard New Sale," *Business Week,* April 13, 1981, 84.

16. Guill, "Bankers Trust and the Birth of Modern Risk Management," 23.

17. "Blurred Vision," *The Economist,* April 8, 1995, 67-68.

18. $5.5^2/6 = 5.05$

19. A basis point is simply 1/100th of a percentage point.

20. $5.51\% - 3.0\% = 2.51\%$; and $2.51(2.75^2/6) = 1.05\%$.

21. David Rowe, "The Dangers of Complexity," Risk Analysis/ www.risk.net, April 2005, www.dmrra.com/publications/Risk%20Magazine/200504%20The%20Dangers%20of%20Complexity.pdf, accessed November 14, 2012.

22. Ibid.

23. Ibid.

24. Ibid.

25. As Tolstoy put it, "All happy families are alike; each unhappy family is unhappy in its own way." Leo Tolstoy, *Anna Karenina,* Chapter 1, p. 1.

26. Saul Hansell, "P&G Sues Bankers Trust over Swaps Deal," *The New York Times,* October 28, 1994, www.nytimes.com/1994/10/28/business/p-g-sues-bankers-trust-over-swap-deal.html, accessed November 15, 2012.

27. This account of the details of the swap arrangement is taken from the succinct account by Carol Loomis, Suzanne Barlyn, and Kate Ballen in "Untangling the Derivatives Mess They Didn't Melt Down the Financial System. But These Red-Hot Instruments Proved Too Tempting for Both Buyers and Sellers. This Is the Story of How Lies, Leverage, Ignorance—and Lots of Arrogance—Burned Some Big Players," *Fortune,* March 20, 1995, http://money.cnn.com/magazines/fortune/fortune_archive/1995/03/20/201945/index.htm.

28. Ibid.

29. Ibid.

30. Hansell, "P&G Sues Bankers Trust Over Swaps Deal."

31. Kelley Holland and Linda Himelstein, "The Bankers Trust Tapes," *Business Week,* October 16, 1995.

32. Ibid.

33. Loomis, Barlyn, and Ballen, "Untangling the Derivatives Mess."

4

Individual Reputation Unhinged from the Firm: Hardly Anybody Goes Down with the Ship

This chapter describes how individual reputation has become distinct from firm reputation. First, it presents the fall of Salomon Brothers as one final example of how the old reputational model used to work. Under that model, unethical or illegal behavior resulted in the collapse both of the firm and of individual employees' careers. Next, this chapter introduces Michael Milken and Drexel Burnham Lambert to highlight three false assumptions of the old model. First, the old model assumed that cheaters never prosper; however, Milken and his colleagues walked away from the wreckage of Drexel with many millions of dollars. Second, it assumed that employees always go down with the ship; however, Milken and his colleagues continued their lucrative careers elsewhere. Finally, it assumed that one's "reputation" combines both corporate and individual facets into a single, unitary thing; instead, despite Drexel's failure, Milken is still revered in many circles.

The traditional reputational model was put to the test by the sales practices of Bankers Trust, and the traditional model passed with flying colors. The reputational model does not predict that big sophisticated financial institutions will never try to fleece their customers. Rather, the reputational model simply predicts that companies like Bankers Trust or Goldman Sachs take a major risk when they try to fleece their customers. That big risk is that the firm doing the swindling and selling will get caught, and that other customers, fearing that they too will be swindled, will shun the real or alleged swindler, leading to major losses and perhaps, like Bankers Trust, to the ultimate demise of the company.

So how do similar titans of Wall Street continue to thrive when venerable progenitors like Bankers Trust and Salomon Brothers disappeared as a direct consequence of the lost reputations that resulted from precisely the same conduct that these firms engage in routinely? An important part of the puzzle is the relationship between reputation and litigation.

Neither Bankers Trust nor Salomon Brothers was litigated out of existence. Bankers Trust was named in many lawsuits as well as in several regulatory enforcement actions by the SEC and the CFTC, but the settlements and fines it paid did not, in and of themselves, threaten Bankers Trust's existence. And far from admitting wrongdoing, Bankers Trust took the position that its clients' losses should be blamed on the clients, who agreed to transactions that they did not understand.

The same is true for Salomon Brothers, another giant, prestigious firm that eventually disappeared without a trace after its reputation disintegrated. Dozens of articles and several books were devoted to the toxic culture at Salomon.[1] One book, *Bonfire of the Vanities,* was a devastating account of life inside a fictional company based on Salomon Brothers. Martin Mayer's book *Nightmare on Wall Street: Salomon Brothers and the Corruption of the Marketplace* is clearly based on the old reputational model. Mayer's basic point was that when the firm's traders manipulated the government bond market in a $10 billion scandal, "they destroyed not only their careers but the reputation of their house in a business where reputation is everything."[2]

In this lies a key to the puzzle. In the old world in which Bankers Trust and Salomon Brothers rose and fell, people conceived of individual and corporate reputations as being inexorably linked, just as Mayer noted. When Salomon Brothers fell, individual careers fell along with it. The people running Salomon Brothers were larger-than-life, even cultish figures—particularly the company's CEO John Gutfreund, its chief economist and oracle Henry Kaufmann, and its bond trading genius Lewis Ranieri. These individuals were closely linked to their firms. The personality and reputation of Salomon Brothers reflected the personalities of these individuals. Without such figures, or equally charismatic and confidence-inspiring replacements, Salomon could not survive. In 1991, when John Gutfreund resigned in the midst of the scandals that rocked the firm, another iconic financier, Warren Buffett, took over the firm. Mayer observes, "If Warren Buffet had not been available to lead Salomon Brothers in August 1991, the firm would have gone under that fall. Foreign banks had already begun to cancel their credit lines to Salomon."[3]

The dramatic fall of Salomon Brothers is perhaps even more epic than the fall of Bankers Trust Company. Bankers Trust had transformed itself over time from a stodgy trust bank to a full-fledged commercial bank to a state-of-the-art investment bank. One might reasonably conclude that transformation in the cultural and ethical norms at Bankers Trust simply accompanied the changes in the bank's strategic focus and business model.

The same cannot be said of Salomon Brothers. For at least three decades, from the 1960s to the early 1990s, Salomon Brothers was the Goldman Sachs of its time. As at Goldman, the best and the brightest Ivy League college graduates flocked there to mingle with the "rocket scientists," the quantitative geniuses from MIT and Caltech, and the gruff traders who had risen, often without the benefit of a college education, from the mailroom or some such place to the trading floor. Salomon Brothers was considered to be the most innovative and aggressive trading firm in the world. Not surprisingly, the traders ran the business during this period. Just as Bankers Trust contributed to the modern world of finance by developing the RAROC model and many important derivatives, including an early form of the Credit-Default Swap, an infamous Salomon Brothers senior trader named Lewis Ranieri was the first to see the enormous, economy-transforming potential of mortgage-backed securities. He is known as the father of mortgage finance. Ranieri's role in mortgage finance was such that in 2009, two decades after he had left Salomon Brothers, Ranieri was selected as one of the people who "Led Us Down the Road to Ruin in the Greatest Financial Crisis Since the Great Depression" in a newspaper poll in which readers were asked who was responsible for the 2007–2008 financial crisis.[4] In this poll, readers put Ranieri ahead of notorious figure Christopher Dodd, the ethically challenged chairman of the Senate banking committee, Joseph Cassano, who led the credit-default swaps team at AIG and whose losses led to the biggest bailout in U.S. history and to a government takeover of AIG, and even ahead of Dick Fuld, whose aggressive approach to business led to the extinction of another great investment bank, Lehman Brothers.

A number of subtle changes in the structure of the finance industry collectively killed the old reputational model. One critical difference between today and the Salomon Brothers/Bankers Trust Company era was that Salomon Brothers and Bankers Trust were creating entirely new businesses, and these businesses were truly enormous in scale. Salomon created the modern mortgage finance industry and the idea of computer-based trading. Bankers Trust Company created the modern approach to risk measurement that now is used all over the world. And, of course, they pioneered the use of the swap as a tool not just for hedging existing risk, but for creating new investment opportunities and entirely new risks. These firms were alone at the top of their industries, just as Drexel was alone at the top of the junk bond industry just before it came crashing down.

The story of Bankers Trust was told in some detail in the preceding chapter; this chapter contains accounts of what occurred at Salomon Brothers and Drexel. These stories will be brief because the stage has already been set: A brilliant, innovative firm led by a strong, charismatic trader creates a new industry and then rises to the top of it. But by now, you already know the ending: These companies could not hold onto their reputations as their businesses evolved, and after brief periods of market dominance, these firms became extinct when their reputations were destroyed.

Salomon Brothers was John Gutfreund's firm. Just as Bankers Trust was a company that reflected the vision, and the aggressive trading mentality, of its CEO, Charles Sanford, Salomon Brothers reflected the similar mentality of its leader, John Gutfreund.[5] As one journalist observed, "It was under Gutfreund's watch that everything started to fall apart."[6] The scandal involved big-rigging in the huge market for U.S. government bonds. In August 1990, Paul Mozer, a Salomon Brothers government bond trader, attempted to corner the market for U.S. sovereign debt, an act of incredible hubris, and a demonstration of just how powerful and dominant the Salomon Brothers trading operation was at the time.

At the time of Mozer's trades, the U.S. Treasury had a rule forbidding any single bidder from acquiring more than 35% of the securities sold in a single auction. Mozer was caught and mildly reprimanded by the firm. Just over a year later, in May 1991, Salomon Brothers tried to corner the market again. Embarrassed by its earlier failure to act against Salomon Brothers, and the attendant bad publicity, the SEC acted this time. The SEC fined Salomon $290 million, the highest fine it had ever levied against a financial services firm.

The reputational market worked much faster than the SEC. By August 1991, Gutfreund had resigned. The firm was on the verge of bankruptcy. Legendary investor Warren Buffett, who had a major stake in the firm, stepped in and took over. Buffett was well aware from the start that in order to restore the business he had to bring clients back, and in order to bring clients back he had to restore Salomon's tarnished reputation. As Buffett observed in testimony at a hearing before the House of Representatives' Committee on Energy and Commerce, shortly after assuming office, "Lose money for the firm and I will be understanding; lose a shred of reputation for the firm and I will be ruthless."[7]

The rest of Buffett's observations also are of use to those of us who study reputation. Buffett also observed that he was taking

> actions that I believe will make Salomon the leader within the financial services industry in controls and compliance procedures. But in the end, the spirit about compliance is as important or more so than words about compliance. I want the right words and I want the full range of internal controls. But I also have asked every Salomon employee to be his or her own compliance officer. After they first obey all rules, I then want employees to ask themselves whether they are willing to have any contemplated act appear the next day on the front page of their local paper, to be read by their spouses, children, and friends, with the reporting done by an informed and critical reporter.[8]

These are among Warren Buffett's most-often-quoted remarks. His point is that employees should not take any action, even if they think that it is within the law, if they would be embarrassed if their family and friends were to learn of it, or if they would be unhappy to see a description of the action in their local newspaper. Equally important is Buffett's explicit recognition that what was wrong within Salomon Brothers was the company's culture. This is noteworthy because few people at the time recognized the important fact that companies such as Bankers Trust, Goldman Sachs, and Salomon Brothers are not just businesses; they are organic communities with their own cultures and their own norms.

What Mr. Buffett did not fully seem to comprehend, however, was how deeply entrenched established norms and cultures can be within a company, and how concomitantly difficult and time-consuming the task of changing people's values and attitudes generally is. In other words, by focusing on Salomon Brothers' damaged reputation, Warren Buffett accurately diagnosed the disease within the company. Curing the disease, however, can turn out to be a very costly, herculean task. Often, as was the case with Salomon Brothers, the patient does not survive the attempt.

Business ethicists attribute the downfall of Salomon Brothers to "its culture, which was directed by the controversial CEO, John Gutfreund. Gutfreund's leadership style helped to mold a corporate culture that eventually resulted in unethical and illegal behavior by its members.... Gutfreund's leadership led to a culture that was tailor-made for greedy and power-hungry employees whose commitment to ethical behavior was suspect."[9]

Salomon Brothers' problem was that their clients stopped trusting them. They developed a reputation for taking advantage of clients and putting their own interests ahead of the people and companies that traded with them. This, of course, is exactly what happened to Bankers Trust. And as was the case with Bankers Trust, Salomon Brothers could not survive the loss of its reputation as an honest counterparty.

Despite their differences, Bankers Trust and Salomon Brothers both were venerable firms with long-standing reputations. In contrast, Drexel Burnham Lambert, the subject of the subsequent chapter, was a young upstart in the world of finance that, at least for a time, fought its way to the top of the industry, becoming the dominant firm in a major new industry, the underwriting, selling, and trading of junk bonds. Under the charismatic leadership of a single trader, the infamous Michael Milken, Drexel rose from obscurity to become the fifth-largest investment bank in the U.S. Shortly after reaching this pinnacle, the firm was forced out of business when it was prosecuted for manipulating the securities it was selling. Drexel, unlike

Bankers Trust and Salomon Brothers, did not fail on its own. It was forced out of business by regulators and the U.S. Department of Justice, which brought criminal charges against it and its most important employee, Michael Milken. Ultimately, Milken pleaded guilty to six felony counts and paid $650 million in fines. The firm was bankrupt not long after, and Michael Milken went to jail.

It was after the fall of Drexel that reputation ceased to matter. Three critical lessons emerged from the Drexel scandal. These lessons revealed seismic faults in the traditional theory of reputation. And these lessons still hold true today and explain why reputation no longer matters to survival and how firms that apparently lack any reputation at all continue not only to survive but to thrive.

Flaw Number One: Cheaters Never Prosper

The first critical flaw in the traditional theory of reputation that the Drexel scandal revealed was the assumption that sharp business practices were only mildly profitable. Drexel showed what we know today: Sharp practices can be enormously profitable. The old theory of reputation was based on the premise that the gains to a business from cheating a particular customer inevitably would be small. Because these relatively small gains inevitably would be less than the costs associated with the reputational loss to the company, rational firms would not cheat their customers.

But Drexel showed that the gains from cheating could be much larger than adherents to the old reputation theory ever had imagined. Modern cheaters potentially can benefit by way of promotions, massive bonuses, and other remuneration that can reach hundreds of billions of dollars. There is even a name for this new kind of massive remuneration: "legacy wealth." Previously, when one thought about compensation on Wall Street, one thought in terms of becoming wealthy, or even very wealthy. Today, when one thinks of a Michael Milken or a Lloyd Blankfein, one thinks of legacy wealth—that is, wealth that is sufficient not only to allow one to live comfortably for one's life, but also to leave sufficient wealth (after taxes) for all one's family to live well in perpetuity on the interest (or even on the interest on the interest). The old model of reputation did not take into account this rather alarming possibility.

Flaw Number Two: You Will Go Down with the Ship

Another flaw in the traditional theory of reputation that we can observe by studying the Drexel scandal is that just as the benefits of cheating were far greater than people previously had thought, the costs of cheating were far less. Two rather amazing facts emerged from the Drexel scandal. First, people can work for companies that had imploded in swindling and cheating scandals and not only survive but thrive, moving on to work for other companies in the same business. Second, and even more astounding, not only are the people who work for firms involved in scandals able to move on to similar work at other companies, but the scandals do not even destroy the futures of the people involved in the scandals.

In other words, the Drexel scandal proved that people's personal reputations are no longer firmly and inexorably linked to the reputations of the firms they work for. Prominent and successful investment bankers, lawyers, and accountants at major national accounting firms now have their own reputations that are entirely separate and distinct from the reputation of the firm with which they are associated. Financial professionals operate under a set of incentives entirely unanticipated by the traditional economic theory of reputation. Under the traditional theory, there was no separation between the reputation of an individual professional and the reputation of the firm for which that professional worked.

In the old days, a professional at a firm tainted by scandal was thought to "go down with the ship." Historically, when information technology was primitive and accurate information about an individual's integrity and competence was difficult to obtain, people's reputations were tied much more closely to the reputations of their firms. Potential clients or regulators or journalists, for example, might never have heard of a single lawyer at a great law firm like Cravath,

Swaine & Moore or Davis Polk & Wardwell, but they knew the firms by reputation and they were confident in drawing inferences about the individual professionals within those firms on the basis of those reputations. Today, of course, potential clients as well as regulators and journalists need not rely on drawing inferences from a firm's reputation in order to reach conclusions about the reputations of particular professionals within the firm. Rather, using databases and modern information technology, one can penetrate the reputational veil of a particular company or firm that offers services within the financial markets, and obtain detailed, particularized information about the individual professional with whom one is working. In other words, on Wall Street, personal reputation has replaced firm reputation as the relevant analytical point of reference. An important implication of advances in technology that have reduced the costs of obtaining information about individuals is that it has made the reputations of companies and firms less important. Somebody who works at Goldman Sachs, for example, might care about the reputation of that firm, but she will care even more about her own reputation. More importantly, should the firm for which one works collapse, as did Arthur Andersen, a major international accounting firm, or Enron, the energy trading firm that imploded in a wave of accounting scandals, individuals untouched by the scandal can move on, often seamlessly, to equivalent jobs in other firms.

The folks involved in the scandals keep the money. Sure, fines have to be paid, and lawyers have to be paid. But swindling often is so enormously profitable that massive piles of money remain. And these piles of money provide a strong incentive to cheat, because not only is getting away with it incredibly profitable, but getting caught is not as bad as people used to think.

This point is strongly reinforced by the demise of regulatory enforcement as a strong, clear reputational signal. For decades, being named as a defendant in a lawsuit for fraud was a devastating blow to one's reputation. Even worse for one's reputation than being named as a defendant in a civil suit was being named as a defendant in a civil suit brought by the U.S. Securities and Exchange Commission, the once-prestigious government agency in charge of regulating the securities industry, including not just investment banks, but also the accountants, financial professionals, and lawyers who "practice before the SEC." Worst of all, of course, was being named as a defendant in a criminal indictment brought by the Department of Justice or by a state prosecutor.

Although the reputational fallout—not to mention the practical repercussions—of being named as a defendant in a criminal indictment is still enormous, civil litigation, even when brought by the SEC, has lost much if not all of its shaming effect on many financial market participants. The vast majority of cases settle. And, for reasons of its own, for years the SEC has permitted defendants to settle even the most seemingly heinous cases without acknowledging that they did anything wrong. Because litigation is so expensive, even huge monetary settlements can be explained away on the grounds that they permit the defendant to "concentrate on its core business" and to "avoid costly and distracting litigation." This has allowed major financial companies to avoid taking any responsibility or blame even for apparently egregious misdeeds. As law professor Peter Henning observed of the SEC's litigation strategy:

> The SEC policy regarding settlements allows the agency to announce a victory, while the defendant does not acknowledge a defeat, so the settlement cannot be used against it by private plaintiffs. It is, if you will, the best of both worlds—the case is concluded favorably for the SEC, which usually issues a news release promoting the penalties, while the defendant does not suffer the consequences of an adverse judgment.[10]

The loss of the "shaming" effect of civil lawsuits has not gone unnoticed. In a highly publicized opinion, a New York District Court judge announced that he was frustrated with business as usual. In a highly unusual move, the judge refused to approve a settlement between the SEC and Citigroup concerning the bank's sale of mortgage-backed securities that reportedly cost investors almost $700 million in losses while the bank garnered a profit of about $160 million.[11] As Professor Henning pointed out:

> The SEC settles most cases, and the resolution usually involves neither an admission nor denial of liability by the defendant, even if a civil penalty is assessed and an injunction issued that prohibits future violations of federal securities laws. It is this failure to have any acknowledgment of wrongdoing that has

gotten under Judge Rakoff's skin, leading him to reject the settlement because it "is neither fair, nor reasonable, nor adequate, nor in the public interest."[12]

The reputations of the individuals who work within companies in the financial world are almost entirely unlinked from the reputations of the companies that employ them. People can work for firms that implode in a tsunami of scandal and, as long as they are not literally in prison or otherwise physically incapable of other employment, after the implosion they calmly and effortlessly move on to other, similar employment. This, of course, makes people much less interested in the reputations of the companies they work for and much less worried about what their colleagues are doing. In other words, it is not that reputation is entirely irrelevant. It is merely that in the financial world, firm reputation is no longer the focal point of reputational analysis.

Another reason firm reputation has been displaced by individual reputation is that, historically, investment banks, law firms, and accounting firms were organized as general partnerships. The hundreds of leading professionals within major firms were general partners under this legal structure. As such, in the old days when a law firm, an accounting firm, or an investment bank failed, people would not just go down with the ship figuratively, in the sense that their reputations would drop with the reputation of the firms for which they worked. Back then—and the importance of this point can scarcely be emphasized strongly enough—financial professionals *literally* would go down with their firms because, as general partners, they would be personally liable, up to the full value of all of their personal assets. Whatever they owned, including but not limited to their homes, cars, yachts, airplanes, helicopters, art, financial and real estate investments, wine cellars, etc., was available to creditors if the companies they worked for became insolvent or were in any way unable to pay their creditors. Investment banks, accounting firms, and law firms were all general partnerships. With this sort of potential liability, it is hardly surprising that all the professionals in the financial firms of the past took an intense interest—and invested considerable resources— in monitoring and other activities that would reduce the risk that the company might fail.

The traditional theory of reputation posits that individuals within firms would invest considerable resources to make sure that their companies stayed well within ethical and legal boundaries in order to protect their own reputations, which were linked symbiotically with the reputations of the companies where they worked. During this period, however, professionals had a separate and distinct motivation for working hard to keep their companies on the straight and narrow path of righteousness: Their own wealth was at stake, because if the firm imploded like Arthur Andersen in 2003, Lehman Brothers in 2008, or law firm Dewey & LeBoeuf LLP in 2012, they were on the hook. All of these firms were, at one time, general partnerships. And each of these firms imploded in a wave of scandal and recrimination that resulted directly from the diminution in monitoring and oversight—and the dramatic increase in risk taking—that was a direct result of the end of the era of the general partnership.

Thanks to significant lobbying, investment banks were allowed first to transform themselves from general partnerships into closely held corporations, and then they were allowed to sell their stock to the investing public, becoming public companies. When the big investment banks like Goldman Sachs, Lehman Brothers, and Morgan Stanley morphed from the general partnership form of business organization into corporations, the partners became shareholders. They were personally responsible only for their own conduct.

While these firms were closely held corporations, and the top officials in these companies owned sizable blocks—indeed, virtually all—of the stock in their own firms, they still stood to lose millions, and sometimes hundreds of millions, of dollars if their firms failed. So they had strong incentives to monitor the performance of their companies. But gradually the big investment banks sold majority interests in themselves to public investors not associated with the company. The bankers claimed that they needed to go public in order to obtain the capital necessary to expand and to remain competitive in increasingly competitive global financial markets. This was the justification that companies like Lehman Brothers and Goldman gave for going public. The individual bankers within these firms claimed that they had to sell sizable portions of their own holdings of stock to the public in order to gain the benefits of diversification and to ameliorate the problems associated with having their savings—their financial capital—tied up in the same firm in which they had invested their professional lives—their human capital.

After these firms went public, they were operated precisely as economic theory predicted. Many of the new managers (who were the former general partners) of these investment banks were transformed overnight from being rich to having enormous "legacy wealth" by virtue of selling their own shares in the company's initial offering of shares to the public. This new wealth was immune from the prying hands of creditors of the investment banks, because these businesses were now corporations rather than general partnerships. These changes created strong new incentives for increased risk taking. These incentives to take risk were exacerbated still further by the fact that the managers of the newly publicly held investment banks now had diversified portfolios, so they were far more insulated from personal financial loss caused by declines in the values of their shares in the companies they worked for.

The transformation of law firms and accounting firms into limited liability partnerships and limited liability corporations was just as dramatic as the metamorphosis of investment banks into public companies. These were new forms of business organizations that enabled the equity owners (still called "partners," or sometimes "members") to avoid personal liability for their firm's and their partners' tort and contract obligations. Statutes permitting these new forms of business organization were enacted in the early 1990s explicitly as a shield against liability. The political pressure for these new statutes came from well-heeled lawyers and accountants who wanted to avoid personal liability for the professional misconduct of their colleagues.

As Robert Hamilton has observed, these new forms of business organization were "a direct outgrowth of the collapse of real estate and energy prices in the late 1980s, and the concomitant disaster that befell Texas's (and other states) banks and saving and loan associations.... Suits were brought...against hundreds of shareholders, directors and officers of failed financial institutions. However, the amounts recovered were small (because these companies were insolvent)... and attention quickly turned to the roles of the lawyers and accountants who had represented the failed institutions.... As a result, several highly reputable law firms...found themselves in deep trouble because of their bank and thrift work during the 'salad days' of the 1980s."[13]

A simple way of putting all of this is to say that all the predictions and implications of the old theory of reputation were strongly reinforced by the liability system that existed at that time. Managers of investment banks wanted to protect their reputations and avoid financial ruin. The way to accomplish both of these goals was to make very sure that the companies where they worked did not take excessive risks and did not implode in a wave of legal or financial scandal.

Flaw Number Three: Corporate Reputation and Individual Reputation Are the Same

The third flaw in the traditional theory of reputation revealed by the Drexel scandal is the assumption that people and companies have a single, unitary reputation. Under the traditional theory of reputation, a reputation is like any other asset: It rises and declines in value in a holistic, unitary way.

Under the traditional approach to reputation, one could, at least in theory, assign a dollar value to reputation: A person who worked for a low-prestige firm would earn less than a person with the same knowledge, work ethic, and talents (what economists would call the same "marginal productivity") who worked at a high-prestige firm because the person working in the high-prestige firm would be able to charge a premium to customers. Customers were willing to pay such a premium because the risks of doing business with the high-prestige firm were significantly less. This account is basically true, but it is very incomplete because it does not capture the reality that in finance, just as in other walks of life, the people who work in firms today exist in several entirely distinct communities.

One might say that people live in a number of different worlds. Their families and close friends constitute one world. Their broader social circle constitutes another world. People who read about finance and follow the SEC's enforcement agenda and form opinions from a distance constitute still another world. And one can be viewed in very distinct ways within each of these worlds. The loss of one's "reputation" that comes from a devastating exposé in a major newspaper or blog often represents the loss of reputation in only a single, distant world. One's day-to-day life among friends, family, and colleagues often is quite a different thing.

One can think of modern investment bankers, top corporate lawyers, and their immediate cohort as a community, with its own culture and norms that are entirely distinct from those that exist outside. These communities are almost entirely insular. The CEO of Goldman Sachs and a prominent financier like Michael Milken have reputations in the small, private worlds they inhabit that are entirely different from the reputations they have in the larger world reached by CNN or MSNBC.

This phenomenon has been recognized in other contexts before. Perhaps most notably, the sociologist Robert Bogdan has studied the lives of the people who inhabited the world of the circus freak shows that were a major facet of American urban and rural life and among the most popular forms of entertainment from about 1840 to about 1940. The stars of these shows were dwarfs, giants, Siamese twins, bearded ladies, people purportedly composed of heads but no torsos, morbidly obese people, and many other highly distinctive individuals.[14] But, as Bogdan observes, the stars of these circus shows did not think of themselves as freaks. Moreover, these performers lived in their own, distinct social environments. In their own worlds, these performers were considered freaks only by the "rubes" in the audience. At home, in the small towns where they lived, and above all, in the communities they formed among themselves, their abnormalities were ignored and they were people just like any other.

The same truth holds for the modern financier. The top Wall Street deal maker might be viewed by the public as a grotesque vision of avarice and criminality, but that is not the world the deal maker actually inhabits. At home in the world the deal maker actually inhabits, at the club, at work among colleagues and competitors, the deal maker is a highly respected and venerated member of the community.

It is this sociological fact that explains the constant stream of embarrassing e-mails in which financiers refer to their customers as "muppets" and brag about how their customers really do not understand the risks involved in the complex financial instruments they are buying. Similarly, Goldman trader Fabrice Tourre, who referred to himself as "Fabulous Fab," was talking to a very close group of friends within the industry when he sent an e-mail pointing out what Wall Street insiders and few others knew in early 2007:

> More and more leverage in the system. The whole building is about to collapse anytime now.... Only potential survivor, the fabulous Fab[rice Tourre]...standing in the middle of all these complex, highly leveraged, exotic trades he created without necessarily understanding all of the implications of those monstruosities!!! [sic][15]

The fact that Wall Street executives live entirely in a world of their own also explains how Lloyd Blankfein, the CEO of Goldman Sachs, was able to describe his work and that of his firm as "God's work" just as his company was about to pay an almost unimaginable $20 billion in compensation to its top executives.[16]

When Blankfein's "God's work" quotation appeared on the front page of the *Financial Times*, the Goldman Sachs public relations team dismissed the remark as merely a lighthearted, tongue-in-cheek throwaway line. But it really wasn't. Blankfein made his remark on November 11, 2009. On October 20, 2009, less than a month before Blankfein's remark, his Goldman colleague Brian Griffiths spoke at St. Paul's Cathedral on the topic "What Is the Place of Morals in the Marketplace?" He went into quite a bit more detail about what it means for an investment banker to do God's work, arguing that when bankers do what is in their own self-interest they actually are helping others: "The injunction of Jesus to love others as ourselves is a recognition of self-interest," Griffiths said, according to Bloomberg News, which noted how his voice echoed around the 365-foot-high domed church's gold-mosaic walls. "We have to tolerate...inequality as a way to achieving greater prosperity and opportunity for all."[17]

Not surprisingly, Griffiths's remarks, like Blankfein's subsequent, more succinct observation, were highly controversial. A responsive article in *Psychology Today* arguing that great inequality is an evil in and of itself observed that people rightly were and should be outraged by this sort of remark: "Wall Street's largest banks turn a taxpayer-funded bailout into [giant] bonuses...while millions of working people lose their jobs and their homes. It's not only the unemployed and homeless who should be outraged."[18]

It is overly simplistic to envision Wall Street bankers as completely avaricious predators who rob their customers in order to help themselves. Often, while Wall Street bankers are enriching themselves, they also are enriching certain favored customers at the expense of other, less-favored customers. When Bankers Trust and Salomon failed, it was because they lost the trust of all of their customers. These firms did not appear to have any favored customers. All customers were "marks."

But Goldman does appear to have some customers who are more favored than others. And as long as a customer manages to stay on the favored list, the profits can be enormous. Chapter 2, "Thriving the New Way: With Little or No Reputation—The Goldman Sachs Story," contained an account of how two apparently less-favored (former) Goldman clients, Deutsche Industriebank AG and Royal Bank of Scotland N.V., wound up losing an enormous amount of money when Goldman sold them the wrong side of big bets on pools of mortgages with the hedge fund Paulson & Company, which Goldman appeared to favor. Unbeknown to its European bank clients, Goldman allowed Paulson to participate in the selection of the very assets it was going to bet would decline in value. While Deutsche Industriebank AG and Royal Bank of Scotland N.V. were hurt badly in the transactions, Goldman Sachs and Paulson both did well. And one must presume that Paulson was happy with the "services" it received from Goldman.

Many, many customers were also very happy with the services they received from Michael Milken and Drexel. Michael Milken is the inventor of what is today the multibillion-dollar junk bond industry. And his story marks the sea change in the world of finance from a world in which reputation was king to today's world, in which reputation is largely, if not wholly, irrelevant.

This chapter demonstrated how an individual's reputation has become unhinged from the reputation of the firm for which the person works. Unlike at Salomon Brothers, where a diminished reputation led to the total collapse of the firm, employees at Drexel Burnham Lambert were able to continue their careers elsewhere. The Michael Milken and Drexel tragedy revealed three key flawed assumptions in the old reputational model: (1) that cheaters never prosper; (2) that employees will always go down with the ship; and (3) that corporate and individual reputations are joined into a single, unitary thing. All three of these assumptions are false.

Endnotes

1. Michael Lewis, *Liar's Poker: Rising through the Wreckage on Wall Street, New York: W. W. Norton, 1989;* Martin Mayer, *Nightmare on Wall Street: Salomon Brothers and the Corruption of the Marketplace,* New York: Simon & Schuster, 1993.

2. Martin Mayer, *Nightmare on Wall Street: Salomon Brothers and the Corruption of the Marketplace*, New York: Simon & Schuster, 1993.

3. Ibid., 221.

4. The Guardian, "Who Led Us Down the Road to Ruin?" January 6, 2009, www.guardian.co.uk/business/poll/2009/jan/26/road-to-ruin-recession.

5. Ronald Sims and Johannes Brinkman, "Leaders as Moral Role Models: The Case of John Gutfreund at Goldman Sachs," *Journal of Business Ethics* 35 (2001): 327-339.

6. Carol Hojnicki, "The Spectacular Rise and Fall of Salomon Brothers," *Business Insider,* July 3, 2012, www.businessinsider. com/salomon-brothers-treasury-bond-scandal-2012-7?op=1#ixzz2CNjhNznV.

7. See Warren Buffett, *Opening Statement of Warren E. Buffett, Chairman of Salomon Inc., Before the Subcommittee on Telecommunications and Finance of the Energy and Commerce Committee of the U.S. House of Representatives*, http://blogs.wsj. com/marketbeat/2010/05/01/buffetts-1991-salomon-testimony/tab/print/.

8. Ibid.

9. Sims and Brinkman, "Leaders as Moral Role Models."

10. Peter Henning, "Behind Rakoff's Rejection of Citigroup Settlement," *New York Times,* November 28, 2011, http://dealbook. nytimes.com/2011/11/28/behind-judge-rakoffs-rejection-of-s-e-c-citigroup-settlement/.

11. Ibid.

12. Ibid.

13. Robert Hamilton, "Registered Limited Liability Partnerships: Present at the Birth (Nearly)" *University of Colorado Law Review* 66 (1995): 1065.

14. Robert Bogdan, *Freak Show,* 1990 (University of Chicago Press).

15. See also *Rolling Stone Magazine,* January 23, 2007, www.rollingstone.com/politics/blogs/taibblog/accidentally-released-and-incredibly-embarrassing-documents-show-how-goldman-et-al-engaged-in-naked-short-selling-20120515#ixzz2CZKTm0hx.

16. Elizabeth MacDonald, "Goldman's Embarrassing Emails," April 22, 2010, Fox Business, www.foxbusiness.com/markets/2010/04/22/goldmans-embarrassing-emails/.

17. Simon Clark and Caroline Binham, "Profit 'Is Not Satanic,' Barclays CEO Varley Says," *Bloomberg News,* November 3, 2009, www.bloomberg.com/apps/news?pid=newsarchive&sid=aGR1F_bjSIZw.

18. Roy Eidelson, "In Praise of Shared Outrage," *Psychology Today,* March, 2010, www.psychologytoday.com/blog/dangerous-ideas/201003/in-praise-shared-outrage.

5

Proof in the Pudding: Michael Milken, Junk Bonds, and the Decline of Drexel and Nobody Else

This chapter tells the story of the collapse of Drexel Burnham Lambert, which was the first significant example of the failure of the old reputational model. First, this chapter introduces Michael Milken, who created the so-called "junk bond" market and helped turn Drexel into a financial powerhouse. Milken and his team underwrote and sold below-investment-grade corporate debt that produced significantly greater returns than investment-grade bonds and helped finance a period of rapid corporate expansion. Second, this chapter describes how Milken became implicated in the savings and loan (S&L) crisis of the late 1980s and early 1990s. The S&L business model had become untenable in the face of rising interest rates, so in an attempt to maintain solvency, the S&Ls began loading their balance sheets with increasingly risky assets, like Milken's junk bonds. After thousands of S&Ls failed, Milken became a convenient fall guy for regulators and ambitious prosecutors. Milken was convicted of six minor trading violations inflated into felonies, and Drexel collapsed soon after. Nevertheless, Milken and his colleagues survived their firm's failure, and proceeded to have successful and lucrative careers elsewhere within the financial industry.

The three fatal flaws in the traditional theory of reputation described in the preceding chapter all can be seen in sharp relief in the story of the dramatic rise—and equally dramatic collapse— of Drexel Burnham Lambert, the house that junk bonds built. The Drexel story is important because it marks the death knell of the traditional economic theory of reputation. The Drexel affair showed the world that the returns from investing in reputation had dropped. For the first time, it became apparent that reputation had become a bad investment.

Michael Milken, the man at the epicenter of Drexel's rise as well as its spectacular fall, continues to prosper. He never led Drexel. Craving independence, Milken chose to work in an office in Los Angeles—a continent removed from the company's New York head-quarters. Milken's earnings from Drexel made him, for a time, by far the highest-paid person on Wall Street. Milken became not just rich, but legacy rich. As such, Milken showed that, at least for the most ambitious and successful, crime pays. Critically, Milken's wealth escaped his indictment and conviction. Not only did Milken keep his wealth, but he did not even have to hide it. Years after his "fall," Milken remained comfortably ensconced in the middle of *Forbes* magazine's broadly read list of the top 400 richest Americans, with a net worth of 2.3 billion dollars as of September 2011.[1] And $2.3 billion certainly is enough to motivate many to take significant risks and even to test the boundaries of the byzantine rules that regulate securities trading and underwriting.

It is very hard to conclude that Milken, despite his place at the epicenter of the scandal that destroyed Drexel, went down with the ship. Many disagree about whether Michael Milken really was a crook.[2] I myself have serious doubts.[3] Innocent or not, however, Milken pled guilty to committing securities fraud in the form of insider trading. But one cannot deny that this was one person convicted of cheating who did prosper.

The second problem that I identified with the traditional theory of reputation is its core assumption that cheating has repercussions even for people in the firm who are not associated with the cheating. Clearly the force of this argument was reduced dramatically when banks, law firms, and accounting firms succeeded in convincing state legislatures to eliminate personal liability for their partners and top managers by allowing them to set up limited liability partnerships, limited liability companies, and corporations. As covered in this chapter, the Drexel case indicates that few top-level professionals who were not personally connected with the scandal really went down with the ship. Even the CEO of the firm—on whose watch Milken's shenanigans occurred—moved on from the scandal and the firm's collapse surprisingly unscathed.

The third flaw in the traditional theory of reputation that was identified in the preceding chapter was the notion that reputation is a unitary thing that might collapse entirely when one is caught engaging in illegal or unethical conduct. The rise and fall and rise of Michael Milken demonstrates that this is not the case.

Michael Milken: The Emperor of Junk Bonds

The house of Drexel was built on what are formally known as "high yield securities," or, more commonly, as junk bonds. For hundreds of years, corporations have been raising money by issuing bonds, which are securities that promise investors a certain periodic rate of interest and a contractually established date (or set of dates) for the return of the investors' principal. Until Drexel came along, the focus of this market was on the largest blue-chip, AAA-rated corporations.

Born in Encino, California, Milken graduated with top honors from the University of California, Berkeley, and went on to study at the Wharton School in the University of Pennsylvania, where he received an MBA. While still an undergraduate at Berkeley, Milken had studied the research of W. Braddock Hickman, a former president of the Federal Reserve Bank of Cleveland. Hickman's major contribution to the field of finance was his analysis of how bonds that lacked investment-grade ratings by the major credit rating agencies and were generally considered to be highly speculative had, for a substantial period of time (1900 to 1943), performed surprisingly well.[4]

As is the case today, the major credit rating agencies, Moody's and Standard & Poor's, evaluated the bonds sold to the public by companies and municipalities. Bonds considered to be relatively safe were then, as they are today, assigned what is known as an "investment grade" bond rating. These ratings include the well-known appellations for high-grade bonds "AA," "AAA," and the less-well-known appellations for bonds considered to be of medium quality, like "BBB."

These investment-grade ratings are supposed to indicate that bonds with such ratings have a low risk of default and can be differentiated from non-investment-grade bonds. Non-investment-grade bonds are those with ratings designations below "Baa3" by Moody's or below "BBB-" by Standard & Poor's. Bonds that fail to earn ratings higher than these traditionally have been considered highly risky and are known colloquially as "junk bonds."

Hickman's research showed that a diversified long-term portfolio of low-rated, non-investment-grade bonds was no more risky, and yet returned higher rates of interest to investors, than a portfolio of top-rated investment-grade bonds. Many later studies using different time periods and different methodologies confirmed Hickman's results: A portfolio of junk bonds offered returns greater than those of a portfolio of investment-grade bonds, even when adjusted for the greater risks associated with holding such a portfolio. Hickman's results held even during times of great economic stress like the Great Depression.

Milken continued to study the performance of junk bonds while at Wharton. When he graduated and entered investment banking at Drexel, the junk bond industry was moribund. Nobody in investment banking had tried to transform the research in non-investment-grade bonds into a strategy for increasing business by underwriting, selling, and trading such bonds.

Milken's career at Drexel began in the 1970s. He turned out to have the ability not only to assimilate financial theory, but also to transform that theory into a successful business strategy. Most of all, Milken was a great salesman. His product was junk bonds. His sales pitch was that the higher a bond was rated, the lower it could fall. Junk bonds did not have far to fall because their ratings were already low. Milken's strategy was strongly confirmed during the major recession that occurred in the mid-1970s, just after Milken began his career at Drexel. In particular, the junk bonds that Milken was touting performed extremely well during the sharp market decline that occurred in 1974, which resulted in major market indexes falling by as much as 50%. The burgeoning junk bond market also fell significantly, but the brave few willing to hold such bonds did extremely well, as the vast majority of non-investment-grade bonds ultimately paid off, and investors with diversified portfolios dramatically outperformed the market. Junk bonds emerged from the 1970s as a respectable investment for the first time. Indeed, junk bonds in general, and Milken and Drexel in particular, were the darlings of the financial world.

During the 1980s, the junk bond market grew from $10 billion in 1979 to $189 billion in 1989, an increase of 34% per year.[5] Whole new industries were financed by Michael Milken and his rapidly expanding junk bond empire at Drexel. Starting with his first deal in 1977 selling junk bonds to raise $30 million in capital for Texas International, a small oil company, Milken's junk bond machine went on to provide the critical funding necessary to launch an astounding number of major U.S. corporations. Among the more famous of Milken's deals while at Drexel were the financing of Turner Broadcasting, which owns CNN, MCI Communications, McCaw Cellular (which is now part of AT&T), and multibillionaire John Malone's Tele-Communications, Inc., which grew to become the world's largest cable television company. Barnes & Noble, Stone Container Corporation, Time Warner, Safeway, and Mattel also received financing from non-investment-grade, high-yield bonds issued by Drexel and Milken.

Milken also used non-investment-grade bonds to finance takeovers and leveraged buyouts (LBOs), including the key mezzanine financing for what was, at the time, by far the largest deal in history, the $25 billion LBO of RJR Nabisco. The Drexel/Milken junk bond machine also engineered a number of major corporate restructurings, spinoffs, and consolidations of distressed companies, including the restructuring of the automobile manufacturer Chrysler, Inc. And investors certainly were not complaining that they were being cheated. According to one estimate, during this period "yields averaged 14.5 percent while default rates averaged just 2.2 percent—a combination that resulted in annual total returns of some 13.7 percent."[6] In fact, investors did not suffer negative returns from junk bonds until Milken was forced out of business at the end of the decade.[7]

Mr. Milken's customer base during the 1980s was described by *The Economist* as "loyal and growing."[8] His main customers were small insurance companies and savings and loan institutions. This customer base proved to be extremely loyal to the man and the company that had transformed their businesses from fledgling also-rans into enormously profitable (if not enormous) financial institutions.

A critical factor in building the loyal customer base that provided a constant source of investment for the junk bonds Milken was underwriting for corporate clients like Turner Broadcasting was the fact that Milken promised to provide liquidity for the bonds he sold. In other words, when savings and loan companies, insurance companies, and other regular customers bought bonds in an initial public offering from Milken, Milken made sure that Drexel provided a reliable, fairly priced secondary market for the bonds after they were sold. Milken offered his customers a liquid market and a way out of investments they no longer wanted. That liquidity attracted mutual funds into the junk arena. Mr. Milken's skill as a market maker was rooted in his knowledge of the bonds issued (which allowed him to price them accurately) and his extraordinary recollection of his clients' holdings (which helped him find new buyers for junk that others wanted to unload).[9]

Milken Was Loved by His Customers, Loathed and Feared by His Competitors

In other words, Drexel's success was largely dependent on the fact that over a relatively brief period—roughly a decade—Milken developed the reputation of being a great person from whom to buy bonds. Milken, of course, had a reputation not only for doing well for his customers and corporate clients, but also for doing extremely well for himself, earning billions in compensation for Drexel and for himself.

Milken charged high fees to his corporate clients, generally three to four times more than the fees that rival investment banks charged for underwriting corporate debt; and although he paid good prices for the bonds he bought in the secondary market for customers, he generally sold them for even better prices, earning significant "spreads" or profits on such trades.

A singular part of the enormous success of Drexel and Milken was the firm's significant market share of the junk bond industry. As one former employee recalled, at the height of its dominance of the junk bond industry, Drexel "was a great place; we had 70 to 80 percent market share." The same trader recalled that, "at Drexel, you didn't pitch business. The phone rang and you picked it up."[10]

Not surprisingly in light of the fact that it had displaced many banks and investment banks as a dominant source of capital for U.S business, Drexel had a lot of powerful enemies. Rival banks were not the only firms to dislike Drexel. Drexel was also high on the enemies list of many U.S. corporations that feared being targeted in a hostile takeover by an upstart rival whose bid was financed by Drexel's junk bonds. At the height of its power, the company "struck fear into the heart of corporate America."[11] And Washington soon noticed the upheaval that Drexel was causing to the old established status quo. Despite the fact that the businesses created by Drexel created far more jobs than were lost in the job cuts that inevitably followed the LBOs and mergers financed by junk bonds, the lost jobs were what got all the attention, particularly from unions. In short, many "Wall Streeters...loathed the upstart bank," calling Drexel employees "junk people."[12]

Where the Drexel People Landed

Writing years later about the "Descendants of Drexel," the influential *The Economist* magazine observed that "with Mr. Milken at its centre, Drexel's Beverly Hills operation became a magnet for the best business-school graduates in the late 1980s. That cohort of financiers is still active. Many of them stayed in Los Angeles after Drexel folded. Almost all have now moved to the asset-management side of the business, although the sell-side skills they developed at Drexel are useful in bringing in money to manage or in arranging outside co-financing for private-equity deals."[13] Examples of how former colleagues at Drexel landed on their feet include Rich Handler, a junk bond trader in Drexel's Los Angeles office who "moved with 35 or so colleagues to Jefferies, a local investment bank." This group, according to *The Economist,* "took their knowledge of high-yield bonds and investors with them. Mr. Handler went on to become the CEO of Jeffries & Co., a major firm with approximately 3,000 employees."[14] Other Drexel alumni include Gary Winnick, a Drexel vice-president who started the Beverly Hills investment company Pacific Capital

Group and was a founder of Global Crossing, the ill-fated cable tele-communications company that achieved a stock market valuation of $23 billion and made Mr. Winnick a multibillionaire before it became one of the larger casualties of the telecommunications implosion of the 1990s.

Another new home for former Drexel employees was the highly successful Apollo Management Company in Century City, Los Angeles, which grew to manage over $55 billion in assets. Drexel alumni at Apollo include John Kissick, Drexel's former head of corporate finance on the West Coast, who took over as head of the junk bond department after Milken left; Antony Ressler, a senior vice president at Drexel who briefly managed the syndication desk; and Leon D. Black. Ken Moelis and nine other Drexel employees left the firm to join Donaldson, Lufkin & Jenrette, with Moelis becoming head of corporate finance. Peter Ackerman, Mr. Milken's right-hand man, left to run the structured finance unit and to help with the recapitalization of Mellon Bank, among other companies. He is now an executive at Rockport Capital, an investment firm based in Washington, making private investments.[15] Other noteworthy Drexel alumni include Warren Trepp, Mr. Milken's chief bond trader, and Dennis B. Levine, the Drexel banker who pleaded guilty to insider trading and who is now president of the Adasar Group, financial advisors in New York.

As *The New York Times* pointed out when looking at what happened to Michael Milken's former colleagues, many Drexel employees who worked in the Beverly Hills office were unsure whether they would ever work in such a "heady environment" again. But, today, "Drexel alumni are...working on Wall Street, running their own investment firms, [and] managing the millions of dollars they were paid more than a decade ago."[16]

Even Fred Joseph, the CEO of Drexel Burnham Lambert at the time of its implosion, moved on to another successful career. Although barred by the New York Stock Exchange from working on Wall Street in any supervisory capacity, Joseph has consistently been employed since Drexel fell apart. During his three-year ban by the NYSE, he was a consultant for Drexel as the firm liquidated its holdings. From 1994 to 1998, he formed his own financial consulting firm, Clovebrook Capital. Then, he became a "senior advisor and managing director at ING Barings.... When ING put that unit up for sale,

Joseph [and others] tried to buy it...but lost out to...an international bank based in Holland."[17]

Then, in 2001, Joseph and a team of investors acquired an investment bank and renamed it after Joseph, calling it Morgan Joseph & Co. (the Morgan is John A. Morgan, the great-grandson of John Pierpont Morgan, who served as the first chairman of the new firm). The business operated along the same lines as Drexel, Joseph's former firm: financing small and mid-size companies, and doing 40 restructurings and debt financing transactions valuing $1 billion in his first two years of operations.[18] During this time, his company's staff grew to 109.[19] Because he was barred from serving as CEO, others held that title, and Joseph, now deceased, served as managing director and co-head of investment banking.

So, clearly the Drexel story is consistent with the hypothesis that financial professionals really do not go down with their ships. As later chapters discuss in more detail, the professionals at fallen companies such as Arthur Andersen and Lehman Brothers similarly moved on to other successful positions similar or identical to the ones they had in their old firms.

Perhaps more than anything, however, the fall of Drexel provides strong support for the point that people in today's information-overloaded world do not have single, unitary reputations. People can mean very different things to very different people. Reputation is not a monolithic thing that could disappear completely when one is caught engaging in illegal or unethical conduct or associates with a firm that does. The story of the rise and fall and rise of Michael Milken provides a pretty clear demonstration that this is not the case. It might well be true that, in some circles, the name Michael Milken is synonymous with greed and sharp dealings with one's customers. But in many other worlds in which Milken operates, he is a hero.

Milken Had Many Reputations, and He Probably Was Innocent

Significantly, Milken is still a hero to many in the field of business and finance. Drexel might have been loathed by regulators and by its competitors, but it was revered by many independent observers, including the billionaire entrepreneurs who got their businesses off of the ground with capital raised by Milken and his Drexel junk bond minions, and the executives of the financial institutions that made significant profits investing in the non-investment-grade "junk" underwritten by Drexel.

Clearly Drexel's reputation was not unitary. The firm had many detractors, but it also had staunch supporters. But it had a great reputation where it mattered: among its clients. For many observers, including the author of this book, the prosecution of Michael Milken was nothing but "the vengeful response by America's business and regulatory establishment to Mr. Milken's phenomenal success." In particular, it is this author's opinion that "as deplorable as Joe McCarthy's attacks on alleged Communists were in the 1950s, the government's attack on Michael Milken during the 1980s was even worse. It was more conspiratorial; it sent more people to jail, and it was, at bottom, an attack on such fundamental American values as entrepreneurship, individual responsibility and, ultimately, capitalism itself."[20]

The influential financial columnist George Gilder wrote that there was no evidence upon which Milken could rationally be convicted, noting that after his release from prison "the entire case against him has collapsed." In his book *Telecosm,* Gilder went on to assert that "Milken was a key source of the organizational changes that have impelled economic growth over the last twenty years. Most striking was the productivity surge in capital, as Milken...and others took the vast sums trapped in old-line businesses and put them back into the markets."[21]

Many observers, including well-known ethicist Norman Barry, characterized the case against Milken as involving technical and "trivial offenses" and described his prosecution as "an affront to the rule of law." Furthering the evidence of the fact that Milken's reputation was not ruined entirely by his conviction, an April 2005 editorial in *BusinessWeek* opined that Michael "Milken's legacy is a favorable one in much of the business community."[22] Along these lines, Irwin Stelzer, a columnist for the *London Sunday Times,* observed that Milken helped revolutionize American industry. Seltzer described Milken's "defenders [as] persuaded that his punishment for violating such rules was more the revenge of the establishment than the just desserts of a willful lawbreaker."[23]

In support of the fact that even successful criminal prosecutions no longer conclusively signal that the convicted felon is really guilty of anything, the venerable Robert L. Bartley, who was at the time of writing the editor emeritus of *The Wall Street Journal,* observed that some politicians caused the savings and loan crisis and the 1990 recession by inflating deposit insurance "and leaning on regulators not to clean up thrift balance sheets. Their fall guy was...Milken and his supposedly malign junk bonds, which [are now] universally recognized as a legitimate financing tool. Mr. Milken was coerced into a plea bargain involving six [minor] trading violations" elevated into felonies.[24]

Along similar lines, Gordon Crovitz, a lawyer and editor at *The Wall Street Journal,* made it clear that Milken had done nothing wrong and that the real crime was the vagueness, complexity, and malleability of the securities laws. Congress encourages "prosecutors to try people even when the law is unclear. Prosecutors identify defendants to go after instead of finding a law that was broken and figuring out who did it."[25]

In certain important respects, Drexel was the first firm that was impervious to the loss of reputational standing, and for this reason, understanding what happened to Drexel is critical to understanding how so many major businesses today, from credit rating agencies to investment banks to law firms, can survive and thrive without the benefit of a reputation for trustworthiness or integrity.

The modern firm that came to be known as Drexel Burnham Lambert did not emerge until 1973, so the firm truly was a parvenu by Wall Street standards. The firm resulted from the marriage of a dowager princess, the venerable Drexel firm—which dated back to 1838 and was highly regarded on Wall Street, but was down to just a couple of corporate clients and almost out of money—to the less prestigious, but far more successful, firm of Burnham.[26]

The firm did not become Drexel Burnham Lambert until 1976, when it merged with a small research firm that was owned by the Belgian merchant bank Groupe Bruxelles Lambert. With that merger Drexel Burnham Lambert emerged as a closely held company, whose largest shareholder, Groupe Bruxelles Lambert, owned 26% of the company, with the rest owned by the company's employees.[27]

Not Even Michael Milken Could Survive the Collapse of the S&L Industry

Michael Milken's fall is inexorably tied to the S&L crisis. Since S&Ls were the biggest customers for junk bonds, when the U.S. real estate market plunged and the S&L industry virtually collapsed, so too did the market for junk bonds, at least temporarily. This temporary collapse was all that Milken's enemies needed in order to pounce. Originally organized to help middle-class Americans achieve the American dream of buying a home, S&Ls specialized in home mortgage lending. To help the industry achieve its goals, the laws applicable to S&Ls (also known as thrifts) allowed them to pay depositors higher rates of interest in exchange for the S&Ls' commitment to use their capital and deposits primarily to make home loans, rather than commercial loans or consumer loans. This model was only stable, however, as long as interest rates were stable.

In the early 1970s the economy suffered a significant recession accompanied by rapid and severe increases in interest rates and high inflation. As interest rates rose generally in the economy, the traditionally moderate interest rates paid by S&Ls became uncompetitive. Savers and investors rushed to move their funds out of S&Ls and into higher-yielding alternative investments. The S&Ls were in a very difficult position because if they raised the interest rates they paid to depositors to competitive levels, they would lose money because market interest rates were actually higher than the interest rates that S&Ls were charging on their mortgage lending.

S&Ls were headed for disaster because their business model no longer worked. Traditionally, S&Ls made money on the "spread" between the modest (but still competitive) interest rates they paid to depositors and the higher (though still attractive) rates of interest they charged borrowers. The industry was doomed when this spread turned negative unless it could shift its business from making home loans to investing in assets that paid higher rates of return. Of course, there is no such thing as a free lunch, and in order to earn higher returns the S&Ls had to take on more risk.

The industrywide problem facing S&Ls became a national economic problem because, like deposits in traditional commercial banks, deposits in S&Ls were insured by an agency of the federal government. Banks were insured by the FDIC; S&Ls were insured by the Federal Savings and Loan Insurance Corporation (FSLIC). With this federally sponsored deposit insurance scheme in place, depositors did not care whether the S&Ls in which they put their money were solvent. And they did not care whether the S&Ls were being run prudently. If their S&L failed, depositors would be repaid by the federal government. So S&L customers looked for high rates of return. They were indifferent to the riskiness of the particular S&L in which they put their money.

S&Ls began competing against each other for deposits by offering higher and higher rates of interest to depositors. To earn a positive spread between their cost of funds—the rates they paid to depositors—and their income from investments, S&L operators had to turn to increasingly risky investments. In 1982, Congress passed a new law, the Garn-St. Germain Act, in a misguided attempt to save the S&L industry and to avoid (or at least to postpone for a few years) the need for a massive, taxpayer-funded bailout of the S&L industry. This statute attempted to "fix" the S&L crisis by allowing S&Ls for the first time to offer checking accounts, to make loans other than home mortgages, and to invest directly in real estate.

The effects of Congress's "fix" were disastrous. S&Ls began to grow quickly as money flowed into them, attracted by the higher rates of interest they could pay not just to savers, but even to people holding checking accounts. S&Ls' balance sheets were becoming riskier, however, as their funds increasingly were being invested in higher-risked assets. In the early 1980s, S&Ls lost tens of billions of dollars in speculative real estate deals.

Michael Milken's junk bonds performed well during the crisis, but the S&Ls were failing anyway, and Milken was a convenient scapegoat. His competitors and government officials started to proclaim that Milken, Drexel, and the non-investment-grade bond industry in general were to blame for the collapse of the S&L industry. Almost 3,000 S&Ls failed during this period, and Michael Milken was wrongfully targeted as the culprit.

Michael Milken Was a Political Stepping-Stone for an Ambitious Unscrupulous NY Politician

The government prosecutor who targeted Milken was Rudolph Giuliani, who used the publicity garnered from his pursuit of Milken as a springboard to become Mayor of New York, and later to launch a series of unsuccessful attempts to garner the Republican Party nomination for President of the U.S.

With enormous fanfare that included a 98-count indictment that was leaked to the press before Milken was arrested, Prosecutor Giuliani tried his case against Milken in the press, where it collapsed. Milken, to avoid the indictment of his brother Lowell, pled guilty to five violations of technical SEC bookkeeping and reporting regulations. He did not plead guilty and was not convicted of any of the more serious charges, such as securities fraud or insider trading. Years later, John Carroll, the lead trial attorney on the case, acknowledged that Giuliani and the prosecution team were "guilty of criminalizing technical offenses.... Many of the prosecution theories we used were novel. Many of the (highly technical) statutes that we charged under hadn't been charged as crimes before."[28]

After settling the criminal case and a large number of civil cases, Milken retained a fortune of hundreds of millions of dollars, and his wife, children, and brother were left with even more, estimated at $300 to $400 million, thereby "ensuring that the Milkens retain their status as one of the nation's wealthiest families."[29] As one journalist noted, it was astounding that "the man who...shouldered much of the blame for the rigged markets and speculative excesses of the '80s... will emerge with a family fortune of perhaps half a billion dollars."[30]

The highly politicized Milken "show trial" had a long-term cost: It significantly eroded the shaming effect of government prosecutions and civil litigation. From a reputational point of view, being sued and pleading guilty, even in a criminal case brought by the federal government, was no longer a death blow to one's reputation. Milken's reputation continues to exist in many dimensions and contexts. He is loved by many, and he probably still is loathed by many others. But, of course, this was the case even before the government's prosecutions were contemplated.

Another legacy of the Giuliani prosecution of Milken is the lesson it taught politically ambitious prosecutors. Other prosecutors, most notably Eliot Spitzer, picked up where Giuliani left off and began to launch their political careers by suing successful Wall Street bankers and their companies. The failure of these lawsuits to reach conclusive results and the high number of settlements and acquittals further eroded the reputational signaling value of litigation against individuals and companies in the financial industry.

At one point, Spitzer accused Hank Greenberg, the CEO of what was then the world's largest insurance company, the American International Group, of fraud. In response, John Whitehead, a former CEO of Goldman Sachs, published an editorial in *The Wall Street Journal* titled "Mr. Spitzer Has Gone Too Far," in which he wrote that something was "seriously awry" with the American system when a state attorney general like Spitzer could level such a serious charge in public without notice and without giving the target of the charge an opportunity to respond or to defend himself. When Spitzer subsequently did file charges against Greenberg, he was forced to drop them because he lacked sufficient evidence to pursue the case.

More recently, the U.S. Chamber of Commerce observed that, beginning with the Giuliani- and Spitzer-era prosecutions, the U.S has been caught in a "vicious cycle" in which "financial regulators are competing more for headlines than ensuring that our markets are competitive."[31]

Drexel Died but Its People Survived

This is the key takeaway point of this chapter: Companies collapsing from scandals used to drag their leaders down with them. In the old days, when Bankers Trust stumbled and fell, its leader John Sanford and his team failed with it. When Salomon Brothers failed, John Gutfreund and his allies and friends also failed. In the case of Drexel, when that firm failed spectacularly, Michael Milken failed at least as spectacularly in a huge show trial that was followed avidly for weeks on television and in newspapers.

A big difference between now and then is that the careers of top financiers are no longer tied to the fate of their financial institutions. In the modern world of finance, nobody—or at least nobody important—goes down with the ship unless they are personally at fault for the reputation-damaging activities of their subordinates. Lloyd Blankfein remained at the helm of Goldman Sachs before, during, and after the lawsuits, congressional testimony, bad publicity, and reputation decline of his firm.

One theory is that Bankers Trust was just ahead of its time. Bankers Trust was among the very first Wall Street firms to transition from a client-centered, reputation-based business model to a counterparty-centered, trading-based business model.

The changes in the nature of large financial firms that transformed the business of finance from a profession into an industry caused seismic changes in all the businesses whose own business models were based on the old reputational model. As the next chapters show, the role of entire industries—particularly the credit rating industry; the old, iconic corporate law firms; and the big audit firms in the accounting industry—was to assist their clients in the financial sector in their quests for reputation. The ancillary industries of law, accounting, and credit rating still exist, of course, but the services that they provide have changed radically. These businesses no longer are tied to reputation building. Today, accounting firms, credit rating agencies, and law firms no longer are in the business of helping firms build their reputations. Now, somewhat ironically, these former "reputational intermediaries" have a new role: They help their old clients, the big banks, to navigate, and where possible to avoid, the costs of regulatory regimes. Subsequent chapters also show how even the stock exchanges that trade financial instruments and the regulators responsible for regulating the financial services industry have changed.

This chapter described the failure of Drexel Burnham Lambert and the subsequent, unexpected success of many of its employees. While at Drexel, trader Michael Milken created a dynamic market for non-investment-grade corporate debt, also known as junk bonds. The junk bond market funded an era of rapid corporate expansion and helped turn Drexel into a financial powerhouse and Milken into a multimillionaire. When thousands of savings and loan companies failed after purchasing Milken's junk bonds, the Drexel trader became a convenient fall guy for regulators and prosecutors. Milken was convicted of six minor trading violations inflated into felonies, and Drexel collapsed soon after. Despite this, Milken and his colleagues kept their fortunes and successfully carried on their careers elsewhere within the financial industry. Their individual reputations had become unhinged from Drexel's in such a way that they continued to be respected and even revered within the financial community.

Endnotes

1. "The Forbes 400: The Richest People in America," *Forbes Magazine*, September 22, 2011, www.forbes.com/profile/ michael-milken/, accessed November 19, 2012.

2. Daniel R. Fischel, "Payback: The Conspiracy to Destroy Michael Milken and his Financial Revolution," *HarperBusiness*, 1995.

3. Jonathan Macey, "The 1980s Villain, Vindicated," *The Wall Street Journal*, July 18, 1995.

4. W. Braddock Hickman, Corporate Bond Quality and Investor Experience (Princeton, NJ: Princeton University Press, 1958); Richard H. Jefferis, Jr., "The High-Yield Debt Market: 1980-1990," *Economic Commentary*, Federal Reserve Bank of Cleveland, April 1990, 1-6.

5. Glen Yago, "Junk Bonds," *The Concise Encyclopedia of Economics*, www.econlib.org/library/Enc/JunkBonds.html.

6. Ibid.

7. Ibid.

8. "Stars of the Junkyard: Drexel Burnham Lambert's Legacy," *The Economist*, October 21, 2010, www.economist.com/node/17306419.

9. Ibid.

10. Jim Casey, former Drexel employee who moved on to JP Morgan Chase, quoted in Nelson Schwartz's "Junk Bonds Are Back on Top," *The New York Times*, October 7, 2010, www.nytimes.com/2010/ 10/08/business/08bond.html?_r=0, accessed November 21, 2012.

11. "Stars of the Junkyard: Drexel Burnham Lambert's Legacy."

12. Ibid.

13. Ibid.

14. Ibid.

15. Ibid.

16. Laura Holson, "Drexel Alumni Move Onward," *The New York Times,* August 13, 2000, www.nytimes.com/2000/08/13/business/drexel-alumni-move-onward.html.

17. Mara Der Hovanesian, "Drexel's Ex-Chief Is Back in Business," *BusinessWeek,* July 13, 2003, www.businessweek.com/stories/2003-07-13/drexels-ex-chief-is-back-in-business.

18. Ibid.

19. Ibid.

20. Jonathan Macey, "The '80s Villain, Vindicated," *The Wall Street Journal,* July 18, 1995.

21. George Gilder, *Telecosm, How Infinite Bandwidth Will Revolutionize Our World* (Simon & Schuster, 2000), 170.

22. "Hank Greenberg and History," *BusinessWeek,* April 10, 2005, www.businessweek.com/stories/2005-04-10/hank-greenberg-and-history.

23. Irwin M. Stelzer, "The Rise and Fall of Enron: The Good It Did Should Not Be Interred with Its Bones," *Weekly Standard,* November 26, 2001, http://datasets.opentestset.com/datasets/Enron_files/full/shapiro-r/The%20Rise%20and%20Fall%20of%20Enron.htm.

24. Dan Stone, *April Fools: An Insider's Account of the Rise and Collapse of Drexel Burnham* (New York City: Donald I. Fine, 1990).

25. L. Gordon Crovitz, "You Commit Three Felonies a Day," *The Wall Street Journal,* Sep. 27, 2009, http://online.wsj.com/article/SB10001424052748704471504574438900830760842.html.

26. Stone, *April Fools.*

27. Ibid.

28. William L. Anderson, "Federal Crimes and the Destruction of Law," Cato Institute, *Regulation,* Winter 2009-2010, 12, www.cato.org/sites/cato.org/files/serials/files/regulation/2009/11/v32n4-2.pdf.

29. Victor Zonana, "Milken to Pay $500M, Serve 40 Months under Settlement," *Los Angeles Times*, February 28, 1992, http://tech.mit. edu/V112/N9/milken.09w.html, accessed November 22, 2012.

30. Ibid.

31. Quote by Tom Quaadman, vice president of the U.S. Chamber of Commerce's Center for Capital Markets Competitiveness, in "Sharp Elbows Among Street Lawmen," *The Wall Street Journal*, August 30, 2012, https://www.uschambersmallbusinessnation.com/article/ sharp-elbows-among-street-lawmen.

6

The New, Post-Reputation Wall Street: Accounting Firms

Historically, the accounting industry, which produces information about clients through audits, functioned on the basis of the traditional economic theory of reputation. Hiring a reputable accounting firm was a way of renting the accounting firm's reputation, which, in turn, lowered that client's cost of borrowing and raising new capital. Both the client and the accounting firm/reputational intermediary benefited: the client from lower borrowing costs and the accounting firm from fees it charged up to—but not greater than—the client's savings.

For accounting firms to charge for their audit services, they had to maintain and invest in their reputations, which would be damaged if they approved fraudulent financial records. The Enron scandal shattered the theory of reputation as applied to the accounting industry. Arthur Andersen accountants at the Enron office relied solely on their work for Enron for their salaries. They also provided lucrative consulting services to Enron, which Enron could use as leverage to ensure favorable audits. The Enron scandal displayed larger, structural problems in the auditing industry. The move from a general partnership structure to limited liability partnerships in the accounting industry lessened the incentive for partners to closely monitor the actions of their co-workers. Auditor independence is vastly eroded by a lack of competition in the auditing world and by the extremely close relationships between auditors and their clients. The Sarbanes-Oxley Act, passed in the wake of the Enron scandal, attempts to address some of the issues affecting auditor independence, but falls short of providing an adequate solution.

The post-WWII financial world flourished hand in hand with the growth of the reputations of the venerable companies that provided the capital for the manufacturing, communications, transportation, and technology companies that fueled the country's phenomenal post-War growth. What new institutions might emerge in the current, post-reputational world is an open question taken up in the final chapter of this book.

Reputations for Hire: The Reputation Industry

The traditional reputation-based world of finance did not just exist in theory. Entire industries, institutions, and lines of business were based on the value of the reputations of the companies within those industries. This chapter describes what I characterize as the "reputation industry" as it used to exist in the days before the death of the reputational model. The next three chapters describe what has happened to this industry in the modern, post-reputational world.

I use the term "reputational industry" to describe products and services specifically designed and engineered for the purpose of lowering the costs of attaining the benefits of a reputation for honesty and integrity. The businesses that provide these services perhaps can best be described as reputational intermediaries. As a matter of basic economics, if a reputational intermediary can figure out a way to increase a client's reputation, and thereby lower that client's costs of borrowing or raising capital, then the reputational intermediary can charge a price for that service as long as the price that the client is charged is lower than the client's cost savings.

The creation of certain industries can be explained only on the basis of this reputational theory. Take, for example, the services provided by the accounting firms that provide audit services for customers. An auditor merely observes. When an accounting firm performs an audit for a customer, it does not create anything new or provide any service that has not already been performed by the company itself. Rather, an audit is the examination and verification of the financial accounts and results that a company already has generated for itself. Audits do not provide information to the companies whose books are being audited for the simple reason that the company already has the information. The purpose of an audit is to confirm the information that a company already has. The audience for the audit opinion is not the client company, but is the client company's investors, suppliers, customers, and other outsiders who deal with the company and are concerned about its financial condition.

In a world of perfect trust, or as economists describe such a world, in an environment of zero information costs and zero transaction costs, there would be no demand for audits. In a world of perfect trust, people would believe the (unaudited) financial statements that companies' own employees generated for themselves. In a world of zero information and transaction costs, there would be no need for audits because it would be costless for investors and others to verify companies' self-generated financial statements.

The traditional economic theory of reputation explains why we observe companies paying for expensive, independent audits of their own financial records. Under the traditional economic theory of reputation, what auditors are offering to their customers is their reputation for honesty.[1] A company's investors, customers, suppliers, and others who might come into contact with the business often must have confidence in the financial condition of the business before they will deal with it. By hiring an independent outside auditor, a company indicates to those outside the firm that it is willing to submit itself to outside scrutiny. This, in turn, sends a credible signal that the company is not cooking its books.

For the traditional economic theory of reputation to work, the accounting firm that performs the audit must have a sufficiently high reputation for honesty and integrity in performing audits so that investors and others dealing with the firm trust it not to conspire with a dishonest client to cover up any financial shenanigans the client might be up to. For this model to work, the auditing firm's reputation must be sufficiently well established and valuable such that the auditing firm rationally believes that it would be irrational for the firm to cheat because the one-shot gains from such cheating if the firm was caught would be lower than the permanent loss to the firm's reputation.

You Don't Have to Trust the Company if You Can Trust Its Auditor

A beautiful thing about the economic theory of reputation as applied in this context is that it describes a strategy that small, new, obscure, and otherwise relatively unknown audit clients can follow in order to ameliorate the costs associated with their lack of reputation. Hiring a well-known auditor with a good reputation effectively allows these sorts of unknown, low-reputation companies to "rent" the reputation of big accounting firms.

It is efficient for audit clients to pay for the services of an outside auditor up to the point at which the actual costs of the audit come to exceed the benefits from getting an outside audit. The benefits come in many forms. Among the primary benefits are being able to borrow at lower rates of interest and raise equity capital at lower cost. Other benefits include being able to recruit high-quality employees more effectively, and being able to persuade employees, customers, and suppliers to deal with the firm on better terms. Outside audits also are often useful in dealing with regulators. And to the extent that the audit firms hired by companies have reputations for probity that are not only better but also broader geographically than the reputations of their clients, outside audits enable audit clients to attract lenders, investors, customers, suppliers, and employees from distant markets.

It is sensible and efficient for audit firms to invest in developing and maintaining their reputations for two reasons. Investing in reputation enables an audit firm to charge more for its services. Without such investments, there would be no demand for the services provided by the audit firm. In other words, according to the traditional economic theory of reputation, the most important component of the services offered by audit firms is the rental of its reputation. If an accounting firm lacks a reputation, clients have no incentive whatsoever to hire the firm, according to the economic theory of reputation, because there are no gains from doing so.

The economic theory of reputation hypothesizes that the accounting firms that perform audits will invest in building and maintaining their reputations. The theory also predicts that accounting firms will compete with one another to develop the best reputations for probity and honesty, because the firms with the best reputations will be able to charge more for their services and will find it easier to attract clients.

High-quality audit services were further ensured by the audit firms' independence from their clients, where independence is measured by the percentage of an audit firm's billings that are derived from a particular client. In a world in which auditors have invested in developing high-quality reputations and in which no single client represents more than a tiny fraction of total billings, high audit quality seems ensured. Under these conditions, any potential gain to an auditor from performing a shoddy audit, much less from participating in a client's fraud, would be vastly outweighed by the diminution in value to the auditor's reputation.[2]

In theory, then, accounting firms are willing to put their seal of approval on a company's financial records only if the company agrees to conform to the high standards imposed by the accounting profession. Investors trust accountants because investors know that any accounting firm that is sloppy or corrupt could not stay in business for long. The long-term loss to the reputation of an independent accounting firm that does slipshod or fraudulent work is much greater than any possible short-term gains the accounting firm might get by cutting corners. Companies that refuse to comply with the auditors' demands for transparency and simplicity in reporting risk being dismissed by their auditors. Being fired by an accounting firm sends a negative signal to investors that often both devastates a company and leads to the dismissal of top management. Outside audits send a strong signal to investors that the company's financial house is in order. From the perspective of audit firms' clients, good audits are good investments because they reduce the cost of capital and increase shareholder wealth. Good audits also increase management's credibility among the investment community. In theory, the capital markets themselves would audit the auditors. If a client's information were inaccurate, auditors would risk being sued by investors. These suits would prove costly, even if they ended unsuccessfully. As such, "public accountants knew they had a lot to lose if their clients' information turned out to be false or misleading."[3]

The theory of reputation also is central to the standard economic theory of auditing. Only auditors with reputations for honesty and integrity are valuable to audit clients. The idea is that, absent a reputation for honesty and integrity, the auditor's verification function loses its value. In theory, then, auditors invest heavily in creating and maintaining their reputations for performing honest, high-quality audits. High-quality audits by independent auditors who have good reputations are assured. The quality assurance is derived from the fact that performing poor-quality audits diminishes the value of the audit firm's investment in reputation.[4]

In the traditional economic theory of reputation, the relationships between auditors and their clients were purely contractual and arms-length. Firms willingly and voluntarily contract for and pay for audit services. The theory does not posit that companies are required to obtain audits. The theory also posits a certain degree of professionalism from auditors. Such professionalism implies that audit firms retained a professional distance and independence from their clients. And, of course, the traditional theory posits that audit firms were prepared to fire uncooperative clients or clients who engaged in fraud, misrepresented their financial condition, or refused to conform their financial reporting to the standards of quality and transparency set by the auditor.

In other words, the traditional theory of reputation predicts that an auditing firm that discovered problems or inconsistencies in a client's financial reporting would insist that such problems or inconsistencies be corrected. If the client was committing fraud by misrepresenting its financial condition or was erroneously reporting its financial condition, the auditor would insist that the client correct its financial statements. If the client refused to conform its financial reporting to the auditor's standards, the auditor would fire the client.

In this environment, being fired by an accounting firm had serious implications for the client being audited because it sent a strong, credible signal to the client's investors that there were unresolved and perhaps unresolvable problems with the client's financial reporting. Significantly, the consequences for the client were more serious than those for the accounting firm. Companies rarely survived such noisy withdrawals because suppliers and creditors would refuse to extend credit unless the company could resolve its problems with its auditors. Shareholders would commence legal action against the company's directors for failure to manage and oversee the company's business in a manner consistent with their fiduciary duties. Regulators would begin investigations, and valuable employees would start looking for jobs in firms whose financial condition was reliable.

On the other hand, an accounting firm that fired an audit client suffered little if at all from publicly disassociating themselves from such clients. The accounting firm would lose only a single client, and that client would be required to pay the accounting firm's bill in any case. Far more significantly, the accounting firm often would actually benefit from having fired the client because its reputation for professionalism and integrity would be enhanced because the firing appeared to have a short-term cost for the company. Potential audit clients who wanted to signal that their financial houses were in order would realize that an audit firm known for firing crooked clients was an ideal firm to retain, because hiring such a firm would send precisely such a signal. Somewhat ironically, in other words, firing crooked clients was a form of good marketing practice for accounting firms operating under the traditional economic model of reputation because auditors who developed strong reputations for firing their clients were likely to attract other clients who were attracted by the firm's reputation, which was enhanced with every such firing.

Arguably, in this environment, there was some remote danger that accounting firms would act strategically vis-a-vis their clients, perhaps by being too strict, in order to advance their own reputational interests at the expense of a client. The point is clear: Under the traditional economic theory of reputation, the client-auditor balance of power was decidedly toward the auditor.

The scholarly literature in both economics and accounting is full of support for the traditional economic theory of regulation. Published research either asserts or sometimes simply assumes that "maintaining a reputation for high quality is of paramount importance for financial services firms generally and auditing firms specifically."[5] Such research reflects the accepted wisdom that "auditor reputation is crucial because the widespread opinion among companies is that reputable auditors perform higher-quality audits and better certify the reliability of the information presented in financial statements."[6]

Enron and the Accounting Firm That Audited It

The traditional economic theory of reputation previously described ended in a fiery death with the epic collapse of the giant energy company Enron. It seems that the scholarly literature was wrong.

Enron was audited by the venerable accounting firm of Arthur Andersen & Co. Enron imploded in a wave of accounting irregularities and improprieties, all of which had been approved or ignored by its auditors. The collapse of Enron and the concomitant indictment and disappearance of its auditor could not be reconciled with the traditional economic theory of auditor behavior because the auditor, Arthur Andersen, sacrificed its reputation and its very existence in order to retain the patronage of a lone audit client.

The Enron saga demonstrated that as accounting firms were growing bigger and increasingly more profitable, their reputations were rotting from the inside out. On the surface, however, Arthur Andersen appeared to be a model of independence operating firmly within the parameters of the traditional economic theory of reputation. Arthur Andersen at first glance appeared to be entirely independent of Enron. The firm had 2,300 other audit clients. None of its clients, including Enron, accounted for more than 1% of Andersen's United States auditing revenue. The percentage of Andersen's business from any single client diminished still further when Andersen's clients were viewed on a global basis. In 2001, the year of Enron's collapse, Andersen's revenues were $9.34 billion, and its anticipated revenue from Enron was $100 million, according to the auditing firm's now-defunct website. Enron became an Arthur Andersen client in 1986. At the time, no firm enjoyed a stronger reputation. An aura of integrity pervaded the firm.

From the moment of its founding in 1913, Andersen worked to develop a reputation for integrity. During the Great Depression, the firm's founder, Arthur Andersen, gave a speech at Northwestern's Business School in which he emphasized the point that "to preserve the integrity of their reports, the accountant must insist upon absolute independence of judgment and action."[7] The key moment in the firm's history and development came quickly. In 1914 the firm's largest client, a Chicago railroad, tried to persuade Andersen to attest to the validity of its financial records despite evidence of significant improprieties. The company did not properly record day-to-day operating expenses, which, if unchecked, would have allowed it to report fraudulently inflated profits.

According to the historical accounts, Andersen responded, "There was not enough money in the city of Chicago to make him approve the bad bookkeeping." As a result, "the small firm lost its big client, but the railroad went bankrupt a few months later, vindicating Andersen and establishing a reputation for independent thinking that would lead to decades of prosperity." Andersen accountants would, "time and again...take bold stands on arcane accounting issues that would anger clients while making Andersen the auditor investors could trust."[8]

In addition to being known and respected around the world for its integrity, Arthur Andersen also was known in its halcyon days for its tight internal controls and for standardized procedures that enabled the firm to speak with authority and conviction. A detailed account of Andersen's history quotes a highly regarded Andersen auditor who ultimately was fired for working too slowly. According to the auditor, every detail in the audit process was standardized. "What you were selling," he said, "was your opinion.... And if you ever cheapened it or if you gave it away, you lost your birthright as a professional.[9]

The former Arthur Andersen auditor just quoted is Mike Gagel, who earned considerable fame and wide respect within the firm. As a junior auditor, he was sent to verify the inventory kept in a Marion, Ohio, storage yard by an Andersen audit partner. The client claimed that it had an inventory of one million bricks in the brickyard. Mr. Gagel counted the bricks pallet by pallet and could verify only 900,000 bricks. His count was 100,000 different from the number claimed by the client. Legend has it that the owner of the factory reacted angrily when Gagel presented his brick count and telephoned Mr. Gagel's boss to complain about the "rookie" auditor. After a third recount, the plant's owner counted the bricks himself and confirmed Mr. Gagel's count. The ensuring investigation revealed that the plant manager had been stealing truckloads of bricks during the night, reselling them, and pocketing the money.[10]

According to the *Chicago Tribune,* Mr. "Gagel's brickyard math is a classic example of the vigilance that made the name Arthur Andersen the gold standard of the accounting profession for decades...." As the culture within the firm changed, and the firm became revenue driven rather than reputation driven, Gagel, along with other Andersen auditors of his generation, was forced into retirement decades earlier than the firm's mandatory retirement age.[11]

The flaw in the traditional economic theory of reputation as it applies to the modern accounting industry was that it put too much stress on the institutional reputations of the accounting firms that were performing the audits on the firms' corporate clients. The theory ignored the importance of the private incentives of the individual people who actually conducted the audits, interacted with the clients, and made the day-to-day decisions about how the financial condition, performance, and results of such clients should be presented to the client's constituencies and to the public and the regulators.

In a nutshell, the traditional economic theory of reputation failed because the institutional reputations of the big audit firms like Arthur Andersen became entirely unhinged from the incentives of the individuals working within such firms. As individuals' careers became separated from the reputations of the accounting firms they worked for, their incentives changed. No better example of this phenomenon can be found than the story of the team of auditors assigned by Andersen to audit Enron. These auditors, led by Andersen partner David Duncan, were loyal to the client and not to the firm. And the firm's failure to reign in the hyperaggressive accounting practices that their Enron team was approving ultimately destroyed the firm.

The traditional economic theory of reputation failed as applied to accounting firms because it did not adjust to reflect considerable changes in the accounting industry over time. Take, for example, the efforts that Andersen made to coordinate, monitor, and offer audit services in a consistent way.

In a sharp break with tradition, at the time that Andersen was monitoring Enron, senior accounting firm partners responsible for monitoring and supervising line audit teams such as those under the immediate control of David Duncan were no longer subject to the same strong incentives to monitor their peers as they used to be.

In fact, under the current legal regime, there are strong incentives within accounting firms (and law firms, for that matter) to remain entirely uninvolved and uninformed about the work that one's colleagues within the firm are doing. This is because, irrespective of the income that partners take from the efforts of others within the firm, the rules of civil liability within modern partnerships insulate partners from liability for professional negligence caused by others within the firm who were not under the partners' direct supervision.

From General Partnerships to Limited Liability Partnerships

Traditionally, accounting firms were organized as general partnerships. Under this legal regime, partners were jointly and severally liable for the professional negligence and malfeasance of their partners. This specter of liability gave partners very strong incentives to supervise, monitor, and correct errors in the work that others within the firm were doing. Partners also had strong incentives to insist that their firms develop and assiduously enforce strict rules against aggressive or risky audit practices. The change by all the major accounting firms, including Arthur Andersen, from general partnerships to LLPs reduced if not destroyed these socially valuable incentives. Today, the limited liability form protects partners in accounting firms and law firms from personal liability. As a result, partners in both accounting firms and law firms have significantly lower, and perhaps even negative, incentives to monitor their colleagues.

The Limited Liability Partnership legislation that swept the country in the 1990s resulted in dramatic changes in the nature of partnership governance. The traditional "basic principle" of the general partnership law that governed law firms and accounting firms required individual partners to be liable for any partnership obligations that exceeded the assets of the partnership. This basic principle was jettisoned. The new LLP form in which law firms and accounting firms operate protects partners' personal assets from attacks by the firm's creditors. The basic concept of eliminating personal liability for partners who do not control or supervise the wrongdoers is now the law in every state.

The move from general partnership form to the LLP form creates disincentives to monitor in law firms as well as in accounting firms. LLP statutes generally impose personal liability on partners engaged in the supervision of the professional activities of others, eliminating the incentive to supervise one's peers.

As a result, professionals who might have provided advice and counsel to their colleagues under the general partnership form may resist doing so in an LLP in order "to avoid taking on potential liability for the work."[12] Consistent with this analysis, it has been reported that after one large law firm converted from general partner form to LLP form, the partners decided to indemnify one another when they took on work for their colleagues' clients in order to provide incentives for partners not involved in a transaction to continue to provide advice and guidance.[13] Although changes in companies' internal rules and procedures might improve monitoring, they do not reduce the incentives of the people running the firm to acquiesce in excessive risk-taking behavior that might lead to more profits.

When combined with today's accounting firm reality—with one partner dominating the work of a client and working on an "eat what you kill" basis—the outcome is perhaps even more troubling. No one supervises partners on particular client cases and partners face financial pressure to hold on to their clients. Their clients, aware of the pressure, exert their own pressure on accountants not to monitor too carefully. As a result, audits have become less reliable. This outcome, though it might have been unintended, was an important consequence of the move within the industries of accounting and law from general partnership form to LLP form.

There has long been a standard response within the large law firm and accounting firm communities to accusations that changes in the liability regime contributed both to the decline in ethical and law-abiding behavior among these firm's clients and to excessive risk taking and reduced monitoring by the professionals themselves. These professional firms maintain that lawyers and accountants retain their traditionally strong incentives to maintain their own professional reputations and, of course, to refrain from allowing anything to happen that might damage their own careers.

The key assumption here is that partners in successful law firms and accounting firms will work hard to prevent excessive risk taking in their own firms and fraud by their clients because these sorts of activities threaten the reputations of all the professionals within the firm by association. In other words, the defense of limited liability in law firms and accounting firms is that professionals retain strong incentives to monitor and prevent wrongdoing in their own firms and among their clients because such wrongdoing threatens to damage or ruin the careers of the professionals in firms like Arthur Andersen that are tainted by wrongdoing.

Proponents of the rules eradicating personal liability for partners' misconduct also defend these "reforms" on the grounds that the giant modern professional associations of lawyers and accountants are so complex and diffuse geographically that monitoring them simply cannot be done. Partners in New York hardly can be expected to monitor the conduct of partners in Houston or Shanghai. The notion that such monitoring could not be effective, much less worth the giant expense, is reinforced further by the dramatic increase in specialization within accounting and law firms. A tax partner rarely if ever will be considered qualified to pass judgment on the work of the environmental law expert or the bankruptcy expert on the floors above and below. The accounting profession has become similarly complex. Every industry has its own individual accounting rules. Accountants who are experts in auditing and providing accounting and tax advice to banks, for example, generally do not audit companies in distinct industries like pharmaceuticals, aerospace, or the automotive industry. Accountants further specialize in distinct areas. Analyzing the costs and benefits of particular legal forms or corporate structures, financial modeling, computerized recordkeeping, tax, compliance with the SEC's accounting rules for public companies, compliance with the requirements of specific statutes like the Sarbanes-O Act, which contains many rules that affect the way audits and other accounting services are delivered, valuation analysis, and managerial accounting are among the more important areas of specialization within the modern accounting industry.

These claims are overblown. In particular, the assertion that lawyers and accountants have incentives to try to make sure that their colleagues behave appropriately lacks support. The reality appears to be that competent professionals within failed firms like Arthur Andersen do not suffer much, if any, personal damage to their reputations when their firms collapse. Rather, they seamlessly move on to the same, or a very similar, job at another firm. In the exceedingly rare event that their firms actually collapse, these professionals often simply move on to rival firms and work for the same clients they worked for previously.

Again, Arthur Andersen provides a convincing example of this modern phenomenon. The ability of former partners of Arthur Andersen to carry on with their careers intact was nothing short of stunning. The general model was as follows. Large corporate clients of Arthur Andersen were, in most cases, quite happy with the particular teams of Arthur Andersen professionals assigned to their accounts. These clients, who generally were entirely remote from Enron, fully recognized the fact that the particular accounting professionals with whom they worked on a day-to-day basis, often for periods of many years, had absolutely nothing to do with Enron's accounting. Virtually no Arthur Andersen professionals outside of David Duncan's team in Houston and its immediate supervisors in Chicago had any knowledge of or connection with Enron or its accounting.

These corporate clients wanted to continue with business as usual with their incumbent team of accountants. And there really was no reason why such clients should not have been allowed to do so. In fact, a steep, time-consuming, and expensive learning curve exists for any new audit team when taking on a new assignment. Any decision by an Andersen client to bring on a new team of accountants would have involved significant expense in direct costs and in diversions of time and resources for the client's audit committee, CEO, CFO, and others in the company's own internal accounting offices. In addition to these costs, changing accountants always involves risk and uncertainty.

New accountants must evaluate the work of their predecessors. Because many decisions about how to treat particular transactions and practices involve subjective judgments, new teams of accountants often disagree with and insist on changes to prior audits. Such changes frequently involve significant uncertainty and regulatory risk for the companies that have engaged the new auditors. In other words, changing auditors is fraught with risk and expense, and companies are extremely reluctant to make such changes unless they absolutely have to.

There is significant evidence that the vast majority of the tens of thousands of Arthur Andersen employees who were left temporarily jobless when Arthur Andersen collapsed in 2002 successfully moved on to other firms. There are many websites that link Arthur Andersen alumni to each other and to other firms, such as www.andersenalumni.com and www.andersenalumni.net, the latter of which seeks "to enable current and former Arthur Andersen employees to maintain relationships, network, search for new employment opportunities, and find current or ex-colleagues from around the world." Membership is free and allows "current and former Arthur Andersen employees to post their resumes, search current job postings, and contact current or ex-colleagues." Other more specialized websites connect particular subgroups of Andersen alumni. Those formerly with the firm's offices in South Florida appear to hold reunions.[14]

The Arthur Andersen Center at the University of Wisconsin continues to thrive and "to promote research that is useful in resolving financial reporting and control problems...and to help address financial reporting issues that are disconcerting to governmental agencies and businesses alike." The Center is "also able to communicate with people throughout academia and the private sector that are interested in financial reporting and control issues."[15]

From a reputational point of view, these websites are interesting because they indicate that former Andersen professionals are not ashamed of their previous association with Andersen despite its indictment and subsequent demise. It appears that the assumption that accountants and other professionals who are associated with firms that have suffered disgrace and been tagged as criminal enterprises suffer along with their firms is not grounded in fact. These professionals do not appear to go down with the ship. In fact, most of these professionals do not appear even to get damp, much less wet, when the ship goes down.

It is practically impossible to trace the whereabouts of all Andersen alumni. It also is impossible to distinguish those partners who have voluntarily left the workforce from those whose retirements somehow are attributable to the collapse of the firm rather than to their own preferences. It also is impossible to know how Andersen's collapse affected the lifetime earnings of the partners. There are many success stories, though.

After Andersen collapsed, the largest of the second-tier accounting firms, Grant Thornton, acquired many former Andersen partners. Grant Thornton took over Andersen's practices in North Carolina and South Carolina and opened a new office in Milwaukee, Wisconsin, headed by five former Andersen auditors and staffed by 36 additional Andersen employees.[16] Former Arthur Andersen professionals started a major consulting firm, the Huron Consulting Group. The firm, which is composed of a "cadre of Andersen refugees and their colleagues," advises companies on the very same sorts of litigation and regulatory issues that plagued Enron. The firm's value grew to above $1 billion, and it employs 1,200 professionals. It has grown into a smaller version of the $1-billion-a-year consulting operations at Andersen.[17] *Bloomberg BusinessWeek* predicted that the 2002 move from Andersen to Huron "may turn out to be the best thing that ever happened" to Gary Holdren, Huron's founder, and to "the other ex-Andersenites who put out their own shingle as Huron Consulting Group Inc."[18]

Where Did All the Enron Partners Go?

The collapse of Enron and the demise of Andersen temporarily stranded the 2,000 Andersen employees in the Washington area. But, as one business journal noted, Andersen's "strong reputation is a key reason the firm's bust created a scramble to snap up its people and practices, rather than leaving scores of unemployed accountants."[19] Andersen alumni from the Washington area alone went on to jobs as chief financial officer or chief accounting officer at prominent firms such as Marriott International, Inc., the Carlyle Group, Cogent Communications, Inc., J.E. Robert Cos., and MuniMae LLC, and to top positions at all the other major accounting firms.

A scholarly study that looked at the help that Andersen alumni provided to each other when the firm collapsed found that half of all Andersen employees moved with a group to another employer. The study also found that this help continued, as former employees used their connections to obtain second and third "post-crisis positions.

Apparently, the dispersion of the network beyond its original domain increased its value as a means of trolling for new positions." The study concluded that the "overwhelming thrust of the interview evidence suggests the social networks at Andersen acted with unusual effectiveness to secure alternative work for Andersen employees...."[20]

Another report, on the fate of the Andersen professionals in the firm's Milwaukee, Wisconsin, office, observed that "Arthur Andersen may be gone, but the overwhelming majority of the accounting and consulting giant's professionals have found gainful employment in the Milwaukee area."[21]

Four accounting firms with offices in Milwaukee hired the majority of former Andersen employees. Deloitte & Touche LLP added 225 Andersen employees. These hires, representing almost all the Andersen tax and audit accountants, doubled the size of Deloitte's Milwaukee office from 160 employees to 385. With the demise of Andersen, Deloitte became the largest audit firm in Milwaukee. Grant Thornton hired more than 50 Andersen alumni, a local firm called Virchow Krause hired 34, and KPMG Consulting Inc. hired 65. The Milwaukee offices of PricewaterhouseCoopers and Ernst & Young added small numbers of Arthur Andersen alumni. Still other Andersen professionals ended up at various regional firms. The effect of the closing of Andersen's Milwaukee office was an opportunity for the auditor's former "competitors to scoop up market share—and skilled staff." The report went on to claim that when Grant Thornton opened a Milwaukee office with three former Andersen partners in June 2002, "the former Andersen partners brought nearly 100 clients with them."[22]

Auditing and Consulting Simultaneously

Another flaw in the traditional economic theory of reputation is that it falsely assumed that accounting firms that perform audits for corporate clients do not provide any other services to the same clients that might generate conflicts of interest. In fact, as the relationship between Enron and Arthur Andersen poignantly illustrated, the big accounting firms historically provided a wide range of other sorts of services, including amorphous "consulting services" that posed severe, sometimes debilitating conflicts of interest.

The massive growth in the provision of consulting services to firms like Enron by firms like Arthur Andersen seriously undermined the independence and objectivity of auditors. During the period before the Sarbanes-Oxley Act put restrictions into place, Andersen and its competitors often realized significantly higher profit margins from the provision of consulting services than from the provision of audit services to the same clients. Increasingly, accounting firms used audit work almost as a loss leader simply to "open the door" to a client in order to pitch their more profitable consulting services.

Worse, the provision of consulting services provided the opportunity for corrupt client firms like Enron to manipulate or intimidate their auditors by engaging in "carrot and stick" or "tit for tat" behavior. Dishonest, unscrupulous, or even "merely" overly aggressive audit clients can reward cooperative auditors who yield to client preferences on the accounting treatment of particular matters with more consulting business. Perhaps even more troubling, consulting clients could threaten to withhold or reduce the consulting business that they give to auditors who refuse to go along with their preferences.

Corporate clients cannot control, much less "ration," the allocation of the auditing services they receive from their accounting firms. Clients need these services and accounting firms either provide them or do not. The same is not true for consulting services, because such services are discretionary. It is quite easy, in other words, for corporate clients to ration the amount of consulting work they allocate to their auditors. The power to withhold or to threaten to withhold highly profitable consulting business from their auditors gives audit clients a power to exert pressure over their auditors in a manner that was never contemplated, much less accounted for, in the traditional economic theory of reputation. In other words, the provision of consulting services by auditors of the kind that Andersen provided to Enron jeopardized their independence and certainly created an appearance of reliance on currying favor with Enron management.

The efforts that accounting firms exerted to remain in the good graces of their clients so that they would not lose consulting led to the appearance either that auditors were captured by their big corporate clients, or, at the very least, that they were susceptible to capture by these clients.

Professor Jack Coffee was among the first to chronicle and analyze these sorts of previously unrecognized conflicts that made accounting firms like Arthur Andersen so susceptible to capture. As Professor Coffee has observed, when clients of an accounting firm are simultaneously audit clients and consulting clients, "the client can then easily terminate the auditor as a consultant, or reduce its use of the firm's consulting services, in retaliation for the auditor's intransigence." Professor Coffee observes that this is a "low visibility response" in the sense that it often goes unnoticed by market participants and regulators because it "requires no disclosure, invites no SEC oversight, and yet disciplines the audit firm so that it would possibly be motivated to replace the intransigent audit partner."[23]

Ultimately, the traditional concept of auditor "independence" became a mere mirage at large accounting firms such as Arthur Andersen.

Replacing the traditional model is a more realistic image modeled on the example of Enron that features aggressive managers at big companies like Enron easily capturing their auditors. In the case of Enron, it has been widely reported that Andersen audit team members consistently succumbed when the company insisted that the accounting firm sign and certify as consistent with GAAP earnings and profit numbers that were generated by very aggressive accounting treatment by Enron's CFO and other managers. In the rare instances in which the local auditors did not accede, they sometimes were overruled by their higher-ups in Chicago. When they refused, their advice sometimes was ignored. Non-Enron auditors apparently lacked sufficient incentives to rein in their Enron colleagues.

Testimony at the Andersen criminal trial and in the Enron securities litigation supports the conclusion that auditors even at large firms like Andersen are susceptible to capture. For example, David Duncan testified that he rejected or ignored advice to change the accounting treatment of the Enron transactions. He needed the client to maintain his pay and status at Andersen. Other members of the Andersen audit teams testified that their negative views of Enron's accounting techniques were also ignored or mischaracterized. In some cases, advice was simply not provided to the client, presumably out of fear that the client would hire another auditor from within Andersen, provide Andersen with poor evaluations of the local audit engagement team, or withhold consulting services. Numerous documents exist that show that Andersen employees knew and were "concerned about, yet covered up or ignored fraudulent accounting practices by Enron."[24]

In the wake of Enron and a host of other accounting-based scandals like Tyco, WorldCom, Global Crossing, and Adelphia, Congress passed the Sarbanes-Oxley Act in 2001 to institute legislative changes to ameliorate the problem of capture. The two most important changes were the implementation of an auditor rotation rule and a restriction to the outside consulting services that auditors can perform.

The auditor rotation rules prohibit accounting firms from placing a person in the role of either lead audit engagement partner or supervising audit engagement partner if that person has worked for the client as an auditor within the past five years. This rule was put in place precisely to address the "David Duncan-style" capture problem. The problem is that the new auditor rotation rules might make the capture problem worse instead of better. After five years, the auditors who are moved from one client to another are going to prefer to be promoted to bigger, more important corporate clients rather than demoted to smaller or less important clients. Client satisfaction is likely to play a major, if not dominant, role in an accounting firm's decision about where to move a partner that must be rotated away from a current account. This, of course, could well make auditors even more intent on pleasing their clients. In addition, there often is intense competition within large accounting firms for internal promotions. A top auditor who follows in the steps of a rival to take over the audit of an important client will have incentives to make the client even more happy and satisfied with the services she provides and the decisions she makes than her predecessor and rival.

The restriction on the performance of outside consulting services also attempted to solve the capture problem that the Enron debacle brought into such sharp focus. However, the rule as finally adopted was full of loopholes and ambiguities, and as of this writing the provision of consulting services by audit firms still is going strong.

Sarbanes-Oxley, or SOX as it often is called, was a compromise between the interest groups battling for a full-scale prohibition on non-audit services and those who wanted virtually no new limitations. The compromise, which is reflected in Sections 201 and 202 of Title II of SOX, generally allows auditors to provide non-audit services, excluding nine particular non-audit services that are listed in the statute. The law says that public accounting firms that do audit work for public companies "may engage in any non-audit service, including tax services," that is not on the list of nine.

SOX bans auditors from selling the financial information systems design and implementation and information technology services that were the source of extraordinary consulting revenue for some accounting firms, particularly the very largest firms such as Arthur Andersen. The Act also bars internal audit outsourcing and "expert" services which were permitted under the SEC's final rules. Services still permitted include reporting on internal controls and of course advising on the appropriate accounting treatment of a transaction or assisting in the preparation of registration statements.

The legislative history is pretty clear. Paul Sarbanes, one of the senators for whom the statute is named, observed in the Congressional Record, "There are a lot of other auditing services, other than the nine I mentioned, that an auditor may want to provide and whose provision we did not preclude."[25] The Committee Report for the Senate bill, which served as the basis for the final act, provides that "the intention of this provision is to draw a clear line around a limited list of non-audit services that accounting firms may not provide to public company audit clients."[26]

Since SOX was enacted, consulting services by auditors have been on the rise yet again. In late 2010 James Kroeker, Chief Accountant of the Securities and Exchange Commission, voiced his concerns about what he feared was the "rebuilding of the consultancy practices within large accounting firms." Mr. Kroeker said, "I trust that the profession will not need to relearn lessons of the past on the serious, adverse effects of under-investing" in the quality of the audit "or failing to strictly maintain the independence of their audit process."[27] Mr. Kroeker ended on a wistful note, declaring—despite all evidence to the contrary—that he is "hopeful that if significant investments are being made to pursue other lines of business within a 'multidisciplinary' [accounting] firm, the potential impact on public trust and public perception of the audit practice is being considered."[28]

Unfortunately, Mr. Kroeker's optimism is entirely unfounded. The problem of auditor independence is actually deeply structural, and it is not at all susceptible to being fixed without significant and currently unforeseeable changes to the industrial structure of the United States. These structural problems are twofold. First, the accounting industry is so concentrated that there is essentially no competition among major audit firms. The traditional economic theory of reputation depends on competition. But in today's world large publicly traded corporate clients cannot distinguish among the major accounting firms on the basis of the quality of their audits because there are no discernible distinctions among the big accounting firms.[29] As I have shown in previous research with Ted Eisenberg, all the big accounting firms—including the late, unlamented Arthur Andersen—historically have had about the same number of clients that have experienced serious accounting irregularities that have required them to restate their financial results. Consequently, even if a company wanted to do so, it could not distinguish itself from its rivals by selecting for itself a particularly honest or "tough" outside auditor.

In addition, auditing has become so technical, specialized, complex, and time-consuming that, in sharp distinction from other professional groups such as doctors and lawyers, accountants who perform audits can have only a single client at a time. Auditing a major corporation is a full-time job for a whole team of auditors. These auditors have offices within the companies they audit, often for years at a time. They have more interactions with their clients than they do with their accounting firm colleagues who are assigned to other accounts.

Under these conditions, it is entirely natural that auditors develop feelings of loyalty and attachment to their clients. As a practical or functional matter, auditors of major corporations are in many ways more like employees of their clients than they are like employees of the audit firms whose business cards they carry around. The client pays their salaries. The clients' evaluation of their performance is critical to their success. The clients are their colleagues and friends on a day-to-day basis. Auditor independence of the kind described by the traditional economic theory of reputation is a thing of the past.

Another significant blow to the traditional economic theory of reputation as it relates to the accounting industry is the simple fact that obtaining an independent outside audit is now a mandatory legal obligation of public companies. It is no longer optional. This, of course, means that there is no signal whatsoever associated with a company's "decision" to have audited financial statements. All public companies have audited financial statements because all public companies are required to have them. The requirement for audits, combined with the lack of auditor independence and lack of competition between large accounting firms, suggests that the outside, independent audit of the theory of reputation does not exist in the modern, post-reputational world.

The accounting industry historically operated under the traditional economic theory of reputation. By producing and certifying information about clients through audits, accounting firms could essentially lend their reputations for accurate bookkeeping to their clients, which lowered clients' borrowing costs. This system was mutually beneficial for both accounting firms and their clients: Firms earned fees for their audits, and clients obtained lower costs of capital.

Under this traditional system, it was imperative that accounting firms maintain and invest in their reputations. If a firm approved or certified fraudulent records, it would ruin both the firm and its employees. However, the Enron scandal destroyed this theory of reputation and revealed larger structural flaws within the accounting industry. It became apparent that Arthur Andersen accountants were deeply intertwined with and dependent on their Enron clients: Andersen accountants relied solely on Enron work for their salaries and were manipulated by Enron's threats to cancel lucrative consulting contracts. The move from a general partnership structure to limited liability partnerships in the accounting industry lessened the incentive for partners to closely monitor the actions of their coworkers, reducing accountant independence and eroding competition. The Sarbanes-Oxley Act addressed some of these issues but failed to provide a completely adequate solution.

Endnotes

1. Ross L. Watts and Jerold L. Zimmerman, "Agency Problems, Auditing, and the Theory of the Firm: Some Evidence," *Journal of Law and Economics* 26 (1983): 613; see also Sung K. Choi and Debra C. Jeter, "The Effects of Qualified Audit Opinions on Earnings Response Coefficients," *Journal of Accounting and Economics* 15 (1992): 229; Rick Antle, "Auditor Independence," *Journal of Accounting Research* 22 (1984): 1; George J. Benston, "Accountant's Integrity and Financial Reporting," *Financial Executive* 10 (August 1975); Brian W. Mayhew, "Auditor Reputation Building," *Journal of Accounting Research* 39 (2001): 599; Brian W. Mayhew, Jeffrey W. Schatzberg, and Galen R. Sevcik, "The Effect of Accounting Uncertainty and Auditor Reputation on Auditor Objectivity," *Auditing: A Journal of Practice & Theory* 20 (September 2001): 49; Norman Macintosh, Teri Shearer, Daniel B. Thornton, and Michael A. Welker, "Financial Accounting as Simulacrum and Hyperreality: Perspectives on Income and Capital," *Accounting, Organizations and Society* 25 (January 2000): 13; Ronald R. King, "Reputation Formation for Reliable Reporting: An Experimental Investigation," *Accounting Review* 71 (1996): 375; George Benston, "The Value of the SEC's Accounting Disclosure Requirements," *Accounting Review* 44 (1969): 515.

2. Theodore Eisenberg and Jonathan Macey, "Was Arthur Andersen Different? An Empirical Examination of Major Accounting Firm Audits of Large Clients," *Journal of Empirical Legal Studies* 1 (2004): 263-300; Jonathan Macey and Hillary Sale, "Observations on the Role of Commodification, Independence, and Governance in the Accounting Industry," *Villanova Law Review* 48 (2003): 1167, 1168.

3. Daniel B. Thornton, "Financial Reporting Quality: Implications of Accounting Research, Submission to the Senate (Canada) Standing Committee on Banking, Trade and Commerce, Study on the State of Domestic and International Financial System," May 29, 2002.

4. Eisenberg and Macey, "Was Arthur Andersen Different?"

5. Srinivasan Krishnamurthy, Jian Zhou, and Nan Zhou, "Auditor Reputation, Auditor Independence, and the Stock-Market Impact of Andersen's Indictment on Its Client Firms," *Contemporary Accounting Research* 23, no. 2 (2006): 465-490.

6. Ibid. See also R. Balvers, B. McDonald, and R. Miller, "Underpricing of New Issues and the Choice of Auditors As a Signal of Investment Banker Reputation," *The Accounting Review* 63, no. 4 (1988): 605-22; R. Beatty, "Auditor Reputation and the Pricing of Initial Public Offerings," *The Accounting Review* 64, no. 4 (1989): 693-709 (cited in Krishnamurthy, Zhou, and Zhou, ibid.).

7. Flynn McRoberts, "A Final Accounting: The Fall of Andersen," *Chicago Tribune,* September 1, 2002, www.chicagotribune.com/news/chi-0209010315sep01,0,538751.story.

8. This account of Arthur Andersen's dealings with the Chicago railroad is drawn from "The Fall of Andersen," *Chicago Tribune,* September 1, 2002, www.chicagotribune.com/news/chi-0209010315sep01,0,538751.story. The story also is recounted in Ken Brown and Ianthe Jeanne Dugan, "Arthur Andersen's Fall from Grace Is a Sad Tale of Greed and Miscues," *The Wall Street Journal,* June 7, 2002.

9. "The Fall of Andersen."

10. "The Fall of Andersen."

11. "The Fall of Andersen."

12. Jonathan D. Glater, "Fearing Liability, Law Firms Change Partnership Status," *The New York Times,* January 10, 2003, at C2.

13. Ibid.

14. http://arthurandersen-sf.com/.

15. http://bus.wisc.edu/centers/arthur-andersen-center.

16. Paul Gores, "Ex-Andersen Partners Land Jobs," *Milwaukee Journal Sentinel,* June 6, 2002, http://news.google.com/newspapers?nid=16 83&dat=20020606&id=YjYqAAAAIBAJ&sjid=9kEEAAAAIBAJ& pg=6308,4843527.

17. "Huron Consulting Group: From the Ashes of Andersen," *Bloomberg BusinessWeek,* June 3, 2007, www.businessweek.com/stories/2007-06-03/huron-consulting-group-from-the-ashes-of-andersen.

18. Ibid.

19. Brian Ruiz Switzky, "Spirit Alive Ten Years After Andersen Demise," *Washington Business Journal,* May 18, 2012, www.bizjournals.com/washington/print-edition/2012/05/18/spirit-alive-10-years-after-andersen.html?page=all.

20. R.D. Sellers, T.J. Fogarty, and L. Parker, "The Legacy of Social Networks in a Failed Public Accounting Firm," June 22, 2011, www.freepatentsonline.com/article/Journal-Managerial-Issues/266346130.html.

21. Peter Millard, "Arthur Andersen Castoffs Stay Close to Home," *The Business Journal Serving Greater Milwaukee*, April 6, 2003, www.bizjournals.com/milwaukee/stories/2003/04/07/focus1.html?page=all.

22. Ibid.

23. John C. Coffee, Jr., "Understanding Enron: It's About the Gatekeepers, Stupid," *Business Lawyer* 57 (2002): 1403, 1404-05.

24. See In re Enron Corp. Sec., Derivative & ERISA Litigation, 235 F.Supp. 2d 549, 679 (S.D. Texas, 2002). For example, Andersen Professional Standards Group partner Carl Bass repeatedly indicated his concern regarding Enron's accounting in e-mails on 12/19/99 and 2/4/00. On 2/1/00, Bass commented on several Enron transactions, saying, "This whole deal looks like there is no substance." Bass was later "removed as PSG advisor for the Enron audit team." Just before his removal, he sent an e-mail asserting that David Duncan and other Andersen employees "were heavily involved in structuring" certain Enron deals and "in decisions to allow Enron to account improperly" for the deals.

25. 148 Cong. Rec. S6327, S6332 (daily ed. July 8, 2002) (statement of Senator Sarbanes).

26. Senate Report No. 107-205, at 18 (2002).

27. James Kroeker, "Remarks Before the 2010 AICPA National Conference on Current SEC and PCAOB Developments," December 6, 1010, www.sec.gov/news/speech/2010/spch120610jlk.htm.

28. Ibid.

29. Eisenberg and Macey, "Was Arthur Andersen Different?"

7

The New, Post-Reputation Wall Street: Law Firms

The legal profession differs in fundamentally significant ways from the accounting profession, though the two share some common characteristics. Lawyers are hired to argue for, protect, and defend the interests of clients. The best lawyers develop new strategies to advance their clients' interests, while the best accountants strictly interpret accounting rules. Lawyers, unlike auditors, are not meant to be independent of their clients. Lawyers display much greater lateral mobility than accountants, with lawyers switching firms frequently. Furthermore, unlike among the top accounting firms, intense competition for clients exists at big law firms, leading lawyers to take increased risks. Lawyers, though, also serve as gatekeepers, or reputational intermediaries, who use their reputations to lend credibility to their clients. The two roles of lawyers—aggressively pursuing their clients' interests and lending a credible, respected reputation to their clients—exist simultaneously. This ambiguity often benefits lawyers. Although scholars have argued that law firms act according to the traditional reputational model, it is highly doubtful that law firms continue to follow this model, if they ever did, for several reasons. Improved information technology, the passage of the securities laws, and the increase in both in-house counsel and specialization of lawyers' functions have decreased lawyers' incentives to monitor their colleagues and, by extension, their firms.

The legal profession shares certain characteristics with the accounting profession, but there are even more important and fundamental differences between the two professions. The most fundamental difference between law and accounting is that lawyers are advocates who are supposed to present their clients' points of view in the most persuasive ways. Lawyers are "hired guns" for their clients.

In contrast, accountants are supposed to retain a professional distance from their clients. As the Chief Accountant of the SEC once said, the profession "cannot be, either in fact or in appearance, that of an advocate for the management of the company it audits." The same regulator suggested that the accounting profession consider changing its "collective vocabulary" in order to strengthen the perception and the reality of auditor independence from its clients. He advised accountants not to "use the word 'client' to refer to the management of companies under audit" because the real client of the auditors of publicly traded companies is the investing public, not the management of the companies.[1]

Unlike accountants, lawyers are advocates. They are not supposed to be independent of their clients. Their job is to argue, persuade, or cajole people into concluding that a client's statements of its financial condition are accurate. At least in theory, the job of the accountant is to make sure that clients' financial statements are accurate, whether the client wants them to be accurate or not. Lawyers are supposed to represent their clients and advance, protect, and defend their interests. The one-sided nature of legal representation is defensible because there is always (or almost always) a lawyer on the other side to take the opposing point of view. The job of the judge is to resolve the disputes between the dueling lawyers according to the appropriate applicable legal and equitable principles.

Turning briefly to the similarities, lawyers enjoy the same insulation from personal liability as accountants. The information market for lawyers has matured even more than has the information market for accountants. Big corporate clients used to hire law firms to do their legal work. Now they hire particular lawyers within law firms. Today a primary responsibility of the in-house general counsels in big companies is to interview, evaluate, and select the particular lawyers who are the best fit to pursue or defend particular lawsuits or regulatory matters and to plan and structure the regulatory, tax, and contract law components of complex transactions.

Another distinction between jobs in top corporate law firms and top accounting firms is the pace of lateral mobility. Lateral mobility for lawyers appears to be much greater than that of accountants. One often sees headlines in legal publications, such as *The American Lawyer,* announcing, "Law Firm Churn Hits All-Time High."[2] The last couple of decades have been described as the "age of mobility" for lawyers, and the "heightened lateral mobility"[3] of lawyers has been called "one of the most conspicuous features of the modern legal marketplace."[4] Large law firms increasingly rely on lateral recruiting to fuel growth and profitability. Top lawyers' careers, to use an analogy used by Jonathan R. MacBride and David J. Samlin, increasingly resemble the careers of professional athletes. In sports, athletes traditionally remained with one team throughout their careers. Now that pro athletes are no longer required to play for the teams that draft them, they regularly move from team to team seeking larger paychecks. Similarly, lawyers used to remain with one firm but now "are the ultimate free agents, seemingly always on the lookout for a law firm that offers them a better opportunity or a bigger payday."[5] Lawyers are "uniquely situated to take advantage of these opportunities." They are largely "at-will" employees who can change jobs whenever they wish. Lawyers are, in addition, usually free to practice law without restrictions after switching firms. In the year ending September 30, 2009, 2,775 partners either joined or left large firms, according to *The American Lawyer.* This was a record, but "because this report merely tracks the partners leaving or joining big firms, this figure represents only the tip of the iceberg as it relates to overall lateral moves throughout the country."[6]

Another distinguishing feature of modern sophisticated legal practice in the financial services area is increased competition among law firms. The legal profession is far more competitive than the accounting profession. There are hundreds of national law firms that compete for clients with the most complex, difficult—and lucrative—cases and issues. There are only a handful of accounting firms that compete for the largest and most complex public company accounting engagements. In addition, individual lawyers personally generate profits to a far greater extent than do accountants. It is hardly a surprise that the most sought-after and intensely recruited lawyers are those whose practice areas are so narrow and specialized—or their skills are in such demand—that they can demand almost any price they want. The goal of the people who run the biggest law firms is "to attract and retain lawyers with the largest books for price-insensitive work." As a result, law firms "increasingly focus on the profits per partner as reported to *The American Lawyer* rather than a long-term business strategy that delivers a highly valued and cost-effective service to clients." This focus, however, has led big firms to ignore "the broad middle market, which pays overhead." As a result, numerous Am Law 200 firms are susceptible to smaller, boutique competitors "with lower cost structures and organizational sizes that permit greater trust, cooperation, a longer time horizon, and ultimately greater value for clients."[7]

Accounting for the Risk?

The implication of this analysis is that big law firms have become significantly riskier than accounting firms and they are growing riskier all the time. Law firms not only merge more than accounting firms, but also simply break apart and go out of business far more often than the big accounting firms. Lawyers face competition not only from lawyers in other law firms (and sometimes from lawyers within their own firms), but also from their clients. Big corporate clients are increasingly moving legal work in-house. Because public companies are required by SEC regulation to have financial statements audited by outside auditors, there is no possibility for this trend to migrate from law to accounting.

These changes have made the practice of law at the highest levels of finance more competitive, risky, and lucrative. One interesting empirical study observed that the largest 100 U.S. law firms have "shifted towards high-end/high stakes practice such as white collar crime, securities enforcement litigation, [and] intellectual property," and have moved away from more traditional practice areas like "general business, regulatory compliance work, trusts & estates," and similar fields. The same study concluded that "the fundamental instability of many large U.S. law firms is evidenced by the large number of Am Law 200 firms in recent years that have collapsed or been wholly absorbed, rather than merged, into other large firms."[8]

The legal and advisory services provided by lawyers are different from the audit and other services provided by accountants in even more fundamental ways. Although intelligence, thoroughness, and attention to detail are important qualities in both professions, the best accountants are those who stay firmly within the lines when they take up their brushes and paint for clients. In sharp contrast, the very best lawyers are those who develop new ways of doing deals or develop new strategies and tactics to advance their clients' interests and to surprise and confound the opposition.

The practice of accounting is much different. "Creative accounting" is a very bad thing. "Creative lawyering" is a good thing. Regulators, lenders, and investors do not want to be known to be associated with accounting firms or accountants that are thought to interpret the accounting rules creatively or aggressively. In contrast, many lawyers pride themselves—and market themselves—as being particularly creative and aggressive in asserting and defending their clients' views.

There is, however, another, somewhat aspirational way of looking at the nature of the services offered by top law firms that stresses reputation in the business model, very much like the role that used to be played by reputation in the accounting industry. Because these two views uncomfortably exist simultaneously, there is no clear understanding of the actual role that U.S. financial lawyers and corporate lawyers that represent public companies are supposed to play. On the one hand, as corporate law professor Stephen Bainbridge has pointed out, the legal profession, as reflected in the profession's strict rules of confidentiality and professional responsibility toward clients, clearly views itself "as advocates, confidants, and advisors, not as gatekeepers like auditors."[9] The corporate officers and directors who retain them and pay their fees also view lawyers in this way.[10]

Resolute Representative and Moral Mediator

The practice of law is schizophrenic because there is another, entirely different way of looking at the role that lawyers play in finance. Professor Bainbridge observes that lawyers are advocates but also that, rather inconsistently, "lawyers often play a reputational intermediary role not dissimilar to that of an auditor."[11] A respected,

powerful lawyer can aid a client in trouble through "the lawyer's reputation for probity and upstanding ethics." Lawyers, especially, Bainbridge asserts, transactional counsel and in-house lawyers, "are well
positioned to intervene by blocking the effectiveness of a defective
registration statement or prevent the consummation of a transaction...." However, Bainbridge notes that lawyers "all too often failed"
in these responsibilites.[12]

This schizophrenia in the way lawyers are viewed—and in the way
lawyers sometimes view themselves—is not really random. This persistent ambiguity serves the interest of the legal profession very well.
The most successful advocates, after all, are those able to convince the
regulators and judges before whom they argue that they are not advocates at all but statesmen who are above the fray and have been called
in not to advocate but to explain. Often lawyers hold themselves out
to their clients as advocates and to the outside world as reputational
intermediaries. In this sense, the schizophrenic way in which the legal
profession is viewed is not due to happenstance. It is merely a convenient self-serving connivance of the profession that would be better
abandoned.

At a minimum, lawyers should be honest about the role they are
playing. It should be clear to judges and regulators when lawyers are
acting as advocates and when they are acting as neutral, "reputational
intermediaries" who are above the fray. In the second case, their role,
like that of traditional reputational intermediaries such as auditors, is
to verify and vouch for the integrity and truthfulness of their clients in
particular contexts and circumstances, such as SEC investigations or
lawsuits for fraud. Often this distinction is clear to all parties. Sometimes, though, it is not.

Attorneys Rise; Accountants Fall

The ambiguity between lawyers' role as advocate and lawyers' role
as reputational intermediary is readily clear in the common situation
of a "true sale" opinion. Companies routinely enter into sales transactions with other firms. Sometimes fraud is involved in these transactions. For example, a company will sometimes succumb to pressure

to show that it is meeting or exceeding its forecasts about how many products it is selling or how much profit it is making in a particular financial quarter. The chief way to fraudulently boost sales and profits is to pretend to sell products, booking profits from such sales, when the products are not really being sold at all. For example, in a scheme known as "channel stuffing," a company transfers its products to a reseller "on consignment," pretending to have really sold the products. Secretly, it agreed to repurchase the products if the reseller is unsuccessful in selling them.

Sometimes, as happened in the Enron scandal, a company will falsely claim to have sold significant assets at high profits to other companies in order to claim fraudulently that its revenues and profits are higher than they really are. At Enron, Andrew Fastow, the company's chief financial officer, created separate corporations, called Special Purpose Entities (SPEs) or Special Purpose Vehicles (SPVs), and arranged for these companies to purchase assets from Enron. Many of these transactions were fraudulent because they did not represent real, arms-length transactions between different companies. Enron or its affiliates actually controlled these companies, so Enron was merely selling its own assets back to itself at inflated prices in order to fool the investing public, creditors, and regulators about its true financial condition. Sometimes Enron would sell assets or enter into deals with companies that really were separate. But Enron would have secret, undisclosed arrangements with these other companies to repurchase the assets later. And Enron often would agree to buy the assets back at prices higher than its previous sales price to compensate the other company for its trouble. Of course, these transactions did not represent true sales of assets either. All of these gimmicks were fraudulent.

Channel stuffing and the other sorts of financial shenanigans described here have been going on for a very long time. Regulators, auditors, creditors, and investors worry about these things happening in the companies in which they are involved. To reduce the risk of these sorts of frauds occurring, outsiders insist that the lawyers involved in these financings issue what is known as a "true sale" opinion. A true sale opinion is an opinion that a transaction that is called a "sale" is really a sale because, as a legal matter, the asset being sold has become "legally isolated" from the seller. Being legally isolated simply means that the seller does not either retain legal ownership of the asset or retain any legal obligation to repurchase the asset after the "sale."

A true sale opinion is an official legal opinion from a law firm that reaches the conclusion that a particular securitization or other financial transaction constitutes a true sale that effectively transfers the seller's right title and interest in the assets to the SPV or other purchaser. People who are buying assets, particularly in complex financings, insist on true sale opinions because they want to be sure that the assets they are buying will not be considered part of the estate of the seller under applicable insolvency law. Thus, if the seller goes bankrupt, its creditors cannot succeed in gaining control of the assets it has bought to satisfy its claim against the seller. True sale opinions also generally contain language that the SPV or other purchaser will be successful in enforcing its ownership of the assets.[13]

True sale opinions are of great interest from a reputational perspective because the lawyers drafting such opinions sometimes are torn between their role as independent verifiers who are offering their reputations in order to help the client persuade onlookers that a particular transaction involves a "true sale" and their role as creative deal-engineers who are paid to structure complex transactions in novel ways that exploit ambiguities and grey areas in the rules governing what are true sales. Issuing true sales opinions has always been considered risky for law firms because if the transactions turn out badly, the law firm that signed such opinions generally is sued along with the seller. For this reason, some firms are reluctant to issue true sales opinions because of liability and ethical concerns.

The stark juxtaposition between the fate of Vinson & Elkins, Enron's primary law firm, which issued fairness opinions associated with disputed Enron transactions, and the fate of Enron's accountants, Arthur Andersen, is worth noting. As recounted in the preceding chapter, Andersen imploded in a tsunami of accusations, civil litigation, criminal indictments, and bad publicity. Vinson & Elkins, by contrast, emerged from the scandal unscathed. In fact, the days following the collapse of Enron, by far Vinson & Elkins's biggest client, have been described as the law firm's Teflon Days.[14]

Vinson & Elkins walked a fine line between trading on its reputation as a top-tier firm and taking off the gloves entirely to champion

Enron's point of view in the many transactions it papered for the corrupt company. Vinson & Elkins had been widely criticized for not blowing the whistle when it grew uneasy with some of Enron's more controversial dealings, such as the notorious LJM partnerships. In a famous letter evaluating certain Enron transactions with SPEs, Vinson & Elkins partner Max Hendricks III described Enron's practice of forming special-purpose entities to keep debt off its books as "creative and aggressive," but added, somewhat oddly, that "no one has reason to believe that it is inappropriate from a technical standpoint."[15] It is not at all clear precisely whom, if anyone, outside of Enron itself and its captured accountant Arthur Andersen, Mr. Hendricks consulted to determine that no one had reason to believe that Enron's accounting was inappropriate.

Ultimately, Vinson & Elkins settled the litigation against the firm, agreeing to waive its claim of $3.9 million for previous legal services to Enron that were as yet unpaid and to pay Enron's bankruptcy estate $30 million in cash for the benefit of Enron's creditors. The settlement was a tiny fraction of the estimated $40 billion lost by Enron's investors. Simple arithmetic favors the conclusion that, even with the $30 million payment and the fee waiver, Vinson & Elkins came out ahead, having billed Enron a total of $162 million in the four-year period between 1997 and 2001 alone.[16] Prior to this small payout, *BusinessWeek* observed, "Amid all the carnage that has surrounded Enron's collapse, one player in the drama has remained remarkably unscathed: Vinson & Elkins." *BusinessWeek* noted that Arthur Andersen collapsed, JPMorgan Chase paid $2.2 billion to settle a shareholder fraud lawsuit, and other banks and outside Enron directors paid almost $5 billion more. No Vinson & Elkins lawyers had to respond to professional misconduct charges by the Texas bar, and Joseph Dilg, the partner responsible for the firm's Enron dealings, was promoted to managing partner. Indeed, Vinson & Elkins, in 2005, broke the $1 million threshold for average partner compensation, becoming the first Texas law firm to do so.[17]

Enron's court-appointed bankruptcy examiner Neal Batson observed in his comprehensive report on Enron's collapse that Vinson & Elkins's opinion letters were "crucial to Enron's ability to complete" various transactions that successfully moved troubled assets off of Enron's balance sheet. The opinion letters allowed Enron to immediately book profits on assets that had not truly been sold and that were worth far less than Enron claimed to have received in the deals.[18] According to *Bloomberg BusinessWeek,* the law firm, while simultaneously providing its "True Sale" opinion letters and other validation for Enron's crooked deals, was not fully comfortable with its role. Joseph Dilg, for example, while getting ready for a meeting with Enron General Counsel James V. Derrick Jr., noted, "We [are] unsure of how opinion rendered satisfies requirements of [the Financial Accounting Standards Board]."[19] A March 1998 V&E opinion letter contained language that "seemed to undermine the whole point of the document." Dilg displayed an understanding of the essential role that the deals sanctioned by the opinion letters played in portraying the financial situation of Enron to investors: "'Large transactions with significant earnings impact,' he wrote in the same set of notes, adding further down: 'Don't want deal to blow up at last moment and cause earnings surprise.'"[20]

An interesting question is whether Vinson & Elkins's aggressive lawyering was ever a risk to the firm. In fact, it seems that its edgy representation of Enron did the firm more good than harm. No risk appears to have existed. Take, for example, an analysis of the various lawsuits against Vinson & Elkins brought by Enron investors. *BusinessWeek* noted of this litigation that the main threat it posed to Vinson & Elkins was to its reputation. Since the firm had restructured as a limited liability partnership in 1992, partners would not face personal liability. Thus, plaintiffs would rely on insurance for compensation.[21]

The better argument is that Vinson & Elkins's reputation was enhanced, not tarnished, by its relentless representation of Enron, notwithstanding the concerns of its own lawyers about the validity and propriety of what Enron was doing. Clients like aggressive lawyers. And, of course, Vinson & Elkins likely is far more concerned with its reputation among its current and prospective clients than it is with its reputation among journalists or other practically irrelevant outside observers.

Thus, law firms and the legal profession lead a double life from a reputational perspective. Regulators, academics, and leaders of the profession embrace and propagate a variant of the traditional economic theory of reputation pursuant to which law firms and lawyers serve as "gatekeepers." Gatekeepers are "reputational intermediaries" whose role is "to assure investors as to the quality of the 'signal' sent by the corporate issues."[22] As John Coffee and others have observed, a gatekeeper is a "repeat player" in the capital markets who enjoys both a reputation for integrity and privileged access to their clients who are issuers (i.e., companies trying to borrow money, either directly or by selling securities or by engaging in related financing transactions).

The Legal Reputational Model

The basic idea, of course, is that, because of their reputations, investors and other counterparties who have never heard of and do not trust a particular issuer *have* heard of and are willing to trust that issuer's highly reputed law firm. Therefore, high-reputation law firms, like accounting firms and investment banks, act in ways consistent with the traditional economic theory of reputation, renting their reputations to their corporate and financial clients.

It seems highly doubtful that this traditional reputational model as applied to law firms is valid any longer, to the extent that it ever was, for several reasons. The first relates to improved information technology. Because of improved information technology, the value of law firms' reputational advantage in relation to their issuer-clients has declined dramatically. Historically, and particularly before the passage of the securities laws, investors would be reassured when issuers (whose names and reputations were entirely unknown to them) hired iconic corporate law firms (whose names and reputations were well known to them). With improved information technology, however, clients have direct access to detailed information about issuers.

A second, and closely related point is that with the passage of the securities laws, particularly the Securities Act of 1933 and the Securities and Exchange Act of 1934, not only could issuers and customers communicate more directly (thereby mitigating the historic asymmetry of the information problem that created the need for law firms to serve as informational intermediaries), but also issuers could credibly assert for the first time that the various claims they were making about themselves, as well as the financial information they were reporting, were accurate. The securities laws passed in the wake of the great stock market crash of 1929 made issuers subject to civil and criminal securities fraud liability if their claims were untrue, or if they knowingly failed to put in clarifying information necessary to prevent any information that was disclosed from being misleading.

It is noteworthy that under the Securities Act of 1933, which governs the disclosures that companies make when they sell securities to the public, disclosures outside of certain formats (i.e., outside of the formal registration statement and its associated prospectus) are strongly discouraged. In addition, disclosures in any format, including oral and written disclosures and any other communications to third parties that are false for any reason, whether as the result of intentional fraud or mere negligence, result in *strict liability* for the issuer, with the remedy being recision.[23] This means that anybody who purchases securities from an issuer in a public offering in which there was a misstatement of a material fact can return them to the issuer and receive the offering price for them.[24] Because issuers are strictly liable for material misstatements or omissions in public offerings, without regard to whether these restatements or omissions were made intentionally or even negligently, demand for independent verification by law firms and other reputational intermediaries was reduced; the issuers' assertions were more reliable.

In addition, underwriters, corporate managers, and directors also are liable for material misstatements or omissions, although they are entitled to the legal defense known as the "due diligence" defense.[25] The due diligence defense provides a method for escaping liability for false or misleading statements or from omissions in disclosure documents.[26] If a non-issuer (recall that the issuer is strictly liable and therefore cannot take refuge in the due diligence defense) can establish that it was appropriately "diligent" in analyzing, verifying, and investigating the statements made by the issuer, it can avoid liability.[27] In my view, the potential liability of underwriters, corporate managers, and directors has reduced the demand for the verification function of lawyers, who charge high prices for providing this service, by imposing the legal requirement that a host of other organizations provide the service. Since customers are forced by the securities laws to pay for these verification services, it stands to reason that many of them will be unwilling to pay law firms again to perform such services.

Moreover, these provisions, along with the antifraud provisions of the securities laws, particularly SEC Rule 10b-5, which makes it illegal to make a false or misleading statement "in connection with the purchase or sale of any security," reduce the incentives for law firms to invest in reputational capital and improve the competitive positions of firms that have not made such investments.[28] The securities laws make it easier for low-reputation firms (firms that have made little or no investment in developing reputation capital) to claim credibly that they will do a thorough and reliable job of vetting the statements made by potential issuers. The antifraud provisions of the securities laws enable low-reputation firms to compete with high-reputation firms because the legal liability created by the securities laws is a substitute for the reputational capital that historically was enjoyed by the venerable law firms of old. After the passage of the securities laws, new firms (like the Venture Law Group, Wilson Sonsini, and others) could enter the market for the first time by claiming, even without having invested in developing reputational capital, that they could be trusted to refrain from associating themselves with unscrupulous clients. These new firms claimed they were trustworthy not because of concerns about reductions in the value of their reputational capital, but instead because of concerns about civil and criminal liability under the securities laws.

The third factor in the decline of law firms' incentives to invest in reputation is the dramatic increase in the sophistication of clients' in-house counsels and the concomitant increased specialization of lawyers' functions. It used to be the case, in decades past, that law firms would handle all or virtually all the legal work for their corporate clients. The big firms would advise on banking law, corporate law, securities law, intellectual property, antitrust, commercial law, international business transactions, franchising law, employment and labor relations, contracts, and torts. These firms would also litigate as well as do the corporate work on behalf of their big clients. Nowadays, in-house lawyers are much more sophisticated in their selection of outside counsel. They develop detailed, highly textured information about individual lawyers rather than firms.

This means that corporate clients no longer choose law firms so much as they choose individual lawyers to represent them in particular matters. This, in turn, means two things. First, investments in law firm reputations are not as valuable as they used to be because it is the reputation of individual lawyers within firms, or perhaps departments of lawyers within firms, instead of the law firms themselves that attracts clients. Second, it means that, to the extent that there is still a payoff to law firms in the form of increased client demand from investing in reputation, this payoff has been reduced because the client demand is likely to be only for the particular lawyer or legal group within the firm that has developed the reputation.

Now that the reputation of individual lawyers has replaced the reputation of law firms, the incentive for lawyers to invest in their own reputations is on the rise, while the incentive of lawyers to invest in their firms' reputations is on the wane. Individual lawyers have become itinerant free agents. They switch firms far more often than they used to. Many switch firms over and over again. Lawyers' incentives to monitor their colleagues has diminished, not only because lawyers no longer have the expertise to monitor other lawyers in the firm with different specializations, but also because lawyers no longer have the incentive to do so. Of course, this incentive has been reduced even further by the replacement of the general partnership, which provided strong incentives for lawyers' accountants and other professionals to monitor their colleagues, with the professional corporation and the limited liability partnership, which eliminates those incentives by removing the risk that lawyers who fail to monitor their colleagues will face liability.

Endnotes

1. James L. Kroeker, Chief Accountant, Office of the Chief Accountant, U.S. Securities and Exchange Commission, "Remarks Before the 2010 AICPA National Conference on Current SEC and PCAOB Developments," December 6, 2010, www.sec.gov/news/speech/2010/spch120610jlk.htm.

2. *Philadelphia Business Journal*, February 24, 2010, http://philadelphia.bizjournals.com/philadelphia/blogs/law/2010/02/american_lawyer_law_firm_churn_hits_all-time_high.html.

3. Leslie D. Corwin, "Response to Loyalty in the Firm: A Statement of General Principles on the Duties of Partners Withdrawing from Law Firms," *Washington and Lee Law Review* 55 (1998): 1055, 1056.

4. William Henderson and Leonard Bierman, "An Empirical Analysis of Lateral Lawyer Trends from 2000 to 2007: The Emerging Equilibrium for Corporate Law Firms," *Georgetown Journal of Legal Ethics* 22 (2009): 1396.

5. Jonathan R. MacBride and David J. Samlin, "The Ethical and Legal Consequences of Lateral Moves between Law Firms," *Chartwell Law Firm Professional Publication,* published in *The Brief,* Volume 40, Number 2, Winter 2011, www.chartwelllaw.com/news_press/documents/brief_v40n2_macbride_samlin.pdf, accessed November 30, 2012.

6. Ibid.

7. Henderson and Bierman, "An Empirical Analysis of Lateral Lawyer Trends."

8. Ibid.

9. Stephen Bainbridge, "Corporate Lawyers as Gatekeepers," essay adopted from Stephen Bainbridge, *Corporate Governance After the Financial Crisis* (Oxford University Press, 2012).

10. Ibid.

11. Ibid.

12. Ibid.

13. www.fasb.org/cs/BlobServer?blobcol=urldata&blobtable=MungoBlobs&blobkey=id&blobwhere=1175817783274&blobheader=application/pdf.

14. See Michael Orey, "Enron's Last Mystery," *Bloomberg Business Week,* June 11, 2006, www.businessweek.com/stories/2006-06-11/enrons-last-mystery.

15. Stephen Traub, "Enron Settles with Vinson & Elkins," *CFO,* June 1, 2006, www.cfo.com/article.cfm/7023131

16. See Michael Orey, "Enron's Last Mystery."

17. Ibid.

18. Ibid.

19. Ibid.

20. Ibid.

21. Ibid.

22. John C. Coffee, Jr., *Gatekeepers: The Professions and Corporate Governance* (2006), 2; see also John C. Coffee, Jr., "Understanding Enron: 'It's About the Gatekeepers, Stupid,'" *Business Lawyer* 57 (2002): 1403; Jonathan R. Macey, "Efficient Capital Markets, Corporate Disclosure, and Enron," *Cornell Law Review* 89 (2004): 394, 405-10; Jonathan Macey and Hillary A. Sale, "Observations on the Role of Commodification, Independence and Governance in the Accounting Industry," *Villanova Law Review* 48 (2003): 1167; William C. Powers, Jr., et al., Report of Investigation by the Special Investigative Committee of the Board of Directors of Enron Corp. (2002): 5, 17, 24-26, available at http://news.findlaw.com/hdocs/docs/enron/sicreport/sicreport020102.pdf.

23. James Spindler, "Is It Time to Wind Up the Securities Act of 1933?" *Regulation* 29 (Winter 2006): 48, 50 (emphasis in original).

24. Ibid.

25. Ibid.

26. Ibid.

27. Ibid.

28. 17 Code of Federal Regulations § 240.10b-5—Employment of manipulative and deceptive devices.

8

The New, Post-Reputation Wall Street: Credit Rating Agencies

Credit ratings are designed to help investors determine how risky a company is by measuring the likelihood that a company would be able to repay its rated debt in a timely manner. Credit rating agencies were, like accounting firms, once reputational intermediaries. However, the credit rating agencies have lost their reputations for independence, objectivity, honesty, and even competence. Credit ratings, given by only three major worldwide firms, no longer contain useful information. However, they still affect securities prices and borrowing costs for companies. Changes in ratings can themselves cause changes in borrowing costs that they are supposed to predict through a series of regulations that have developed over the past three decades. These regulations began with the designation of SEC-approved nationally recognized statistical rating organizations, or NRSROs. The NRSRO designation created a regulation-driven demand for credit ratings that was dissociated from the actual utility of the ratings. With this artificially created demand, credit rating agencies could increase profits by increasing the number and decreasing the quality of the ratings they issued. Furthermore, companies would choose the rating agency that would issue the most favorable rating, essentially buying off the credit rating agencies. Credit rating agencies issued high ratings to a large number of extremely complicated, structured financial instruments in the years before the 2008 financial crisis. Because of the false confidence these inaccurate ratings provided, the agencies have justifiably been blamed for the financial crisis. However, credit rating agencies have largely escaped legal liability, at least in the United States. Despite new legislation in the Dodd-Frank Act that attempts to curb the influence of and reliance on credit ratings, investors still seem to use the ratings, even though they are now known to be largely useless. This continued use seems to stem from two factors. The lemming effect, or going along with the crowd, provides one reason. The other reason is that the complicated way of measuring risk in financial markets using the beta coefficient causes investors to use credit rating agencies as a simple, easy signal when investing.

Credit ratings from credit rating agencies such as Moody's and Standard & Poor's are supposed to assist investors. The ratings are designed to help determine the risk of the company that is being rated as expressed by the likelihood that the company will be able to repay its rated debt in a timely manner. The higher the rating assigned to a company or a particular debt issue, the better the odds of repayment.

Credit rating agencies, like the big accounting firms discussed in Chapter 6, "The New, Post-Reputation Wall Street: Accounting Firms," were, once upon a time, pure reputational intermediaries. According to the traditional economic theory of reputation, credit ratings have no value whatsoever unless the credit rating agency that issues the rating is trusted and respected by the investing public. Credit rating agencies first emerged in the United States during the rapid westward expansion in the early years of the Republic. The capital funds required for investment were in the East Coast capitals of Boston, Philadelphia, and New York. Increasingly, new investment opportunities were in the distant western regions of the country. Credit rating agencies first emerged to provide information to investors on the East Coast about opportunities in the "Wild West."[1]

The fundamental implication of the traditional theory is that if investors and others do not trust the information content in the ratings produced by credit rating agencies, the rating agency itself is doomed. If the business community does not trust the ratings generated by a credit rating agency, it will not let those ratings influence investment decisions. At some point, the companies that used to buy ratings from the agency will no longer find the cost of procuring these ratings to be worth the expense. When this happens, according to the theory, the credit rating agency loses its only source of revenue and must exit the industry.

On the other hand, if the investing community has confidence in a credit rating agency, investors will be acutely interested in the ratings.

Ratings will influence investment decisions, with investors being willing to pay more for highly rated securities and less for securities that the rating agency considers risky and therefore assigns a lower rating. As Amanda Bahena has pointed out in her excellent e-book on the financial crisis, "When they are comparing financial instruments promising the same yields, investors are more willing to invest in the higher-rated instrument."[2] Of course, this is true only to the extent that investors actually believe that the higher-rated financial instrument is more valuable than the lower-rated one. In other words, if a company or its securities are low-rated, the company "must provide investors with additional incentives, such as higher interest rates, to convince them to invest."[3] There is evidence that ratings "directly affect the cost of raising capital."

However, when a small number of huge rating agencies become massively powerful, as they have in the United States and throughout the developed world, analysis of the quality of the information produced by the credit rating agencies becomes difficult and the results are quite muddy. The credit rating industry is dominated by three companies globally, and by just two firms in the U.S. The U.S. credit rating agencies are Standard and Poor's (S&P) and Moody's Corp. The non-U.S. company is the British rating agency Fitch Ratings, which is a distant third in market share. Together these firms dominate the market, accounting for over 95% of the ratings of companies and securities issues.

Rating the Raters

Despite the enormous size, prevalence, and visibility of the major credit rating agencies, the three companies and their ratings are subject to significant shortcomings. A big problem regarding ratings is what are known as "feedback effects." If ratings change borrowing costs for companies, not because they reveal new information, but simply because they raise borrowing costs for other reasons, then ratings don't tell us very much. Worse, a ratings downgrade can raise borrowing costs for companies for no good reason and even force companies out of business simply because investors and lenders shun the company because of the downgrade.

For example, in the real world, credit ratings are ubiquitous. In many, if not most, loan agreements and bond covenants, a credit downgrade is what is known as an "event of default."

Loan contracts and bond covenants generally hold that, in an event of default, the lenders and bondholders immediately have the right to demand repayment regardless of the original maturity date of the instrument in the initial agreement. Accelerating the due date for these obligations frequently forces the borrower into insolvency and always causes problems for the company that has experienced the event of default. In other words, even a perfectly healthy company likely will find itself in big trouble or even fail when it experiences a ratings downgrade, as lenders demand immediate repayment of debts that might otherwise not have been due for years in the future. Events of default also raise the issuer's borrowing costs and extinguish any contractual obligations that lenders might have had to make loans to the company in the future. MIT professor Gustavo Manso points out the feedback-effect problem caused by credit ratings in a paper. Though credit rating agencies should, he notes, give "an independent opinion on the credit quality of issuers," credit ratings can "themselves affect the credit quality of issuers." This occurs because "market participants rely on credit ratings for investment decisions." Professor Manso provides an example: "A rating downgrade may lead to higher cost of capital for the borrowing firm because...of rating triggers in financial contracts."[4]

There are studies that show that credit ratings affect companies' borrowing costs. Some interpret these statistical results as evidence that credit rating agencies enjoy strong reputations in the community.

Not surprisingly, many of these studies are authored by the credit rating agencies themselves. But others are not. Independent researchers have demonstrated that, as one set of MIT scholars succinctly put it, "the lower rated the bond, the higher the borrowing costs."[5] But the interpretation of these results as somehow proving that credit rating agencies are trusted and respected simply because their ratings affect borrowing costs is highly doubtful.

For one thing, the feedback effect previously described shows that changes in ratings can *cause* the very increase in borrowing costs that they predict. It seems pretty hard to argue with the notion that if a ratings downgrade forces a firm into bankruptcy by automatically accelerating the date on which all of its loans must be repaid and canceling lenders' obligations to make new loans, then ratings downgrades will have a statistical impact on the companies whose securities are downgraded, even if the downgrades have nothing to do with the actual financial condition of the company.

In other words, because ratings downgrades often are a "condition of default" in lending agreements and other debt instruments, a downgrade can, and often does, actually cause the company receiving the downgrade to experience the very financial distress that the downgrade "predicts." The problems caused by the fact that ratings downgrades trigger defaults all by themselves pale in comparison to the problems caused by the fact that thousands of different regulations and internal rules within companies that make investments severely restrict or prohibit investors' holdings of lower-rated bonds.[6] These regulations are the primary source of the feedback effect. In fact, the credit rating agencies have terrible reputations for accuracy. The demand for credit ratings is driven not by ratings quality but by regulation. The scholar Frank Partnoy, in a series of articles and books, has chronicled how regulation has come to drive the market for credit ratings.

For credit rating agencies, the feedback effect was caused by the fact that thousands of regulations require, in various ways, that the biggest institutional investors, such as pension funds and mutual funds, must invest only or at least primarily in "investment grade" instruments or in securities with even higher ratings. SEC regulation, in the form of the NRSRO designation, has created an artificial demand for ratings, despite their lack of usefulness to investors.[7] These regulations also transformed the ratings industry from a competitive industry into an anticompetitive cartel.[8]

NRSROs and a Downgrade in Quality

These regulations require that investors limit their investments in companies to those whose debt is rated by one of the small number of companies designated by the SEC as NRSROs. The SEC uses

NRSRO credit ratings to determine how much capital broker-dealer firms must maintain when they hold debt securities under Rule 15c3-1 of the Securities Exchange Act of 1934 (the "Exchange Act").

For years the ratings of NRSROs were used to measure the credit risk of short-term instruments in the regulation of money market funds under Rule 2a-7 of the Investment Company Act of 1940 (the "1940 Act"), which is the regulation that governs money market mutual funds. Money market funds are a species of mutual funds that invest in short-term, high-quality, highly liquid securities. Money market funds were developed as an alternative to the checking account. Like checking accounts, money market funds are a safe place to invest, but they also generally offer somewhat more competitive rates of return than traditional commercial bank checking accounts for funds that customers want to have immediate access to or want to hold in savings only for a relatively short period.

The NRSRO problem started years ago when money market mutual funds grew in size and popularity. The SEC became concerned that for marketing purposes mutual funds might try to trick investors by calling some of their funds "money market mutual funds" even though they did not invest exclusively in the high-quality and high-liquidity assets that investors had come to associate with mutual funds that called themselves money market funds. To address this perceived problem, in 1975, the SEC developed the concept of the nationally recognized statistical rating organization to identify particular companies supplying credit ratings that could be relied on by the Commission for regulatory purposes. The Commission originally adopted the term "NRSRO" in 1975 solely for the purposes of defining the term "money market fund" in order to limit the ability of mutual funds to claim that their mutual funds were "money market mutual funds." Under the rules, funds may only refer to themselves as MMFs if, among other requirements, their assets were rated "in one of the two highest short term rating categories" by two NRSROs.[9]

But the use of the NRSRO designation did not long remain the exclusive provenance of money market mutual funds. Soon the requirement that a company or securities issue be rated "in one of the two highest short term rating categories" by two NRSROs came to drive the world of corporate finance.

For example, issuers of certain debt securities that received an investment-grade rating from an NRSRO were entitled to register under the Securities Act of 1933 (the "Securities Act") on the shorter, simpler Form S-3. Banking and other regulators similarly rely on NRSRO credit ratings to protect the capital of financial institutions. Thus, many regulated financial institutions can only purchase certain types of securities if they have received an investment-grade rating from an NRSRO.[10] At the state and local levels, thousands of such regulations were created that steered or commanded investors to look to the ratings given by the SEC-recognized NRSROs when purchasing securities. The regulation in the Code of Federal Regulations that reads "an insured state savings association...may not acquire or retain any corporate debt securities not of investment grade" is both typical and illustrative of this type of regulation.

The result of this regulatory morass was that issuers who wanted to sell their securities had no choice but to pay for ratings, because if their securities did not have ratings, few if any investors would be legally eligible to buy them. In this environment, quality quickly became irrelevant. Credit rating agencies could increase profits not by raising quality, but by cutting costs. One way to cut costs, of course, is to offer lower, less competitive salaries, hiring cheaper, less competent or well-credentialed personnel. After the demand for their ratings had become unlinked from the quality of those ratings, credit rating agencies could do this without bearing a cost. Another way to cut costs is to invest less in technology and information gathering. Still another way was to rely on the clients being rated to do the very modeling required to generate a rating. All of these things have occurred in the credit ratings industry, and all of them contributed to various degrees to the decline of the quality of the ratings generated by the credit rating industry.

Besides cutting costs, another way the rating agencies increased profits was by expanding the number of companies and issues they rated. The SEC's rating agencies had no incentives to decline to rate a strange or exotic bond whose structure made no sense. These rating agencies also had no incentive to offer low ratings under the old regulatory regime. This led to a new, strange, and perverse sort of regulatory competition: Those rating agencies that rated quickly and predictably and generously and were the friendliest and easiest to work with were the most in demand. And it appears that rating agencies could be bought by the companies whose securities they were rating. In the years before the collapse of the mortgage market, there was explosive growth in the number of mortgages issued and in the issuance of mortgage-backed securities rated by the NRSROs.

Understanding Structured Issues

Far more important to the rating agencies, however, was the explosive—indeed, exponential—growth in what are called "structured issues," including such complex derivative instruments as credit derivatives, credit default swaps (CDS), and collateralized debt obligations (CDOs). Credit default swaps are contractual obligations that require one party to make a payment to another party if an "event of default" occurs in a security (known as the reference security). Wall Street traders can create infinite numbers of CDSs because these securities are, essentially, merely bets on the financial performance of a security. So, just as an infinite number of people can bet on the outcome of an Italian soccer match or a U.S. football game, so too can an infinite number of people bet on whether a security will default.

CDOs are a particularly complex way of packaging and selling credit risk. In a CDO the cash flows generated by a portfolio of bonds is split up—"spliced and diced"—in several ways, and multiple classes of securities known as tranches, whose payoffs are linked to the payments of different cash flow patterns, are created. Each tranche, in other words, is entitled to different priorities of payments in a different order. Each tranche also has its own distinct set of contractual rights in case of default.

Just as there is no end to the number of CDSs that could be created, there also is no end to the ways in which CDOs, CDSs, and other complex derivatives could be combined, mixed, and matched. JP Morgan, a leader in the field of creating complex derivatives, came up with the idea of combining CDOs and CDSs in a single, massively complex financial instrument that has been dubbed "the most sublime piece of financial engineering that was ever developed" and even "Frankenstein's monster."[11] These financial instruments grew to dominate, and, for a time, to cripple, the U.S. economy. They also were a huge boon to the new, post-reputation credit rating agencies for two reasons. First, they created a huge new market for credit ratings. CDOs and mortgage-backed securities had to be rated in order to be sold. The more complex the instrument, the greater the need for a top rating by a credit rating agency was to the successful marketing of the security. Second, not only did many of the most complex derivative instruments have to be rated themselves, but the individual securities that made up the portfolios had to be rated as well. This increased the demand for ratings. Then, incredibly, many of these complex derivative instruments allowed the issuer to change the makeup of the underlying portfolio, substituting securities in and out as long as the new securities being substituted in had a credit rating at least as high as the old ones being removed from the portfolio.

As Jesse Eisenger observed early on, these new products provided incentive to financial firms and banks "to take on riskier loans than they should have; helped increase leverage in the global financial system; and exposed a much wider array of financial firms to the risk of default."[12] None of this would have happened without the help of the credit rating agencies, which received, justifiably, the lion's share of the blame for the financial crisis of 2007–2008.

There is no escaping the conclusion that the credit rating agencies were the sine qua non cause of that financial crisis, lawyer-speak for the fact that, but for the actions of the credit rating agencies, the financial collapse of 2007 and 2008 would not have occurred. As noted economic historian Larry White observed, "When the histories are written of the U.S. subprime residential mortgage debacle of 2007–2008, and the world financial crisis that followed, the three large U.S.-based credit rating agencies—Moody's, Standard & Poor's (S&P), and Fitch—will surely be seen as central parties to the debacle; and rightly so."[13]

Prior to the financial collapse, the credit rating agencies were, literally, doing a "land office" business, but they were not doing it competently or well. Martin Fridson, in a careful empirical study of the rating agencies' performance in the financial crisis, began by stating that "it would be impossible to defend the agencies'...ratings of mortgage-related collateralized debt obligations" since "89% of the investment grade mortgage-backed securities ratings that Moody's awarded in 2007 were subsequently reduced to speculative grade."[14]

Interestingly, Fridson's findings not only show that the rating agencies performed poorly, but they also show that the quality of the credit rating agencies' performance declined markedly when they jumped with both feet into the business of rating the tsunami of complex securities and derivatives that were related to the mortgage boom. It certainly appears that the credit rating agencies were corrupted by vast new business and potential profits made possible by the derivatives boom. Fridson observes in his study that, in general, the agencies' performance on corporate and municipal issues was "reasonably good, with a relatively high correlation between ratings, defaults and losses, and net returns."[15]

The big credit rating agencies' finest hour came in the weeks and months leading up to the giant stock market crash of October 1929 that precipitated the Great Depression. Significantly, in advance of the crash, both Standard Statistics and Poor's Publishing, the predecessors of what we now know as Standard & Poor's, advised their clients to liquidate their securities portfolios.[16] In the months leading up to 2008, no such event occurred.

The empirical evidence is consistent with the hypothesis that "between 2001 and 2008 the agencies lowered their standards, causing many CDO tranches to receive undeserved Triple-A ratings."[17] This does not appear to be mere coincidence. It appears that issuers, in fact, bought off the credit rating agencies. The rating agencies sold their reputations for a pot of gold. They did this because their reputations were no longer of any value to them and because the pot of gold had become enormous.

Downgraded Ratings

It seems likely that the decline in the quality of ratings preceded the new millennium by at least a couple of decades. In 1975, Standard & Poor's suspended its ratings of New York City bonds. But this decision was an embarrassment, not a triumph for the rating agency, because the suspension of the Big Apple's rating lagged rather than preceded the market. Standard & Poor's merely was closing the door and turning out the lights after everybody had already left the building. The decision to suspend New York's rating lagged behind the decision by Bankers Trust Company, and then by every other major bank in the world, to decline to participate in underwriting New York City debt. Even Standard & Poor's concedes that its decision to withdraw the City's rating was "triggered by the reluctance of major underwriters to help the city sell or roll over its debts."[18] In fact, S&P had assigned New York City debt a high "A" rating until Bankers Trust Company decided that it would no longer underwrite the city's short-term "Tax Anticipation Notes." The ratings change provided no new information to investors or to the market.

The SEC and a myriad of other lawmakers had promulgated rules that ensured that credit ratings would be in demand by issuers even if the agencies producing such ratings had lost all credibility and respect. Explaining the drop in the reliability of ratings in the years before the financial collapse, Fridson notes that it appears clear that the rating agencies succumbed to the conflicts of interest they faced between their mission to give objective, unbiased ratings and their interest in maximizing profits for their own investors. As Fridson explains, the rating of the senior tranche in a mortgage-related CDO is essential to a deal involving the CDO, for "the issuer is not an existing company with a new need for capital. Rather, the prospective offering has come about because an underwriter has structured a financing around a pool of mortgages." The deal, though, will fall through if investors will not buy the senior tranche and "accept a comparatively low yield in exchange for a very high level of perceived safety." This safety comes through a Triple-A rating. If bankers do not think this rating is possible, "they will not even bother to commence work on the deal. In that case, the CDO will not be created and the rating agencies will receive no revenue."[19]

We now have persuasive evidence that one important set of reputational intermediaries, the credit rating agencies, was less effective in evaluating one set of customers—those seeking ratings of structured assets—than its traditional customers, corporations, and municipalities seeking ratings of their notes and bonds. The suspicion is that because customers seeking ratings of structured assets paid higher fees and accounted for a disproportionately large share of rating agencies' profits, the agencies exercised a lower standard of care in evaluating the risks of such debt issues.[20]

We now know, of course, that the ratings were inaccurate. As Frank Partnoy has observed, there is a great deal of evidence indicating that the information generated by the rating agencies was both stale and inaccurate.[21] The truly abominable performance of the credit rating agencies in their ratings of a whole host of debt issues, including Orange County, Mercury Finance, Pacific Gas & Electric, Enron, WorldCom, and most recently General Motors and Ford, amply illustrates the point, as do a plethora of academic studies showing that credit ratings changes lag the market.[22]

The Enron case provides a particularly vivid illustration of the poor quality of the credit ratings of the big NRSROs. Neither Standard & Poor's nor Moody's downgraded Enron's debt below investment-grade status until November 28, 2001, four days before the firm's bankruptcy, when the company's share price had plunged to a paltry 61 cents. Enron's $250 million in rated senior unsecured debt had declined in value from 90 cents to 35 cents on the dollar in the month preceding its downgrade. In other words, the market rejected the investment-grade rating on Enron's debt before the credit rating agencies exercised their power to downgrade it.[23]

Somewhat ironically, credit rating agencies even performed poorly in doing the job for which the NRSRO designation originally was created: making money market mutual funds safer for investors. During the financial crisis of 2007–2008, the SEC noticed that the most important class of securities held by MMFs, the short-term notes issued by large corporations, "had a 'high quality' rating from a NRSRO until shortly before the default." Though several money market mutual funds held these notes, the shareholders did not suffer any harmful effects "because each fund's investment advisor purchased the defaulted commercial paper from the funds at its amortized cost or principal amount."[24]

One important question remains, however: Did the clients of the credit rating agencies *know* that the ratings were inaccurate? If so, then the reputations of the rating agencies had already been destroyed before the crisis. One thing is sure: It is impossible to find any neutral observer or industry expert who really believes that credit ratings were of any use to anybody during the financial crisis.

A more rigorous way to address this question is to observe the market's response to changes in ratings. If credit ratings have reputational content, then when a rating changes, the price of the bond should change in tandem, with higher ratings leading to higher prices and lower prices leading to lower ratings. On the other hand, if even big ratings changes do not lead to price changes in the securities being rated, we must conclude that people are ignoring the ratings and that they have no useful, informational content. And this appears to be the case.

In one important empirical study the researchers looked at bond downgrades and upgrades by the two largest credit rating agencies, Moody's and Standard & Poor's. These researchers studied 125 ratings changes of a letter grade (for example, from AAA to AA). Interestingly, the authors found that the average upgraded bond borrowing cost (interest rate) is close to the average for all bonds before the upgrade and does not vary much after the rating change. The authors conclude that large credit upgrades do not decrease a bond's borrowing cost but that large credit downgrades increase a bond's borrowing cost. For example, if a credit rating went down from BBB to BB, its borrowing costs were increased by almost 50%.[25]

The finding that improvements in credit ratings do not lead to better securities prices is consistent with the observation that credit ratings agencies lack informational content. The finding that when credit rating agencies lower a rating, the downgrade leads to lower securities prices does not detract from this conclusion because downgrades that do not have informational content still will cause price declines if and to the extent that regulations forbid investors to hold securities with the new, lower ratings. Because this is the case, the downgrades will force price declines not because they have informational content, but because the downgrades require investors to sell in order to remain in compliance with applicable law and pertinent provisions of various financial contracts.

Objective observers did not dispute the fact that credit ratings were inaccurate. The fact that credit rating agencies caused the financial collapse also is beyond dispute. The dismal realization that the market's complete addiction to credit ratings not only caused the financial crisis, but also remained a source of extreme fragility—the Achilles heel of the financial world—finally dawned on Congress. As SEC Chairman Mary L. Shapiro stated, "In passing the Dodd-Frank Act, Congress noted that credit ratings applied to structured financial products proved inaccurate and contributed significantly to the mismanagement of risks by financial institutions and investors." Chairman Shapiro described the newly proposed SEC rules regarding credit ratings as "intended to strengthen the integrity and improve the transparency of credit ratings."[26]

In light of the massive harm either caused by or enabled by the credit rating agencies, it is no wonder that frustrated investors have sued all the credit rating agencies, claiming that they were harmed because they relied on ratings that allegedly were either negligently or even fraudulently prepared. In the U.S. at least, the credit rating agencies have dodged legal liability for their ratings failures by hiding behind the skirts of the free-speech clause of the Constitution that is contained in the First Amendment. As Floyd Norris noted in his widely read column, "The rating agencies have long managed to turn aside litigation by asserting they have a free-speech right to their opinions, whether or not they turn out to have been correct."[27]

But looking at the outcome of an investor lawsuit against Standard & Poor's in Australia, Mr. Norris observed that after the financial crisis, judges seem to be becoming less willing to keep giving "get out of jail free" passes to the credit rating agencies. Legal protection might be starting to break down. In particular, in late December 2012, a federal judge in Australia found that Standard & Poor's was liable for issuing the top investment-grade rating of AAA for a product she described as a "grotesquely complicated" piece of financial engineering. In a massive tome of an opinion comprising more than 4,000 pages of prose, the judge "meticulously traced how S.&P. came to issue a top rating."[28] Her conclusion was that no "reasonably competent ratings agency" would have awarded the rating that S&P gave to this particular structured finance product, called a constant proportion debt obligation (CPDO).[29]

As Mr. Norris observed in his *New York Times* piece, although the amount of the monetary damages was relatively small, around $14 million, "the danger to the firm's reputation—and the fact that the ruling could prompt other suits—potentially could be much greater."[30]

The securities that Standard & Poor's rated were like hundreds and perhaps thousands of other securities, rated AAA but nonetheless involving "a gamble, and a particularly risky one in that it effectively called for increasing the amount wagered if one bet lost money, on the theory that over time everything would work out." However, if losses continued to accumulate, the investor could "lose as much as 90 percent of the initial investment."[31]

The huge potential losses ended up materializing.[32] The investment involved a "casino strategy" of betting more and more whenever one lost previous bets, and, as the court observed, "If you hit a losing streak your net worth can become very low, however most of the time you will be able to 'bet yourself out of the hole.'"[33] The court held that buyers of CPDOs did not realize what was happening. The investors depended on S&P's ratings, and the agency rated the CPDOs AAA. This rating supposedly "meant the agency thought that there was less than a 1 percent chance of losing money."[34]

Many of the cases against credit rating agencies involved the use of flawed statistical models, most of which contained unrealistic assumptions that real estate prices in various regions were uncorrelated or that real estate prices would never decline. In this deal, however, S&P did not even model the CPDOs before rating them, but instead, it simply adopted the model used by the bank [ABN AMRO] that issued the CPDOs and was paying Standard & Poor's for the rating. The court also found that Standard & Poor's did not "bother to verify the assumptions in the model." The judge also analyzed the assumptions used by the bank and the rating agency, finding "that in many cases they were far more optimistic than history justified."[35] Apparently, in assigning this rating, Standard & Poor's did identify one assumption used by the bank in its forecasting model, but never "bothered" to make the necessary adjustment.[36] And the Australian judge found that, even if the adjustment had been made, "there was no way that even the bank's model would have justified the AAA rating."[37]

Tradition and Simplicity Outweigh Reputation

The evidence in the case reveals that the whole idea of reputation in the credit ratings industry has become twisted and perverse. The credit rating agencies understood that the structured finance instruments such as credit derivatives are what the agencies considered to be a "one-rating market." A one-rating market is a market in which the financial instrument being rated either achieves AAA rating or is never brought to market. If it is not brought to market, the issue is never rated. The bank that invented the new instruments makes no money on the security, and, significantly, neither does the credit rating agency. The evidence reveals a Standard & Poor's official stating that the firm had been "highly successful in this area [rating credit derivatives] based on our responsiveness [to issuers] and consistency of approach." He goes on to worry about Standard & Poor's reputation, calling it "seriously at risk" and "in effect in tatters." The official anticipated "the repercussions of this to feed through to all areas of our synthetic business—effectively handing our market share and revenues to Moody's and Fitch on a plate."[38] As Mr. Norris tellingly observed, the official was not worried about the firm's reputation among those who relied on the firm's ratings. Instead, "it was the banks whose approval he deemed to be critical. That memo had its desired effect. Within days S.&P. decided it could resume giving AAA ratings to CPDO's...."[39]

Finally, in 2010, Congress passed a law to deal with the credit ratings problem. The Dodd-Frank Act requires the SEC (and all federal agencies) to remove references to credit ratings within one year of passage. This means, for example, that the SEC had to change its rules about who can legally refer to themselves as a money market mutual fund to eliminate the reference to credit rating agencies.[40] Specifically, the Dodd-Frank Act also requires every federal agency to review existing regulations that require the use of an assessment of the creditworthiness of the security or money market instrument and any references to credit ratings in such regulations; to modify such regulations identified in the review to remove any reference to, or requirement of, reliance on credit ratings; and to substitute with a standard of creditworthiness as the agency shall determine as appropriate for such regulations.[41]

The SEC suspended its own NRSRO designation provisions after passage of Dodd-Frank. But NRSROs continue to dominate the financial world. In other words, even though the credit rating agencies have lost both their reputations for accuracy and much of their regulatory protection, there remains a high demand for their ratings by issuers. It is curious why these issuers still are willing to pay money for ratings.

Historically, the best explanation for the mysterious fact that credit rating agencies simultaneously enjoy great success while providing no information of value to the investing public is that the SEC inadvertently created an artificial regulatory demand for the services of a small number of favored rating agencies when it misguidedly invented the NRSRO designation. This designation has, over time, caused an artificial demand for ratings, despite their lack of usefulness to investors. Even now that the rating agencies' collective "cover" has been blown, the rating agencies continue to dominate the financial markets. Demand for ratings has not diminished.

What remains is in some ways a "lemming effect." Lemmings are small rodents that, according to myth, sometimes blindly march to their deaths over high cliffs because they unquestioningly follow the pack. Going along with the crowd, also known as the lemming effect, appears to be an entrenched genetic survival trait in humans. The lemming effect has been used to explain financial bubbles. Indeed, the lemming effect appears to affect securities prices and financial markets particularly strongly, and for good reason.

If a securities trader learned that suddenly millions of other traders were going to buy or sell a particular stock simultaneously, that trader would be perfectly rational to try to effectuate purchases or sales of the security before the stampede. Likewise, perfectly rational traders, knowing that credit ratings are a load of malarkey, would still follow ratings closely and trade on the basis of ratings if they thought that all the other traders in a market were doing the same. And this is where we are with respect to credit ratings. After so many decades of slavish reliance on credit ratings, ratings are now a signal to investors to start marching like lemmings in a particular direction. And as long as one thinks that other investors are following the silly signal, it is quite rational for investors to pay assiduously close attention to credit ratings.

Another way of thinking about it is that we are caught in a massive collective action problem. Our economic system would be much safer and more stable if credit ratings were ignored because our markets' slavish reliance on ratings is the major source of the asset bubbles and the cycles of boom and bust that have been plaguing the economy for decades. But no single market participant can afford to ignore credit ratings as long as that market participant expects everybody else to pay close attention to ratings.

The lemming effect is what causes the feedback effect discussed earlier in this chapter. Even though ratings lack meaningful or timely informational content about the companies and securities being rated, they still move stock prices because they cause herd behavior. This feedback effect has been reinforced by the many decades in which the herd behavior itself was caused by regulation.

Another reason credit ratings are still followed has to do with the complex role of risk in financial markets. Basic corporate finance teaches us that when investors are deciding whether to buy or sell particular securities or particular portfolios of securities, they focus on two factors: risk and return. Successful investors are those who maximize returns and minimize risk. A rational investor looking at two securities that pose the same level of risk always will choose the security with the higher returns. And, by the same token, a rational investor choosing between two securities that promise the same rate of return always will choose the security with lower risk.

Risk and return are the way all professional investors, from mutual fund managers to hedge fund entrepreneurs to pension fund managers, are evaluated by markets and within their own organizations. Imagine, for example, two portfolio managers who work in the same mutual fund complex. Suppose further that the two managers have assembled portfolios with exactly the same risk profile. The superior portfolio manager is the manager whose portfolio has experienced the higher rates of return over the relevant period of observation. Likewise, if the two rival portfolios have garnered the same returns over the applicable period, the portfolio manager who has assembled the less risky portfolio of securities is the one who has done the better job.

Because both risk and return must be analyzed when we are analyzing the performance of a particular portfolio or investment strategy, obviously, there must be some mechanism for measuring both risk and return if we are to analyze the performance of competing managers or strategies with any competence or validity. The good news is that returns are quite easy to measure objectively and accurately. One can measure securities returns in real time. Huge data banks are available for measuring historical returns. In fact, one database alone, maintained by the Center for Research in Securities Prices (CRSP) at the University of Chicago's Booth School of Business, provides complete and accurate historical share price data on virtually all equity securities.

The bad news is that whereas returns can be measured easily, risk cannot. People intuitively understand returns. Returns are tangible, extrinsic, and visible. It is easy to see when a security's price has moved from one price to another. It is easy to see when a company is paying high dividends or making interest payments dependably. It is far harder to measure risk. Risk is more intrinsic.

The basic tool for measuring risk is something called the "beta coefficient." The idea of measuring risk by using beta is well entrenched among experts in investing and finance, but the concept is largely unknown outside of the world of investing and finance.

Risk as measured by beta is a lot more complicated than returns as measured by, well, returns. Beta is defined as "the ratio of the covariance of the market's returns and security's returns to the variance of the market's return." But experts acknowledge that the standard definition "does not really provide any intuition around beta."[42] Another way of expressing beta is that beta equals (the ratio of the security's volatility to that of the market's volatility) times (the correlation of the security's returns to the market's returns). One expert claims, rather hopefully, that "thinking about beta in these terms provides more intuition."[43]

Certainly, professionals understand stock betas. It is far less clear, though, that beta as a measure of risk is well understood by average investors. In any case, beta is certainly not as intuitive or straightforward as credit ratings. Beta is essentially a measure of the historical volatility of a particular stock or portfolio of stocks when compared against the market as a whole for a particular period. Even properly understood, the concept of beta is complex, and determining the beta of a particular stock or portfolio is not entirely objective. Calculating beta, in other words, requires subjective judgment calls.

Specifically, to determine beta, one must choose a benchmark portfolio against which to calculate the beta of a stock or portfolio of stocks. Comparing the price movement of a stock or portfolio of stocks to a volatile market can make the volatility of the stock or portfolio of stocks being studied appear to be rather tame. Comparing the price movement of a stock or portfolio of stocks to a stable, nonvolatile market can make the volatility of that stock or portfolio of stocks appear to be rather volatile in comparison. Choosing different historical periods as the point of reference also will affect the calculation of beta for a stock or portfolio of stocks. Including a highly volatile period, for example, can reduce the apparent risk of a stock or portfolio as measured by beta. Further, betas of individual stocks are rather volatile over time, which simply means that the beta of the same company or portfolio changes a lot when measured over different periods. For these reasons, experts understand that when it comes to incorporating betas into one's work, "it is important to use them with skepticism."[44] Experts also caution that "it is always important to understand how a derived metric is calculated so you can make your own assessment as to how you should use it when making an investment decision."[45] This is excellent advice for professional investors, but it hardly is practical for ordinary investors to understand how a "derived metric" such as a beta coefficient is calculated.

Thus, in addition to the feedback effect and the lemming effect discussed in this chapter, another reason we continue to rely on ratings even now that the rating agencies have been discredited and are even being gradually removed as reference points in regulation is best explained by the well-known "under the streetlight joke," which is frequently told by economists. Basically, we still rely rather irrationally on credit ratings because they are so easy to spot. The joke explains the phenomenon:

> Late one evening, a man who was walking his dog comes upon an economist who is searching the ground under a streetlight. The passerby asks the economist what he is doing.

"I'm looking for my lost keys," says the man searching the ground. "I dropped them on my way home from that bar down there," he says with a slight slur.

The passerby offers to help search for the keys, but after several minutes of searching under the streetlight they have no luck.

"Are you sure you dropped them here?" asks the passerby.

"Oh, I have no idea if I dropped them here," says the economist, now swaying ever so slightly. "All I know is that I think I'm pretty sure that I dropped them somewhere on this street on my way home."

"Then why are you only looking under this street light?"

"Well," replies the economist very slowly, blinking with the effort. "Because this is where I can see the best."[46]

So it appears that we are stuck with credit ratings as a central feature in economic life, despite their unreliability. In other words, the credit rating agencies have managed to survive long after their reputations for accuracy and integrity died their quiet, unheralded deaths.

Historically, companies that utilized the public markets for debt and equity utilized credit rating agencies for the same reason they utilized the services of accounting firms: They wanted their financial condition to be verified by a credible, independent source; that is, by a highly reputable source. Demand for the services of rating agencies derived from the fact that companies lowered their capital costs when they subscribed to the services of credit rating agencies, and the savings from such lower capital costs were greater than the costs of the subscription fees charged by the credit rating agencies for assigning a rating to a company's securities. Ultimately, however, like the accounting firms, the credit rating agencies have lost their reputations for independence, objectivity, and even competence.

Genuine demand fueled by market forces was displaced by ersatz demand fueled by regulatory requirements. Just as happened in the market for audit services, regulation led to the cartelization of both of these industries. As cartelization occurred, companies were given little if any choice about whether to do business with credit rating agencies, just as such customers have no choice about whether to deal with the big four accounting firms. Over time, we observed a marked and undeniable diminution in the quality of the services of credit rating agencies, but no corresponding drop in the demand for these services. Regulation replaced reputation. And when steps finally were taken to reform the regulation, it was too late. Investors had become lemmings, searching together under streetlights where nothing of use was to be found.

Endnotes

1. Amanda Bahena, "What Role Did Credit Rating Agencies Play in the Credit Crisis?" March 2010 e-book, http://blogs.law.uiowa.edu/ebook/uicifd-ebook/part-5-iii-what-role-did-credit-rating-agencies-play-credit-crisis.

2. Ibid.

3. Ibid.

4. Gustavo Manso, "Feedback Effects of Credit Ratings," November 17, 2011, MIT/American Economics Association Research Paper, www.aeaweb.org/aea/2012conference/program/retrieve.php?pdfid=266.

5. Paul Asquith, Thomas Covert, Andrea S. Au, and Parag A. Pathak, "The Market for Borrowing Corporate Bonds," MIT Research Paper, October 20, 2011, p. 23, available at http://economics.mit.edu/files/7477.

6. Manso, "Feedback Effects of Credit Ratings."

7. Frank Partnoy, "The Siskel and Ebert of Financial Markets? Two Thumbs Down for the Credit Rating Agencies," *Washington University Law Quarterly* 77 (1999): 619-714.

8. On the effects of cartelization in the credit rating industry, see, generally, Claire A. Hill, "Regulating the Rating Agencies," *Washington University Law Quarterly* 82 (2004): 43. Hill calls particular attention to reforming the industry by "encourag[ing] a less concentrated market structure." Ibid., 45. For empirical evidence on the perceived poor quality of credit rating agencies, see "Rating the Rating Agencies: The State of Transparency and Competition: Hearing Before the Subcommittee on Capital Markets, Insurance, and Government Sponsored Enterprises of the House Financial Services Committee," 108th Congress, 2003, 101-122, available at http://financialservices.house.gov/media/pdf/108-18.

pdf. Reduced competition in the accounting industry, largely as a result of pressures on accounting firms to consolidate in response to the SEC's auditor independence rules, has "reduced the accounting firms' incentives to differentiate their products on the basis of quality." Jonathan Macey and Hillary A. Sale, "Observations on the Role of Commodification, Independence and Governance in the Accounting Industry," *Villanova Law Review* 48 (2003): 1167, 1177.

9. 17 Code of Federal Regulations § 270.2a-7(a)(12)(i).

10. Statement of Amy Lancellotta, Senior Counsel, Investment Company Institute for the SEC Hearings on Issues Relating to Credit Rating Agencies (November 21, 2002), available at www.sec. gov/news/extra/credrate/investcoinstit.htm.

11. Jesse Eisenger, "The $58 Trillion Elephant in the Room," *Upstart Business Journal,* October 15, 2008, Philip Toledano, http://upstart. bizjournals.com/views/columns/wall-street/2008/10/15/Credit-Derivatives-Role-in-Crash.html?page=all.

12. Ibid.

13. Lawrence White, "Credit Rating Agencies and the Financial Crisis: Less Regulation of CRAs Is a Better Response," *Journal of International Banking Law and Regulation* 25 (2010): 170-179.

14. Martin Fridson, "Bond Rating Agencies, Conflicts and Competence," *Journal of Applied Corporate Finance* 22, no. 3 (2010): 55-64.

15. Ibid.

16. This fact is highlighted on Standard & Poor's website. See www. standardandpoors.com/about-sp/timeline/en/us/.

17. Ibid.

18. Standard & Poor's History of Standard & Poor's, 1966-1970, www. standardandpoors.com/about-sp/timeline/en/us/.

19. Ibid.

20. Ibid.

21. "Legislative Solutions for the Rating Agency Duopoly: Hearing Before the Subcommittee on Capital Markets, Insurance, and Government Sponsored Enterprises of the Committee on Financial Services," 109th Congress, 2005, 2 [hereinafter Partnoy] (statement of Frank Partnoy, Professor of Law, University of San Diego School

of Law), available at http://financialservices.house.gov/media/pdf/109-42.pdf.

22. Ibid., 2 ("Numerous academic studies have shown that ratings changes lag the market...."); see also "Rating Agencies and the Use of Credit Ratings Under the Federal Securities Laws," 68 Federal Register 35,258 (concept release June 12, 2003).

23. Jonathan R. Macey, "Efficient Capital Markets, Corporate Disclosure, and Enron," *Cornell Law Review* 89 (2004): 394, 405-06.

24. "Revisions to Rules Regulating Money Market Funds," SEC Release No. IC-17589 (July 17, 1990) at text preceding n.18.

25. Asquith, Covert, Au, and Pathak, "The Market for Borrowing Corporate Bonds."

26. "SEC Proposes Rules to Increase Transparency and Improve Integrity of Credit Ratings," May 18, 2011, www.sec.gov/news/press/2011/2011-113.htm.

27. Floyd Norris, "A Casino Strategy, Rated AAA," *The New York Times*, November 8, 2012, http://www.nytimes.com/2012/11/09/business/judge-in-australia-finds-flaws-in-sps-triple-a-rating-strategy.html?pagewanted=all&_r=0".

28. Ibid.

29. See Bathurst Regional Council v. Local Government Financial Services Pty Ltd (No 5) [2012] FCA 1200.

30. Norris, "A Casino Strategy, Rated AAA."

31. Ibid.

32. Ibid.

33. Ibid.

34. Ibid.

35. Ibid.

36. Ibid.

37. Ibid.

38. Ibid.

39. Ibid.

40. See Conference Report to H.R. 4173, Title IX, Section 939A.

41. SEC, Credit Rating Agencies, www.sec.gov/spotlight/dodd-frank/creditratingagencies.shtml, SEC Rules related

to the removal of the "NRSRO" designation can be found at www.sec.gov/rules/proposed/2011/33-9186.pdf; www.sec.gov/rules/proposed/2011/33-9193.pdf; www.sec.gov/rules/proposed/2011/34-64352.pdf; and www.sec.gov/rules/final/2011/33-9245.pdf.

42. Jim Pyke, "The Challenges of Using Beta to Measure Risk," *Seeking Alpha,* May 23, 2011, http://seekingalpha.com/article/271235-the-challenges-of-using-beta-to-measure-risk.

43. Ibid.

44. Ibid.

45. Ibid.

46. See "The Street Light," http://streetlightblog.blogspot.it/2006/10/why-street-light.html. The "under the streetlight" joke comes in several versions. Here is another:

Late at night, a drunk was on his knees beneath a streetlight, evidently looking for something. A passerby, being a good Samaritan, offered to help.

"What is it you have lost?" he asked.

"My watch," replied the drunk. "It fell off when I tripped over the pavement."

The passerby joined in the search but after a quarter of an hour, there was still no sign of the watch.

"Where exactly did you trip?" asked the passerby.

"About half a block up the street," replied the drunk.

"Then why are you looking for your watch here if you lost it half a block up the street?"

The drunk said: "Because the light's a lot better here."

See Joke Buddha, www.jokebuddha.com/joke/Under_the_street_light_1.

9

The New, Post-Reputation
Wall Street: Stock Exchanges

Organized stock exchanges, particularly the NYSE, used to play an important reputational role in U.S. capital markets. Stock exchanges no longer play such a role, but, unlike in the cases of accounting firms and credit rating agencies, regulations are not to blame for the demise of stock exchanges as reputational intermediaries. Instead, stock exchanges lost this status because of a secular change in the nature of their products and services. Today, stock exchanges are businesses that compete for the business of trading securities on behalf of customers. Traditionally, being listed in a major stock exchange was a seal of approval for a company. Besides this reputational signal, stock exchanges offered three other services: liquidity, monitoring trading to prevent cheating such as insider trading, and off-the-rack corporate governance rules for listed companies. Traditionally, incentives existed for exchanges to monitor trading activity, because insider trading forced exchanges to increase their bid prices, thereby decreasing trading volume and decreasing trading revenue. Furthermore, companies had incentives to follow the rules set by exchanges, because an exchange could respond to prohibited behavior by delisting the company. In the days when the exchanges dominated the trading market, this delisting would be catastrophic for a company and would signal to investors that they should not invest in the company. In addition, exchanges provided a centralized, efficient monitoring system. Today, the SEC has standardized the exchanges' monitoring function. Increased competition from over-the-counter trading markets such as NASDAQ and a myriad of other exchanges has eliminated the consequences for a company that is expelled from stock exchange membership, thus eradicating the ability of stock exchanges to enforce their own rules by making sanctions irrelevant for firms that break exchange rules. These days delisting hurts the exchange that delists a company more than the company that is delisted because the exchange loses listing fees and trading revenues, while the delisted firm simply migrates to another exchange. For this reason, stock exchanges delist clients only when they absolutely are forced to do so. In today's environment, stock exchanges are no longer reputational intermediaries.

As recounted in Chapter 6, "The New, Post-Reputation Wall Street: Accounting Firms," and Chapter 8, "The New, Post-Reputation Wall Street: Credit Rating Agencies," accounting firms and credit rating agencies lost their reputations for several reasons, but ossifying regulations that relieved these businesses of the need to compete were a primary factor in the destruction of their reputations. Stock exchanges are a bit different. Regulation bears little if any of the blame for the demise of stock exchanges. Stock exchanges lost their status as reputational intermediaries because of secular changes in the nature of the product they offered. This secular change occurred because of secular changes in the nature of their services.

Although many academic lawyers continue to claim, hollowly and with nobody sensible listening very hard, that accountants and auditors continue to enjoy stolid reputations, it is very hard to find anybody willing to make the argument that stock exchanges continue to serve as reputational intermediaries the way credit rating agencies and accounting firms did long ago. Today when economists and policymakers think of stock exchanges, they correctly envision these entities as businesses that compete for the business of trading securities on behalf of customers. Stock exchanges make money by charging commissions on trades and sometimes in other ways as well, such as by selling some of the data that they collect about the trades that occur on the exchange and by charging "listing fees," which are the fees charged to companies for allowing the stock to be traded on the exchange receiving the fees.

Today the "product" that stock exchanges offer to the companies whose shares are traded on the exchanges is the provision of "liquidity." Investors value the ability to sell the securities they own in a quick and risk-free environment. But historically the dominant stock exchanges such as the New York Stock Exchange and the Tokyo Stock

Exchange offered a much more interesting and complex array of services. Briefly examining the history of stock exchanges reveals how reputation used to be part of the constellation of services offered by exchanges.

Unlike accounting firms and credit rating agencies, which historically operated in competitive environments (highly competitive for accounting firms; less competitive for the credit rating agencies but still competitive), the major stock exchanges began their corporate lives as monopolists. Changes in technology and in the structure of markets have transformed the stock exchanges from monopolists into firms that compete in an increasingly competitive space. Also, understanding how the array of products offered by stock exchanges has changed is fundamentally important to understanding why reputations have come to play an increasingly less important role in stock exchanges' business.

Stock exchanges are businesses like any other: They supply services to listed companies in exchange for the fees that come with listing. Listings are what stock exchanges competed for historically. Listings were lucrative not only for the initial and periodic fees they brought to the exchange, but also for the trading revenue. Historically, the shares of companies that listed on an exchange like the NYSE traded on the NYSE almost exclusively. The broker-dealer firms that were members of the Exchange—and all of them were members—were required by rules called "Off Board Trading Restrictions" to trade the shares of listed companies exclusively on the NYSE.

Even before the founding of the NYSE, traders had been congregating informally outside of the Tontine Coffee House at the corner of Wall Street and Water Street in lower Manhattan (when it rained, the brokers went inside the coffeehouse). The Buttonwood Agreement, signed on May 17, 1792, formalized their relationship. The Agreement, named for the large "buttonwood" (now called sycamore trees) outside the coffee shop where traders gathered in good weather, formalized the relationship among this historic coterie of stock traders. The Buttonwood brokers, as they were known, eventually sent a delegation to examine the constitution of the Philadelphia Stock Exchange, which was then the biggest stock exchange in the U.S., because Philadelphia was at the time the largest and most important city in the U.S. The business model used at the stock exchange in Philadelphia was the model for the NYSE (it was then called the New York Stock and Exchange Board).[1] The Buttonwood Agreement bound the signatories, all of whom were full-time stockbrokers, to conduct business at a single location, a rented room located at 40 Wall Street in Manhattan (moved in 1865 to the corner of Broad Street and Wall Street after the first location was destroyed by fire). The requirement that the men signing the Agreement show up for every trading session ensured that casual traders and passive investors could not join the club.

In its early years the NYSE traded stocks on a rotating basis. At 11:30 a.m. every business day the president of the Exchange called out the name of each listed stock in alphabetical order. When the name of the stock was called, the brokers would call out the prices at which they were willing to buy (bids) or to sell (asks) the stock. When trades were completed in the first stock, the president would call out the next. There were 30 listed stocks at that time. Trading was completed by about 1:00 p.m. All trades were to be settled, stock certificates delivered and paid for, by 2:15 p.m. of the following business day.[2] The stockbrokers, who now had become members of the club/ Exchange, were assigned chairs (hence the reference to exchange seats) and were required to be present for each session.[3]

The Buttonwood Agreement offered something for everyone. For the signers the Agreement was extremely attractive because it put an end to the fierce competition among brokers who kept cutting the commissions they charged their customers for buying and selling their stocks for them. The Buttonwood Agreement required members to eschew public auctions for securities. The Agreement also set a floor of .25% on the commissions that brokers could charge their customers. The signatories also agreed to give preferential treatment to each other when trading stock. The members/signatories of the Agreement would get first preference in case they were competing to buy or sell a stock with non-members offering the same price for the shares.

From the point of view of the larger economy in general and people investing in the stocks traded on the NYSE in particular, there also were certain advantages to establishing a single, central physical location at which stock trading was known to occur. From investors' perspective, the physical location of the NYSE in lower Manhattan solidified that location as what is known in game theory as a Schelling point (also known as a focal point).[4] Schelling points are points of common reference. Following the examples in Schelling's book, game show hosts would tell various contestants that they would win a prize if they could succeed in meeting one another on a particular day somewhere in New York City. The contestants would not be told when or where on the day in question they were to meet. They had to guess the time and place of the rendezvous.

In the game, each player tries to intuit (guess) the time and place that her fellow contestants will select. Successful players chose natural focal points in space like Grand Central Station or The Empire State Building. These contestants also chose focal points in time, usually noon. The buttonwood tree and the Tontine Coffee House became focal points for securities traders.

The vital importance of a focal point for trading stocks is difficult to comprehend in today's world of computers and instant global communication. The fact that the New York Stock Exchange played a critical role in solving an acute communications problem among traders becomes clear when we look at the situation at the time of the founding of the NYSE in May 1792. The telegraph was not invented until 1844. The first transatlantic cable was invented in 1866, the first stock ticker in 1867.[5]

The telephone was first displayed to the public in the U.S. and Europe by Boston University professor Alexander Graham Bell in 1876, 84 years after the Agreement founding the NYSE was formalized.[6] The NYSE was quick to jump on the new technology. A mere 2 years later, in 1878, that newfangled invention was installed on the floor of the NYSE.

The economic role of the major stock exchanges like the NYSE originally was serving as Schelling or focal points for traders. As technology developed, the need for central physical locations at which securities could be traded subsided and eventually disappeared. Today virtually all securities trading takes place via electronic communications networks and digital communications.

The NYSE still has its historic trading floor, but mainly for histori-cal reasons. For example, in the fall of 2012, when Hurricane Sandy threatened the East Coast of the U.S., many businesses in lower Man-hattan closed their doors temporarily to wait out the storm, and the New York Stock Exchange suspended its physical floor trading opera-tions. However, the Exchange announced that it would be open for trading as usual. The Big Board simply moved its trading to its propri-etary, fully electronic trading platform called Arca.

The idea of a physical stock exchange is essentially obsolete. Today, as the International Monetary Fund has pointed out, stock exchanges serve more functions than providing a physical location. They establish rules to oversee trading and communication regarding the trading. The exchanges "are closely linked to the clearing facilities through which post-trade activities are completed for securities and derivatives traded on the exchange."[7] The exchange "centralizes the communication of bid and offer prices to all direct market partici-pants," who can decide to either accept the offer or make a different offer. When a trade is complete, the exchange then relays that infor-mation throughout the market. This creates "a level playing field that allows any market participant to buy as low or sell as high as anyone else as long as the trader follows exchange rules."[8] With the develop-ment of electronic trading, exchanges no longer need to be physical locations, and many trading floors are closing. The NASDAQ Stock Market, Eurex, and the London Stock Exchange are fully electronic. The NYSE runs both floor and electronic trading, as do derivative exchanges like the CME Group.[9]

Even though there is no longer a need for stock exchanges to have a central physical focal point location, there remain certain advan-tages to having all trades occur on a single system or forum. An orga-nized exchange, even if its "location" is virtual rather than physical, can disseminate complete information about trading patterns virtu-ally instantaneously by electronic means. The rapid dissemination of information for exchange-listed securities lowers the search costs for market professionals who need price information quickly in order to make trading decisions.[10]

At the same time, stock exchanges operate in increasingly com-petitive environments. By the time their original product, the single, fixed physical "Schelling Point" in space and the prearranged time of operation at that location, became unnecessary and obsolete, stock exchanges had evolved to provide a bundle of other services. Chief among those services was the provision of reputation for listed companies. Indeed, the NYSE was firmly in the Reputation Business even before accounting firms and credit rating agencies, and long before the creation of the Securities and Exchange Commission or the invention of modern securities regulation in the form of the Securities Act of 1933 and the Securities Exchange Act of 1934, which regulate the issuance and trading of securities on public markets including the NYSE.

The big credit rating agencies did not come along until the twentieth century. At that time the credit rating agencies did not exist as information intermediaries. Audits existed, but they did not provide public audits until the early part of the twentieth century.[11] Significantly, until the early twentieth century, when the credit rating agencies and the accounting firms took over these roles, the stock exchanges provided the important service of reputational intermediary in the financial markets.

The Credit Rating Agencies

The history of credit ratings can be traced to 1860. Prior to this date, independent third-party analysis of the burgeoning railroad and construction industries in the U.S. was very limited.[12] In 1868, a father and son team, Henry Varnum Poor and Henry William Poor, started publishing *The Manual of Railroads,* which, for the price of $5.00, offered information targeted at investors in railroads. The first issue sold all 2,500 copies that were printed.[13] In 1906, another company, called Standard Statistics, was founded. Standard Statistics began to publish and sell, in an annual bound volume, news and information about industrial companies in addition to railroads. The information in the book was kept on 5- by 7-inch cards, which enabled the company to update on a continuous basis the information published in the bound volume.[14] Standard Statistics grew rapidly and in 1914 its owners bought a controlling interest in Moody's Manual Company.

It then began negotiations to buy the Poor's rating company, which at that point was called "Poor's Railroad Company." Both Moody's and Poor's, like Standard Statistics, provided financial information in book form. Eventually, Moody's Manual Company and Poor's Railroad Company merged together, and the combined firm was named "Poor's Publishing Company."

Standard Statistics remained a distinct company. In 1922, Poor's Publishing began rating corporate bonds and municipal securities. In 1923, Standard Statistics launched the first stock market index.[15] This eventually developed into the well-known S&P 500 index, which remains today among the most important stock market indexes.

Poor's Publishing eventually went bankrupt. Standard Statistics merged with Poor's Publishing in 1941, creating the modern Standard & Poor's Corp. In that year S&P rated 7,000 municipal bonds and several hundred corporate bonds.[16]

Moody's Investor Services, then called "John Moody and Company," first published information and statistical data about the securities issued by selected companies in 1900. It was not until the 1920s that Moody's began providing ratings for corporate and government bonds. Fitch's was founded in 1913, when it began publishing two books, *The Fitch Stock and Bond Manual* and *The Fitch Bond Book.* Fitch did not start assigning the now-famous letter-grade (AAA through D) rating system that has become the basis for ratings throughout the industry until 1924.[17]

The Accounting Firms and the Audit of Public Companies

As Sean O'Connor has observed in a historical account of the audit, it was not until the early twentieth century that audits were even directed at the general public. Before that, audits were "simply a private engagement of an accountant or bookkeeper by an investor or manager to check up on the books of a debtor or subordinate."[18] Audits were primarily done for internal purposes within the companies that commissioned such audits. A "distinguishing feature of these audits," was that the company that commissioned them "had the full authority to hire, fire, and/or pay the auditor."[19] This is a sharp distinction from the current situation as it developed in the first two decades of the 1900s. In other words, audits were not directed at the investing public. As Professor O'Connor observes, there were no clearly identifiable third-party beneficiaries of the audits that were performed before the twentieth century. Even in cases where the auditor and the client acknowledged some third-party beneficiary (e.g., a bank or another creditor), there was no formal contractual relationship between the auditor and the third-party beneficiary. In the first two decades of the twentieth century, though, some major corporations experimented with "public audits," or "public disclosures of private audits that they had commissioned for internal or shareholder purposes," that created large classes of third-party beneficiaries.[20] It was not until the twentieth century that audits assumed a "public profile."[21]

It was in this context that auditors came to serve the role of reputational intermediaries, and, at least for a while, "a fairly ideal environment for the development of a reputational marketplace existed" for auditors and "[c]ompanies apparently were beginning to believe that obtaining the 'independent' certification of the company's financial statements would give them an edge in the increasingly crowded equity markets of the Roaring Twenties."[22]

Stock Exchanges as Reputational Intermediaries

The major stock exchanges here and abroad served as reputational intermediaries until they were replaced in that role by credit rating agencies and accounting firms. Listings were a sort of "Good Housekeeping Seal of Approval." Certainly, the New York Stock Exchange long marketed itself as offering such a seal of approval, albeit to an increasingly skeptical audience.[23] Stock touts still portray a stock exchange listing as a selling point for the stocks they are peddling. For example, the head of marketing for a New York service that provides "marketing services to ultra-high net-worth family offices and individuals" still uses the time-worn Good Housekeeping Seal of Approval metaphor to explain the value of an exchange listing reputation. The individual describes getting listed by a major stock exchange as being similar to undergoing a "vetting process" that "looks into all of the nooks and crannies." The individual regards a listing on the NYSE as proof that the company has "passed a fairly substantial due diligence process." An NYSE listing "is indeed a joyful day for a company." The listing gives the company credibility and "provides gains in visibility and liquidity, which may reduce the cost of capital for the firm." The individual cites studies that "have shown that after a move to the NYSE, merger and acquisition activity of a company increases." These factors usually have a favorable influence on stock price.[24]

But it is highly doubtful that the New York Stock Exchange continues to serve as a reputational intermediary. The list of companies listed on the NYSE that have imploded in various fraud schemes and accounting scandals is enormous. Many of the biggest corporate meltdowns, from Enron to WorldCom, were NYSE-listed stocks. A list of the major corporate scandals would include Adelphia, Cendant, Enron, Global Crossing, Sunbeam, Tyco, Waste Management, and WorldCom. All but two of these companies (Adelphia and World-Com) were listed on the NYSE.

NYSE Euronext, as the Exchange now is called, is lobbying for new laws that make it easier for firms to obtain a Big Board listing. They also are lobbying for relaxed listing standards for foreign issuers from places like Russia and China where corporations operate under lax corporate governance rules and few, if any, established ethical norms. The NYSE is concerned about its inability to attract listings away from London and other rival venues due to its more stringent disclosure and audit rules. It would like to weaken or to jettison such rules in order to make itself more attractive to non-U.S. firms, which for decades have been its major source of growth.

Despite the fact that U.S. investors have lost billions of dollars on U.S.-listed Chinese companies in numerous accounting scandals, the NYSE continues to market its listing services in that country. Developing countries have taken particular note of the NYSE's recruiting efforts. As reported in the Economic Times (India) and in the Arab News,[25] but not in any U.S. news outlets, NYSE Euronext's head of international listings, Albert Ganyushin, courts foreign companies with a sales pitch he used in December 2012 in Moscow. Ganyushin told the companies that over the previous three years, it has been "much easier to list in the US as a foreign company than a US company—you can follow your home corporate governance practices, you don't have to have an independent board, you don't have to report in US GAAP."[26] Marketing pitches like this mark the end of the NYSE as a reputational intermediary for listed public companies.

As the New York Stock Exchange developed in the nineteenth and early twentieth centuries, it ultimately came to offer a robust package of distinct, albeit complementary, services to its clients, the companies listing their shares for trading on the Exchange. These services consisted of the following four components, each of which had value to customers:

1. The provision of liquidity.

2. Close monitoring of exchange trading for indications of insider trading, price manipulation, and other forms of cheating.

3. Standard-form, off-the-rack corporate governance rules for listed companies that reduced transaction costs and had a strong, positive reputational and signaling effect for the listed companies.

4. A reputational signal that informed investors that any company listing its securities for trading on the NYSE was of high quality and was committed to transparency and ongoing scrutiny by the exchanges.

On the NYSE, liquidity historically was ensured by the fact that essentially all the trading in listed companies' stock had to take place on the floor of the Exchange. The sheer number of buyers and sellers and the huge volume of trading were sources of liquidity for NYSE-listed stocks. The specialist system also provided liquidity for listed stocks. The Exchange rules provide that the Exchange will assign every listed company to a particular person, the specialist, who is responsible for maintaining a high-quality secondary market in the stock of her assigned company. Specialists match buyers and sellers who appear at the same time. They also, as a general rule, constantly maintain an inventory of shares of the stocks assigned to them so that they instantaneously can supply stocks to buyers who appear when no corresponding seller is immediately available.

The original system previously described, which assigned stocks to trade at specific times or when called from a list, broke down when interest in trading many stocks became so significant that there was a strong demand for trading throughout the day, rather than at certain specific times that had to be kept short to accommodate the growing list of stocks being traded. Under the new system, which developed in the late nineteenth century, brokers began to specialize in specific stocks. These brokers naturally would congregate to particular locations within the Exchange itself. These points were Schelling points for particular securities within the larger Schelling point that was the Exchange itself. Eventually, this system evolved into what became known as the "Specialist System."

Each NYSE stock was, and is, assigned to a "specialist," who has an obligation to facilitate trading in the stock of the listed company that is assigned to him. Specialists are responsible for making continuous, high-quality two-side markets for the stocks assigned to them.

The specialist system, in other words, was created to establish a reliable, trustworthy trading environment in which investors in the listed stock were assured that they could buy and sell their stock at a moment's notice. In other words, specialists provided liquidity. Their privileged access to trading information regarding their assigned stock, and the spread between their bid prices and their offered prices, provided the returns necessary to support the specialists in their roles as liquidity providers.

Monitoring of exchange-listed securities was closely linked to the specialist system. Shenanigans like insider trading and stock price manipulation damaged investors, but they damaged specialists and the exchanges even more. As the most active traders in their assigned stocks, specialists are deeply threatened by insider traders and manipulators because these fraudsters buy when the specialists' price is too low and sell to the specialists when their price is too high. Such trading, in other words, causes specialists to lose money.[27] To make up for their expected losses to insider-traders and manipulators, specialists must increase the "spread" between their bid prices and their offered prices. These higher costs reduce trading volume, hurting the exchanges' revenue. Not surprisingly, in light of these facts, the exchanges have strong incentives to monitor the trading activity that occurs in their listed shares. Because investors benefit from monitoring against trading fraud and manipulation, to the extent that such investors believe that better monitoring occurs on an exchange than off the exchange, shares listed on exchanges that enjoy reputations as effective monitors of trading will thrive.

Another historical reason why stock exchanges provided monitoring of secondary market trading, and why the companies issuing securities or individual investors did not provide such monitoring, is that there are significant economies of scale associated with centralized monitoring of stock trading.[28] These economies of scale exist because it is more efficient for a single entity, such as an exchange, to monitor the stock trading of many companies. And the same technology used to monitor a single stock can monitor stock trading in thousands of companies simultaneously. For example, a single computerized surveillance system can monitor trading in many companies. It makes little sense to have individuals or a single company create such systems for trading the stock of a particular company when an exchange or a governmental organization can provide this service simultaneously for thousands of companies from a single computer platform.

The centralized monitoring function traditionally performed by the exchanges has been usurped by regulators such as the Securities and Exchange Commission and the Commodities Futures Trading Commission. Under federal law, insider trading and stock price manipulation are just as illegal off the exchange floor as they are on the floors of the exchanges. And the SEC, along with the organized exchanges' various rivals, monitors these sorts of activities as assiduously as do the exchanges. Certainly there is no evidence that companies experience less fraud or less manipulation as a result of being listed on an exchange.

Another reputational benefit provided by stock exchanges was the provision of off-the-rack legal rules. Standardized off-the-rack rules reduce transaction costs for companies and investors. These rules used to be provided by stock exchanges but are not any longer. Stock exchanges predate the jurisdictional competition for corporate charters that exist among the states. Historically, the stock exchanges provided the internal rules of corporate governance for big companies that now are provided by federal laws, such as Sarbanes-Oxley, the

Securities Act of 1933, the Securities Exchange Act of 1934, and by the corporation codes in states like Delaware. Today there are no significant differences between the corporate governance rules of companies whose shares trade on the NYSE and those that trade on the over-the-counter NASDAQ Stock Market.

In days gone by, when a public corporation listed on a stock exchange, that corporation was making a credible commitment to abide by the set of corporate governance rules that the stock exchanges required of all registrants that were designed to maximize shareholder wealth. In other words, listing on an exchange like the NYSE sent a strong reputational signal.

The New York Stock Exchange, for example, told prospective listing companies that "the prestige and worldwide recognition associated with [being] a 'New York Stock Exchange listed company' is a distinct advantage not only to investors, but also with lenders, suppliers, customers and prospective employees."[29] The NYSE, from a reputational perspective, was striking in that it acted both as a reputational intermediary and as a mechanism by which companies that were trying to signal that they were playing by a particular set of rules could offer a credible commitment to the investing public that they would continue to abide by these rules in the future.

The commitment was made credible by the threat of delisting, which historically had draconian effects on companies because of the lack of alternative trading venues for shares in public companies. Over time, however, advances in technology and the development of markets have weakened the primacy of the traditional exchanges. A whole host of competitors for the traditional stock exchanges have emerged. And now exchanges compete for listings and it appears clear that they will list every company that can pay, as long as the regulators will permit it. Particularly attractive to stock exchanges are companies with high trading volumes, because such high trading volumes generate the most trading fees.

As technology has developed, over-the-counter trading, particularly electronic trading, became a superior, low-cost substitute for costly exchange listing. But exchanges, particularly the NYSE, continued to thrive as reputational intermediaries, at least for a time. As recently as three decades ago, it would have been unimaginable for companies that were eligible for listing on the venerable and prestigious NYSE to choose a competing venue. Historically, companies desperately needed the reputational cache associated with an exchange listing. Today, however, it is common for companies to choose the NASDAQ National Stock Market or even non-U.S. venues over the New York Stock Exchange.

Prominent companies such as Automatic Data Processing (ADP), Amazon.com, Amgen, Apple, Dell, Fifth Third Bancorp, Google, Intel, Microsoft, News Corporation, Oracle, Starbucks, and Sun Microsystems, all of which easily met the NYSE's listing requirements when they went public, decided to opt out of listing on the NYSE in favor of being traded on the NASDAQ stock market. And of course, the biggest public offering of the twenty-first century, Facebook, chose NASDAQ over the NYSE. There does not appear to be any reputational cost associated with this choice. The NYSE historically was "where the blue-chip, larger, more traditional companies have listed. The high-growth tech companies have gravitated toward NASDAQ. Over the last year, those lines have become blurred."[30] SEC regulations have saved the stock exchanges from being entirely eradicated by the competition unleashed by technological progress by passing regulations that restrict exchanges from trading in securities listed on other exchanges (NYSE shares cannot be traded on NASDAQ or other exchanges and vice versa).

The competition among stock exchanges today is much like the competition among airlines in the days when the Federal Aviation Administration fixed ticket prices and cargo prices. Until 1978, fares and other prices had to be approved by the government, which insisted on standardized rates. Airlines therefore could not compete over prices. Airlines competed instead to offer the most lavish services to customers at the fixed prices approved by the government.

An important nonprice vector along which the stock exchanges compete is advertising. Exchanges provide "free" co-branded advertising. To be more precise, competing exchanges provide advertising whose price is built into the listing fees that companies pay. This advertising is co-branded in the sense that the name of both the company and the exchange are displayed in the advertising simultaneously.[31] NASDAQ gives listed companies publicity in a very prominent way, showcasing listed companies and their products and services on its own seven-story electronic billboard in New York's Times Square, which of course, in addition to being one of the world's "top tourist destinations," is the scene of a huge New Year's Eve celebration broadcast worldwide on multiple channels.[32] For its part, the NYSE has deals with 30 U.S. and non-U.S. television stations and networks that broadcast stock market reports from the floor of its exchange, and the NYSE has erected digital billboards on Highway 101 in Santa Clara and Redwood City, California, in Silicon Valley, the capital of the U.S. tech industry.[33]

Traditionally, firms moved from one trading venue to another (from the NASDAQ to the NYSE) because they had grown and viewed the move as a promotion from the over-the-counter markets that catered to start-up companies, to the NYSE, which was the venue of choice for mature, successful companies. Decisions by highly successful companies, such as Google and Microsoft, to remain in the over-the-counter markets, along with the ability of a few venerable firms such as Hewlett-Packard to be simultaneously listed on both the NYSE and NASDAQ (due to quirks in the regulatory system), illustrate the change in the traditional ordering and the decline of the reputational model.

Modern stock exchanges are subject to vigorous competition from various sources, including both rival exchanges and alternative trading venues. Major competitors are companies that have organized what are known as "black pools" or "dark pools," which are private stock trading venues operated by financial institutions including Goldman Sachs and Citigroup, as well as by a number of independent companies. In the middle of 2012 there were around 20 black pools. Other major competitors for the NYSE include IntercontinentalExchange, Inc. (commonly referred to as ICE), the NASDAQ OMX Group, Inc., Ares Capital Corporation, CBOE Holdings, Inc., Apollo Global Management and Apollo Global Investment Corporation, and Main Street Capital Corporation. All of this competition has strained the exchanges' capacity for self-regulation and undermined their incentives to regulate in the public interest with respect to issues related to the corporate governance of their members.[34]

Moreover, the available evidence indicates that organized exchanges do not even act as stand-alone regulators of their own listed companies anymore. There is no longer a reputational advantage associated with an exchange listing. Modern technology, the securities fraud rules, and the SEC's unwillingness to allow exchanges any leeway in the way in which different exchanges regulate listing firms all have combined to eviscerate the ability of competing trading venues, particularly that of the NYSE, to compete by serving as a reputational intermediary for listed firms.

Instead, today all trading venues are better understood as mere conduits for the SEC, which coordinates the corporate governance regulations that ostensibly are promulgated under the exchanges' authority as self-regulatory organizations. The available evidence here consists largely of a series of episodes in which the exchanges failed to self-regulate, often followed by a coordinated regulation led by the SEC. Self-regulation by the exchanges is in general dysfunctional in significant part because securities are often traded simultaneously in multiple venues, thus inhibiting the ability of exchanges to unilaterally enforce regulations.[35] As the *Special Study on Market Structure, Listing Standards and Corporate Governance* pointed out years ago, the SEC "encourage[d] exchanges 'voluntarily' to adopt given corporate governance listing standards and in the process has urged the exchanges, listed companies and shareholders to reach consensus on those standards."[36] This pattern continues to this day. The SEC now coordinates the regulatory price fixing among the exchanges' self-regulatory organizations with respect to every facet of the exchanges' relationships with listed companies. Thus, the SEC has undermined the traditional way in which exchanges competed with one another by serving as a reputational intermediary by providing and enforcing efficient corporate governance rules to enhance the reputations of listing firms.

As I have pointed out before, a powerful example of the reputational demise of the NYSE is the Exchange's inability to enforce its most powerful rule concerning corporate governance. This was the rule requiring listed firms to limit themselves to having only one class of common stock outstanding, and to providing that class of stock with no less and no more than one vote per share of stock.

At the height of the 1980s takeover wave, when corporate managers wanted to insulate themselves from takeover, they violated this rule by adopting so-called "dual class" capital structure.[37] The NYSE found that when it threatened to delist major companies that violated this rule from the Exchange, the companies, like General Motors and Dow Jones, Inc., responded by agreeing to delist, a result that would have imposed significantly higher costs on the NYSE than on the listed companies being "punished" by being delisted. Delisting would cause the NYSE to lose listing fees and trading revenue, while the listed companies would simply move their listings to a rival venue like the NASDAQ Stock Market at no cost to themselves. Thus, the traditional sanction—delisting—that the NYSE deployed when it wanted to enforce its own rules no longer constituted a meaningful threat to member firms. As the *Los Angeles Times* pointed out at the time, "In the 1920s, when the one share, one vote rule entered the exchange's rule book, it had a *de facto* monopoly over stock trading." The article quotes former SEC Commissioner A.A. Sommer Jr., who said "there was no place else a first-class company could go to be traded." In this competitive environment, he continued, "no company was going to withdraw from the New York Stock Exchange." Now however, "it has scarcely escaped the Big Board's notice that the trading technology of the over-the-counter market has so improved that companies threatened with delisting now greet the news with equanimity."[38]

Unable to enforce its own accounting rules, the NYSE lobbied the SEC to prevent these companies from delisting or, barring that, to require the NASDAQ to adopt a one-share-one-vote capital structure in order to eliminate the incentive to delist for companies desiring a dual class voting structure. In other words, as the Exchange began to face competition for listings, it began to lose the ability to enforce its own rules of corporate governance. This, in turn, meant that companies listing on the Exchange could no longer claim that such listing provided a credible commitment to be bound by the Exchange's rules.

Evidence abounds that exchanges are failing to meet their regulatory mandates. For example, in 2000, the Justice Department and the SEC sanctioned the American Stock Exchange, the Philadelphia Stock Exchange, the Chicago Board of Options Exchange, and the Pacific Stock Exchange (which is owned by an ECN, ArcaEx) for not enforcing their own internal rules for the trading of options. The four exchanges agreed, without admitting or denying wrongdoing, to spend $77 million on new surveillance technology and enforcement initiatives. In 2003, the SEC investigated and disciplined the New York Stock Exchange for failure to properly regulate against trading in front of customer orders and other actions by Exchange members that harm investors. Later that same year, the SEC Office of Compliance, Inspection and Examinations wrote a confidential report that, according to *The Wall Street Journal,* concluded that self-regulation at the NYSE "does not adequately discipline or deter" securities law violations by Exchange members.[39] And in late 2004 the SEC was preparing enforcement actions against three other exchanges, the American Stock Exchange, the Philadelphia Stock Exchange, and Chicago's National Stock Exchange. The SEC has "evidence that some...firms that oversee the buying and selling of securities at these exchanges withheld valuable pricing information from the public or traded for their own accounts before filing public orders." These firms "allegedly took advantage of their knowledge of price trends to get better deals for themselves, shortchanging other investors."[40]

These are all clear examples of the fact that self-regulation, even by venerable entities such as the New York Stock Exchange, is systemically dysfunctional in today's environment. The SEC is pressuring the exchanges to engage in self-regulation because the exchanges are required to police trading on their floors aggressively, which they do not do. But the problem is that the exchanges no longer have the proper incentives to engage in self-regulation with respect to many issues. These incentives have been replaced by the need to survive by attracting order flow from rival trading venues.

In previous work with Maureen O'Hara, I have argued that exchanges traditionally provided a vector of services to investors and issuers, including standardized rules, monitoring of trading, clearing and settlement, liquidity, and a signaling function.[41] Delisting rules allowed the exchange to preserve the value of the reputational signal associated with listing on a particular trading venue. This enhanced the exchange's self-regulatory role by allowing it to expel errant firms, thereby enforcing the norms of the exchange. Furthermore, investors could rely on the integrity of firms listed on the exchange because their trading signified having met these underlying standards. Whether such signal-based rules are still sensible is debatable.

Increasingly, investors have myriad sources of information regarding firms' prospects, suggesting less reliance on the listing venue. A second complicating factor is that where a firm trades is now often divorced from where a firm lists. These factors undermine the traditional reputational content of listings. Despite a seemingly unending string of corporate scandals, few firms are actually delisted for aberrant behavior. The intense competition between exchanges for listings is largely responsible for stock exchanges' reticence to delist. Such competition means that the stock exchanges hurt themselves and not the companies they threaten to delist. This, in turn, renders the threat of delisting hollow and unconvincing, both to listed firms and to the investing public.

Stock exchanges, formerly an important reputational signal in U.S. capital markets, no longer play such a role. As more competition between exchanges has emerged and regulations have ensured the illegality of practices such as insider trading on and off exchanges, traditional exchanges such as the NYSE can offer fewer essential services to firms. Firms, as a result, have less incentive to remain listed on an exchange, and often the consequences of delisting are greater for the exchange than the firm. Thus, the reputational signal formerly associated with an exchange listing has been lost.

Endnotes

1. Jerry Markham and Daniel Harty, "For Whom the Bell Tolls: The Demise of Exchange Trading Floors and the Growth Of ECNs," *Journal of Corporation Law* 33, no. 4 (2008).

2. Elizabeth Oltheten, "Introduction to Stock Market Investment," University of Illinois online course, available at http://business. illinois.edu/broker/course/lesson09/x1b.htm, accessed December 5, 2012.

3. James E. Buck, *The New York Stock Exchange: The First 200 Years* (1992), 16.

4. Thomas Schelling, *The Strategy of Conflict* (Cambridge: Harvard University Press, 1960), 57.

5. NYSE/Euronext, Technology Timeline, www.nyse.com/about/ history/timeline_technology.html, accessed December 5, 2012.

6. Matthew Josephson, *Edison: A Biography* (Wiley, 1992). Although Alexander Graham Bell certainly deserves credit as a great inventor,

another inventor, Elisha Gray, independently developed a device that could transmit speech electrically. See About.com/Inventors, http://inventors.about.com/od/bstartinventors/a/telephone.htm.

7. Randall Dodd, "Markets: Exchange or Over-the-Counter?" International Monetary Fund Finance and Development, www.imf. org/external/pubs/ft/fandd/basics/markets.htm, accessed December 5, 2012.

8. Ibid.

9. Ibid.

10. Jonathan Macey and Hideki Kanda, "The Stock Exchange as a Firm: The Emergence of Close Substitutes for the New York and Tokyo Stock Exchanges," *Cornell Law Review* 75 (1990): 1007-1052.

11. Sean O'Connor, "Strengthening Auditor Independence: Reestablishing Audits as Control and Premium Signaling Mechanisms," *Washington Law Review* 81 (2006): 536, 525-593.

12. Standard & Poor's, "A History of Standard & Poor's," 1860-1940, www.standardandpoors.com/about-sp/timeline/en/us/, accessed December 5, 2012.

13. Ibid.

14. Ibid.

15. Ibid.

16. Ibid.

17. "A Brief History of Credit Ratings Agencies," Investopedia, August 13, 2009, www.investopedia.com/articles/bonds/09/history-credit-rating-agencies.asp#axzz2EAlPi98Z, accessed December 5, 2012.

18. Sean O'Connor, "Be Careful What You Wish For: How Accountants and Congress Created the Problem of Auditor Independence," *Boston College Law Review* 45 (2004): 741, 756-758.

19. O'Connor, "Strengthening Auditor Independence."

20. Ibid.

21. Ibid.

22. Ibid., 538.

23. Andrew Ross Sorkin, "The Big Board Tunes Out Its Own Rules," *The New York Times,* DealBook, April 25, 2011, http://dealbook. nytimes.com/2011/04/25/the-big-board-sets-aside-its-own-rules/, accessed December 5, 2011.

24. Dave Goodboy, "This Biotech Stock Could Become 'the Next Big Thing...,'" June 15, 2012, www.streetauthority.com/growth-investing/ biotech-stock-could-become-next-big-thing%E2%80%A6-459336, accessed December 5, 2012. The author of this excerpt, Mr. Goodboy, was identified as "vice president of marketing for intrendX llc, a New York City–based marketing service to ultra-high net worth family offices and individuals. He also works with Adria Partners LLC, a bond lease real estate fund. Dave is well versed in technical analysis, tape reading, niche strategies, fundamental analysis and stock picking. His knowledge base runs deep and wide in currencies, equities, derivatives and index futures." www.streetauthority.com/ users/dave-goodboy, accessed January 21, 2013.

25. http://economictimes.indiatimes.com/topic/For-the-last-three-years-it's-much-easier-to-list-in-the-US-as-a-foreign-company-than-a-US-company-you-can-follow-your-home-corporate-governance-practices,-you-don't-have-to-have-an-independent-board,-you-don't-have-to-report-in-US-GAAP,/; *Arab Times,* New York Exchange Courts Russian Companies, December 2, 2012, www.arabnews.com/ new-york-exchange-courts-russian-companies.

26. Ibid.

27. David Haddock, Jonathan Macey, "Regulation on Demand: A Private Interest Model, with an Application to Insider Trading Regulation," *Journal of Law and Economics* 30 (1987): 311-52.

28. Jonathan Macey, "From Fairness to Contract: The New Direction of the Rules Against Insider Trading," *Hofstra Law Review* 13 (1984): 9, 59.

29. New York Stock Exchange Listing Standards Manual of 1989, 3.

30. Kathleen Pender, "Will Facebook List Its Shares on the NYSE or the Nasdaq?" *The New York Times,* February 9, 2012 (quoting Richard Repetto, analyst with Sandler O'Neill + Partners), www.sfgate.com/business/article/Will-Facebook-list-its-shares-on-NYSE-or-Nasdaq-3160992.php.

31. Ibid.

32. Ibid.

33. Ibid.

34. Jonathan R. Macey, *Corporate Governance: Promises Kept, Promises Broken* (2008), 112.

35. See Jonathan R. Macey and Maureen O'Hara, "From Markets to Venues: Securities Regulation in an Evolving World," *Stanford Law Review* 58 (2005): 563, 575, 577-79 ("As a purely descriptive matter, the available evidence is inconsistent with the assertion that rival trading venues compete to produce corporate law rules. Rather, the accurate depiction of the competitive situation is that the SEC coordinates the regulatory standards of the exchanges and the Nasdaq in order to prevent competition among these trading venues from occurring at all.").

36. Robert Todd Lang et al., "Special Study on Market Structure, Listing Standards and Corporate Governance," *Business Lawyer* 57 (2002): 1487, 1503.

37. See SEC Office of Chief Economist, "Update—The Effects of Dual-Class Recapitalizations on Shareholder Wealth: Including Evidence from 1986 and 1987," Table 1 (July 16, 1987). See also Jeffrey N. Gordon, "Ties That Bond: Dual Class Common Stock and the Problem of Shareholder Choice," *California Law Review* 76 (1988): 1, 4. Gordon counts more than 80 public firms that have "adopted, or proposed to adopt, capital structures with two classes of common stock." Ibid. In footnote 2, Gordon adds, "One recent estimate is that since 1985 the number of companies with dual classes of stock has risen from 119 to 306." Ibid., n. 2. See also Linda Sandler, "Class Struggle: Dual Stock Categories Spur Powerful Debate over Stability vs. Gain—Shares with Multiple Votes Annoy Corporate Raiders and Many Investors Too—If You Don't Like It, Sell," *The Wall Street Journal,* May 17, 1988, 1.

38. Michael Hiltzik, "Assault on Principle of One Share, One Vote Stirs Growing Concern," *Los Angeles Times,* May 18, 1986, http://articles.latimes.com/1986-05-18/business/fi-21072_1_shareholder-rights/2, accessed December 5, 2012.

39. Floyd Norris, "Option Boards Are Censured by the SEC," *The New York Times,* September 12, 2000, C1.

40. Landon Thomas, Jr., "SEC Steps In as Fines Are Planned on Five Firms," *The New York Times,* October 17, 2003, C1.

41. Jonathan Macey and Maureen O'Hara, "The Economics of Stock Exchange Listing Fees and Listing Requirements," *Journal of Financial Intermediation* 11 (2002): 297.

10

The SEC and Reputation

The traditional theory of regulation posits that regulation and reputation work hand in hand. Regulators bring criminal or civil charges against fraudsters, and these charges send a signal to investors that the company or individual cannot be trusted. However, regulation no longer serves this function. Prosecution is increasingly viewed as a political tool that ambitious prosecutors use to advance their careers. Regulators now need to satisfy interest groups and political overseers. The SEC exemplifies the way that modern regulation undermines rather than strengthens the role of reputation in capital markets. Not only do SEC regulators seek to enhance the power of their organization, but many also aim to advance their own careers. A revolving door exists between the SEC and powerful positions at top law firms and banks. Many SEC employees take positions at these firms. As a result, SEC regulators have incentives to develop expertise in highly technical areas, which increases their demand at firms and banks. The SEC therefore lacks regulators who have expertise and interest in identifying forms of simple fraud, such as Bernie Madoff's famous Ponzi scheme. The resulting regulatory environment over-enforces highly technical rules, such as front-running, and under-enforces simple fraud, thereby undermining the reputational signaling of SEC action. In addition, all major investment banks and accounting firms have been involved in litigation, destroying the ability of investors to use regulation as a means of identifying good or bad companies. The firms also settle nearly all the cases brought against them without admitting wrongdoing, further complicating the information that investors can infer from regulation. As a result, regulation has become decoupled from reputation in modern financial markets.

The fall of Drexel marked the beginning of the end for the traditional economic theory of reputation. This seems true regardless of whether one believes that junk bonds are good or bad for the economy or whether one believes that their progenitor, Michael Milken, was a hero or a villain. The story of Drexel is the story of an investment bank that was very successful for a time and that collapsed in ways wholly inconsistent with the traditional economic theory of reputation. The alleged evildoers made fortunes, and these fortunes were not confiscated. While the firm, Drexel Burnham Lambert, collapsed, its flesh-and-blood employees went on to other successful careers. Individuals' reputations had become completely unhinged from those of the companies for which they worked.

Perhaps most important, regulation did not play the role it was supposed to play in the Drexel collapse. The traditional theory of regulation posits that regulation and reputation work hand in hand, almost symbiotically. Civil and criminal charges brought by regulators are a primary means by which fraudsters are identified. Such charges send a concrete signal about wrongdoing that presumably marks the death knell of the company and the individuals identified as culpable.

Unfortunately, this no longer is the case. As in other countries, prosecutions in the U.S. increasingly are viewed as political tools by which ambitious prosecutors can advance their careers and fulfill their goals of obtaining higher office. Rudolph Giuliani was not the first prosecutor to use his prosecutorial agenda to advance his own career. But he was among the first to show how successfully this could be done against the most powerful Wall Street firms. Eliot Spitzer followed directly in Giuliani's footsteps. And, as of this writing, there simply are no Wall Street firms that have not been sued and fined significantly for misdeeds. The suing of a Wall Street firm no longer sends any signal at all other than that one has attracted the attention of regulators. It might be that the firm being investigated has engaged in sharp dealings with its customers. Alternatively, the company might be an attractive target for political reasons, or, as discussed later, a person or company might be targeted by regulators and prosecuted for bureaucratic reasons. The bottom line is that regulation and reputation no longer work symbiotically to help keep Wall Street firms honest. Rather, regulation has entirely lost its value as a signal of weak reputation.

Succeeding In and Out of the SEC

A large part of the problem is that, just as Wall Street operators have reputations that are separate and distinct from those of the firms in which they work, regulators also have reputations of their own. Moreover, regulatory agencies are bureaucracies that need political support in order to survive. Regulators face strong pressure not only to "do the right thing," but also to satisfy powerful political overseers and various influential interest groups. Regulators also have incentives to do things that advance their own careers and to advance the power of the bureaucracies for which they work.

These problems are exacerbated by the fact that often it is difficult even for experts to tell what the right thing is. As a practical matter, it is impossible for the public to fully understand the consequences of the actions taken by regulators. These sorts of information problems, which economists refer to as "rational ignorance" problems, coupled with the high costs to individual citizens of galvanizing into effective political coalitions to fight waste and favoritism toward special-interest groups, mean that it is extremely difficult to monitor regulators, which in turn means that regulators have considerable freedom to pursue their own interests rather than the public interest however one might define the term.

The point of this chapter is to evaluate the relationship between reputation and regulation. Basically speaking, regulation no longer supplements or reinforces companies' investments in reputation. Rather, the regulation of modern financial markets increasingly has undermined the value of investments in reputation.

The SEC, Wall Street's primary regulator, exemplifies the way modern regulation undermines rather than strengthens the way reputation functions in the capital markets.[1] There is considerable support for the hypothesis advanced by scholars that SEC officials maximize along two vectors. First, like many bureaucrats, officials at the SEC attempt to maximize the power and the budget of the Commission. At least to some extent, their careers are linked to the power and prestige of the agency they work for, in the sense that as the agency's power and prestige rises or falls, so too does the relative power and prestige of the people working within the agency. This observation appears to apply with particular force to "career bureaucrats," or those officials whose ambition is to rise as high as possible within the power structure of the bureaucracy itself.

Not all SEC officials spend their entire careers at the Commission. In fact, the SEC has one of the highest rates of turnover of any administrative agency in Washington. It is extremely common for SEC officials to move to top legal jobs at large law firms that practice before the SEC, and, increasingly, to senior positions within the financial firms that the SEC regulates. There are many examples of this revolving door in operation. In recent years, without exception, all the people leading the SEC's most important branch, the prestigious Division of Enforcement, have moved on to jobs as lawyers or in-house counsel to the very firms they used to regulate. One former SEC Director of Enforcement is a partner in the giant law firm of Davis, Polk & Wardwell, which represents many clients before the SEC in a wide variety of contexts.

That person's predecessor as Enforcement chief now is the general counsel at JP Morgan Chase, which, of course, routinely is involved in regulatory issues before the SEC in various contexts, including the enforcement context. The predecessor at the SEC of the person who became general counsel to JP Morgan Chase went on to serve in the same position—general counsel—at Deutsche Bank. Other top SEC officials have gone on to other major law firms and also to other regulated entities, including Credit Suisse and Morgan Stanley. One scholar observed that somebody studying the SEC "could be forgiven for thinking that the whole point of landing a job as the SEC's Director of Enforcement is to position oneself for the better paying one on Wall Street."[2]

One way for SEC staffers to garner top-paying jobs on Wall Street is to develop practice specialties in highly technical fields in which there are few experts. After developing such a specialty, the lawyers within agencies can make themselves even more desirable in the private sector by ratcheting up the enforcement of the technical rules that they have mastered. In other words, from the point of view of the people working within the SEC, technical rules are better than nontechnical rules because SEC alumni who are expert in highly technical areas are in particularly high demand. And the more vigorously such technical rules are enforced, the higher the demand for SEC alumni will be.

This rather perverse incentive system has produced a regulatory environment in which there is overenforcement of highly technical rules and underenforcement of simple, old-fashioned fraud. This in turn has undermined, to a large extent, and perhaps completely, the reputational or signaling effect of SEC enforcement actions. To the extent that SEC enforcement actions are brought in order to provide a platform for SEC officials to demonstrate their technical mastery of particular regulatory fields—and to demonstrate that SEC regulators increasingly are directing their attention to the precise regulatory fields in which the bureaucrats have expertise—the signal sent by SEC regulatory action is no longer even related to the target of the regulatory action. Instead, the signal these days relates to the regulators themselves, who are signaling to the job market that they have the precise skill sets that regulated entities require.

For example, perhaps the most common—and certainly the most venerable—form of securities fraud is the Ponzi scheme. In a Ponzi scheme, the crooks perpetrating the fraud promise investors that they are investing their money in some clever way, and then they simply steal some of the investors' money rather than investing it. To perpetuate the scheme, however, the operators of the Ponzi scheme will take some of the money invested by subsequent investors and use it to pay back earlier investors in order to create the impression that the successful investments are actually being made. As long as the fraudsters running the Ponzi scheme can continue to collect increasingly large sums of money from new investors so that they can repay earlier investors, the scheme can continue. Eventually, however, like all houses made of cards, Ponzi schemes ultimately collapse when they grow beyond a certain size. As increasingly large numbers of investors demand their money back, eventually, the fraudsters are unable to collect enough new money to meet the expectations of existing investors for the return of their money.

The famous fraud of Bernard Madoff was a Ponzi scheme, albeit an exceptionally large and long-lived one. Madoff collected money from investors while claiming to be allocating it to safe investments that, despite their low risk, garnered very strong annual returns. In fact, Madoff wasn't making any such investments at all. Instead, he was running a classic Ponzi scheme, stealing a lot of the new money, but using some of it to repay existing investors in order to keep the fraud going. Madoff's scheme was so successful that, while billions in wealth vanished, a number of early minority investors managed to get all of their money back—including interest (though most of this "lucky" minority later was sued by the Trustee of Madoff's estate to recuperate some money in order to pay back some of the billions owed to later investors).

The SEC badly bungled the Madoff fraud. The Commission ignored repeated warnings of likely problems with Madoff's investment scheme and was later forced to acknowledge the fact that "no one can or should defend, excuse or deflect responsibility for the SEC's handling of the Madoff matter."[3] In the months following the implosion of Madoff's Ponzi scheme, the SEC suffered a public relations nightmare when headline news stories emerged that the SEC had received numerous specific warnings over the years about the likelihood that Madoff's investment business was a major fraud.

The SEC's internal watchdog, the Office of the Inspector General, conducted its own investigation of its failure to uncover the Madoff fraud. The results were highly embarrassing to the SEC:

> The SEC received more than ample information in the form of detailed and substantive complaints over the years to warrant a thorough and comprehensive examination and/or investigation of Bernard Madoff and BMIS [his company, Bernie Madoff Investment Securities] for operating a Ponzi scheme, and that despite three examinations and two investigations being conducted, a thorough and competent investigation was never performed.[4]

The SEC's Office of Inspector General found that during the 16-year period of the fraud, between June 1992 and December 2008, the month that Madoff actually confessed to federal prosecutors, the SEC received a total of six separate complaints that raised significant, specific red flags concerning Madoff's investment operations and handling of investors' funds. Particularly stunning was the fact that over the years, Madoff falsely claimed to have placed hundreds of thousands of specific trades with various financial institutions that were subject to the SEC's jurisdiction. The SEC's investigators never bothered to investigate whether any such trades ever occurred.

In other words, the SEC could have uncovered the Madoff fraud merely by asking the financial institutions that Madoff claimed to be buying from and selling to for verification of the trades that Madoff was claiming to have made. Had the SEC asked these financial institutions, UBS and the Royal Bank of Scotland, they would have learned immediately that Madoff never engaged in the transactions that he claimed to have made on behalf of investors. This, of course, is the classic sign of a Ponzi scheme. Apparently, Madoff was aware that the SEC bureaucracy was particularly inept at handling inquiries of non-U.S. financial institutions such as UBS and the Royal Bank of Scotland, so he simply claimed to be placing his fictitious trades with non-U.S. firms. The SEC also was aware of press reports dating back several years before the discovery of the fraud that raised doubt about whether it was possible legally to earn the consistently high returns that Madoff claimed to have earned.[5]

The SEC has few incentives to investigate the simple but effective sorts of fraud schemes that Bernard Madoff masterminded because there are few career payoffs to doing so. Sophisticated banks like JP Morgan Chase and Goldman Sachs might have their ethical shortcomings, but they have never been known to run—or even been suspected of running—Ponzi schemes or other sorts of simple frauds. Consequently, there are few if any future career payoffs to SEC staffers from developing expertise and gaining experience in identifying such simple frauds. In fact, it turns out that one of the teams of SEC investigators sent to look into the allegations about Madoff's fraud failed to discover the fraud because they had no interest, experience, or expertise in uncovering simple frauds.

Apparently, this particular group was expert in dealing with a more sophisticated sort of fraud called "front-running," a type of fraud one does observe with some frequency among established banks. Front-running occurs when a securities dealer receives an order from a customer to purchase or to sell an unusually large block of securities. The purchases of significant blocks of securities typically drive prices up, and the sales of significant blocks of securities typically drive prices down. These price effects are attributable to various factors including normal supply-and-demand pressures. Another explanation for these price effects is that market observers and participants logically infer that large purchases of securities reflect an expert analyst's or trader's positive assessment and evaluation of a company and that large sales of securities similarly reflect an expert's negative assessment and evaluation of a company.

The securities firms that receive these buy and sell orders can profit at their customers' expense by front-running, which simply describes the practice of trading ahead of a customer's order. Front-running, in other words, involves buying before executing a large buy order on behalf of a customer or selling before executing a large sell order on behalf of a customer. This enables the securities firm to make profits on the securities purchased ahead of the customer and to avoid losses on the securities sold ahead of the customer.

Front-running trading hurts customers and is illegal. When front-running takes the form of buying, it is illegal because such purchases can, and often do, hurt the customer by driving up the prices of the very securities that the customer is buying before the customer's buy orders are executed. When front-running takes the form of selling, it is illegal because such sales can, and often do, hurt the customer by driving down the prices of the securities that the customer wants to sell before the customer's sell orders are executed.

Securities firms face frequent accusations of front-running, so the demand for lawyers and compliance officials who can monitor and control—and defend against accusations of—such activity is strong and constant. It is, therefore, not surprising that a team of SEC officials would have expertise in this sort of investigation rather than in investigating the sorts of simple fraud that actually hurt ordinary investors. In 2009, six Wall Street firms paid a total of $42 million in fines for having engaged in front-running by trading in front of customers' orders during the seven-year period between 1999 and 2005. One of these, the electronic broker E*Trade, paid a fine of $34 million. According to the SEC, E*Trade Capital Markets LLC and the five other, smaller firms, "failed to meet their basic obligation as specialists to serve public customer orders over their own proprietary interests while executing trades."[6]

There have been persistent rumors about front-running at all the major investment banks, including Goldman Sachs, which consistently have been denied. Goldman Sachs, however, for years actually notified its customers of the possibility of front-running in the contractual Terms and Conditions of Use that clients had to accept before gaining operational access to the Goldman Sachs website. Goldman Sachs notified its clients who used its portal for trading, "Your use of the products and services on this website may be monitored by...Goldman Sachs, and...the resultant information may be used by GS for its internal purposes...."[7]

In trading for its own account (now restricted by law under the so-called Paulson rule, which is part of the Dodd-Frank Wall Street Reform Act of 2010), Goldman has never hidden the fact that its goal was to make money by buying low and selling high, that is, buying customers' securities before they rise in value and selling securities to customers before they decline in value. In a famous colloquy with regulators, Goldman CEO Lloyd Blankfein explained: "In our market-making function, we are a principal. We represent the other side of what people want to do. We are not a fiduciary. We are not an agent."[8] Market making remains legal under the Dodd-Frank Act.

The topic of front-running received new publicity when Goldman Sachs's proprietary trading operation (called Fundamental Strategies) sent out an e-mail to Goldman's clients that was interpreted as notifying them that the firm routinely engaged in a form of front-running. As *The New York Times'* Andrew Ross Sorkin described the issues raised in the letter, "Goldman and other firms have come under criticism for trading ahead of, or at odds with, its own clients."[9] The letter informed clients that the company might occasionally "discuss with you Trading Ideas generated by our Fundamental Strategies Group." The firm, according to the letter, in an effort to deal with "conflicts of interests appropriately," sent the letter to clearly establish how the Fundamental Strategies Group worked with other parts of Goldman and how that affected Trading Ideas. The firm informed clients that it might trade in response to Trading Ideas "before we have discussed those Trading Ideas with you." Furthermore, it might continue to make trades "out of any position, based on Trading Ideas, at any time after we have discussed them with you." Likewise, Goldman told clients that it would discuss Trading Ideas with other clients "both before and after we have discussed them with you."[10]

The letter continued, advising clients that they "should not consider Trading Ideas as objective or independent research or as investment advice." Goldman clearly stated in the letter that it would not be acting as an advisor while talking with clients about Trading Ideas, and that it was the clients' "responsibility to seek appropriate advice." The firm protected itself in the letter from liability resulting from information in Trading Ideas, claiming "we...accept no liability, other than for fraudulent misrepresentation, if" the information in the Trading Ideas turned out to be inaccurate.[11]

In Goldman's defense, it is important to recognize that Goldman's distribution of this e-mail to its clients is indisputable proof that Goldman is not trying to hide its business practices. It is certainly no secret that Wall Street firms such as Goldman are in business to make money. There is nothing wrong with that. It is also no secret that Goldman makes money by risking its own capital in trading and underwriting, as well as by earning fees and commissions from customers that are generated by giving advice to these customers and by executing trades on behalf of these clients.

It is extremely difficult to manage the simultaneous provision of trading services, in which the "client" is a counterparty and one trades at the customers' expense, and brokerage services, in which the client is looking to the investment bank for information, advice, and technical assistance. The rules governing these areas are very technical. Officials at the SEC have incentives to focus on enforcing the most technical rules because doing so maximizes their career prospects both inside and outside of the agency. In stark contrast, however, as the Madoff saga painfully reminded us, there is little professional payoff to SEC officials from focusing on simple, old-fashioned, garden-variety fraud like Madoff's giant Ponzi scheme.

The current practice of the SEC of bringing highly technical cases that might or might not actually involve wrongdoing against a company or an individual seems to inevitably be one of the reasons why there is no longer much, if any, negative reputational signal for these companies and individuals who are targeted by the SEC. Another reason there is no longer a reputational signal associated with the SEC's enforcement actions is that the vast majority of such cases settle, regardless of how egregious the behavior of the defendants might have been, without any admission of wrongdoing. Since litigation is so expensive, companies and individuals that the SEC targets routinely explain away large SEC settlements as necessary in order to avoid expensive, distracting, and time-consuming litigation.

Two more reasons exist that help explain the lack of reputation signal of SEC enforcement actions. First, for a lawsuit to send a reputational signal, the lawsuit must contain some information that allows market participants such as potential customers to distinguish the target of the lawsuit from the other companies or individuals in the same industry. But nowadays, lawsuits contain no such information because there simply are no investment banks, credit rating agencies, or accounting firms that can be distinguished from their rivals on the basis of the fact that they have a clean litigation record. All the major financial companies have sued and settled private litigation alleging similar, and often identical, sorts of bad behavior. All four of the major accounting firms have had clients who have been involved in accounting fraud.[12] It simply is not possible for clients, regulators, or the public to distinguish among the major accounting firms that audit public companies on the basis of quality distinctions.

Second, because all the major investment banks have been sued for fraud by some governmental entity, including the SEC, such suits no longer send much of a signal. For example, not long ago, the city of Cleveland, Ohio, sued 21 investment banks including Deutsche Bank, Goldman Sachs, and Merrill Lynch for creating a "public nuisance" by marketing and selling inappropriate and misleading home mortgage loans. The loan defaults and the foreclosures of the houses that collateralized these loans have ruined entire neighbourhoods. The banks named as defendants bought subprime mortgages from lenders who had bought them from the marketers or "loan originators" who dealt directly with the customers. The banks then packaged the mortgages into securities and sold the securities that were backed by the mortgages to investors.

Many other municipalities, including the City of Baltimore, Maryland, have sued major banks and investment banks for manipulating the key interest rate, known as LIBOR (London Interbank Offered Rate), that is used to determine the interest rates on floating-rate mortgages and other loans to benefit themselves. Baltimore has sued JP Morgan Chase, Bank of America, Barclays, Citibank, and Deutsche Bank, claiming that these banks acted illegally to depress LIBOR during the financial crisis. One large bank, Barclays, already has acknowledged its role in manipulating LIBOR, and it appears that the Bank of England, Britain's central bank, knew about and might have been involved in the plan.[13] Other settlements, some in the billions, are likely on the way.

Likewise, all the major credit rating agencies have handed out inflated, inaccurate ratings to the special-purpose entities that issued the complex mortgage-backed securities that led to the financial crisis. In 2010, the U.S. Permanent Subcommittee on Investigations found that the ratings given by the two biggest credit rating agencies in the United States, Moody's and Standard & Poor's, on the key securities that fueled the financial crisis, residential mortgage-backed securities, or RMBS, and collateralized debt obligations, or CDOs, were biased in the sense that the credit rating agencies allowed the financial institutions whose securities they were rating "to impact their analysis." The report concluded that the rating agencies "did it for the money."[14] The report argues that the big credit rating agencies were the catalysts for the 2007–2008 financial crisis. They gave their top ratings to highly speculative securities backed by home mortgages months after the housing market started to collapse, and then, in July 2007, began wholesale downgrades. The report postulated that "perhaps more than any other single event, the sudden mass downgrades of residential mortgage-backed securities and collateralized debt obligation ratings were the immediate trigger for the financial crisis."

Congress contemplated radical reforms for the agencies during the drafting of the Dodd-Frank law, but the final draft of the bill included no major reforms. The SEC's response to the rating agency debacle was complete capitulation to the big industry incumbents.

During the financial crisis, Wall Street firms exerted tremendous pressure on credit rating agencies to give top ratings to their exotic derivative securities that they were manufacturing by the billions. For example, an August 2006 e-mail cited in the Senate Subcommittee on

Investigations Report said that the rating agencies were like hostages to the big banks who had essentially kidnapped them. The employee said that the rating agencies suffered from what he called "a kind of Stockholm syndrome." The Stockholm syndrome is a psychological condition thought sometimes to afflict people who are captured or kidnapped. The syndrome's major symptom is that the captive begins to identify with his captor, adopting the captor's goals and values. The SEC sometimes appears to be suffering from the same malady with respect to the firms it regulates. Sure they sue the companies they regulate, but they settle amicably without requiring any admission of guilt and then the SEC's top officials move on to comfy jobs in the industry they used to regulate. After a few years in these jobs, these SEC alumni cordially negotiate more cozy settlements with their old colleagues.

The SEC's regulatory actions demonstrate how regulation and reputation have become decoupled in U.S. financial markets. Employees at the SEC have incentives to specialize in very technical types of fraud, such as front-running, instead of simple fraud that is more likely to hurt average investors. Such specialization allows employees of the SEC to be highly sought after by large law firms or financial institutions, increasing their job prospects after they leave the SEC. Being sued by the SEC no longer signals any useful information to investors about the firm, as all large financial firms are periodically sued and almost all settle the litigation. As a result, SEC regulation and reputation no longer work symbiotically in U.S. capital markets.

Endnotes

1. Jonathan Macey, "Administrative Agency Obsolescence and Interest Group Formation: A Case Study of the SEC at Sixty," *Cardozo Law Review* 15 (1994): 909.

2. Michael Lewis and David Einhorn, "The End of the Financial World as We Know It," *The New York Times*, January 4, 2009, WK9.

3. U.S. Securities and Exchange Commission, Office of Investigations, "Investigation of Failure of the SEC to Uncover Bernard Madoff's Ponzi Scheme" (2009). See also U.S. Securities and Exchange Commission, "2008 Performance and Accountability Report"

(2008); "Oversight of the SEC's Failure to Identify the Bernard L. Madoff Ponzi Scheme and How to Improve SEC Performance," Hearing Before the Senate Committee on Banking, Housing and Urban Affairs, 111th Congress, 22-23 (2009) (statement of Robert Khuzami, Director, Division of Enforcement, U.S. Securities and Exchange Commission, and John Walsh, Acting Director of Compliance Inspections and Examinations, U.S. Securities and Exchange Commission, available at http://banking.senate.gov/public/index.cfm?FuseAction=Hearings.Hearing&Hearing_ID=7b38b6a3-f381-4673-b12c-f9e4037b0a3f).

4. U.S. Securities and Exchange Commission, Office of Investigations, "Investigation of Failure of the SEC to Uncover Bernard Madoff's Ponzi Scheme," 2009, 20-21.

5. Ibid., 98.

6. Jonathan Spicer, "SEC Charges E°Trade, 5 Others, for Front Running," Reuters, March 5, 2009, www.reuters.com/article/2009/03/05/etrade-sec-idINN0530515020090305?rpc=44. The five other firms that were served the civil injunction were Automated Trading Desk Specialists LLC, Melvin Securities LLC, Melvin and Company LLC, Sydan LP, and TradeLink LLC.

7. A copy of the Terms and Conditions of Use discussed here may be found at http://1.bp.blogspot.com/_FM71j6-VkNE/Sktz-Ie3rNI/AAAAAAAADwg/IJWaKHlGTxU/s1600-h/GS+frontrunning.jpg.

8. Lloyd C. Blankfein, Chairman and CEO, Goldman Sachs, Testimony at the First Public Hearing of the Financial Crisis Inquiry Commission, January 13, 2010, 27, http://fcic-static.law.stanford.edu/cdn_media/fcic-testimony/2010-0113-Transcript.pdf.

9. Andrew Ross Sorkin, "Goldman Acknowledges Conflicts with Clients," *The New York Times,* DealBook, January 12, 2010, http://dealbook.nytimes.com/2010/01/12/goldman-executive-discloses-conflicts-policy/.

10. Ibid.

11. Ibid.

12. Theodore Eisenberg and Jonathan Macey, "Was Arthur Andersen Different? An Empirical Examination of Major Accounting Firm Audits of Large Clients," *Journal of Empirical Legal Studies* 1 (2004): 263-300.

13. Michael Fletcher, "Baltimore Takes Lead in Suits Against Banks over Alleged Libor Manipulation," *Washington Post,* July 11, 2012, www.washingtonpost.com/business/economy/baltimore-takes-lead-in-suit-against-banks-over-alleged-libor-manipulation/2012/07/11/gJQAN3V7dW_print.html.

14. United States Senate Permanent Subcommittee on Investigations report "Wall Street and the Financial Crisis: Anatomy of a Financial Collapse," April 13, 2011, www.hsgac.senate.gov//imo/media/doc/Financial_Crisis/FinancialCrisisReport.pdf?attempt=2.

11

The SEC: Captured and Quite Happy About It

The reputation of the SEC, similar to the reputations of auditors, credit rating agencies, and stock exchanges, has declined in recent decades. The SEC protects sophisticated investors, such as those susceptible to complex frauds like front-running, instead of small investors who are victims of simple fraud. This pattern occurs largely because of incentives for SEC employees to gain expertise in regulating complicated fraud, which increases the likelihood that they will be hired by a big law firm or Wall Street firm in the future. The SEC appears to be captive of the large credit rating agencies. Dodd-Frank, with its creation of the Office of Credit Ratings, has only exacerbated this problem by creating new incentives for employees to specialize in these areas and then secure employment with the credit rating agencies. The SEC's action in suing the small credit rating agency of Egan-Jones shows the extent of the organization's captivity. The SEC's practice of suing all participants in a particular industry, though sometimes necessary, does not help investors determine which firms are "good" and which are "bad." This undermines the incentives for firms to invest in reputation and causes the SEC's regulatory actions to create the impression that there is no way to distinguish among the various companies in an industry because they are all equally sleazy. Furthermore, the SEC purposely keeps rules regarding illegal actions such as insider trading vague and in flux. These rules increase the power of the SEC and allow government lawyers to choose prosecution targets. As a result, the SEC has damaged both its own reputation and the reputation of the financial institutions that it is supposed to safeguard and secure.

Problems at the SEC: Is the SEC Simply "Captured" or Is It Suffering from "Stockholm Syndrome" Too?

For its part, the SEC seems to be suffering from a Stockholm syndrome of its own. While the credit rating agencies appear to have been captured by issuers during the financial crisis, the SEC appears to have been captured even more completely by the big credit rating agencies. Not long ago the SEC suspended a proposed rule that would have subjected credit raters to increased liability. The SEC was forced to suspend this rule because when the major credit rating agencies learned of the new rule, they refused to allow their ratings for asset-backed securities to be published or quoted in SEC filings. As *The New York Times* reported, "The SEC quickly caved and suspended the rule. Meanwhile, the rating agencies have begun a guerrilla campaign of behind-the-scenes lobbying to weaken the commission's efforts to carry out other parts of Dodd-Frank."[1]

In other words, the SEC gave a vote of confidence to the big credit rating agencies just when they should have been encouraging investors to ignore and not rely on the rating agencies. This seal of approval for the rating agencies by the SEC was entirely inconsistent with Congress's expressed goal in the Dodd-Frank Act of weaning the investing public off of its addiction to ratings.

It is not surprising that the SEC has been captured by the credit rating agencies. The major credit rating agencies are a significant source of support and employment for SEC alumni. The Dodd-Frank Act is likely to have exacerbated this problem. Dodd-Frank creates a new SEC Office of Credit Ratings. This office is charged with administering the SEC's rules that relate to the practices used by the credit rating agencies in determining ratings.[2] With the establishment of this office, SEC staffers will have even stronger incentives—and more opportunities—to specialize in the care and feeding of the credit rating agencies in the hope of future employment.

The SEC's seemingly relentless campaign against a weak, fledgling new entry into the credit rating industry provides a striking example of the lengths to which the SEC is willing to go to protect the powerful incumbents in the credit rating industry. The fledgling new entry is a firm called Egan-Jones Ratings Company. Pressured by Congress, in 2008 the SEC grudgingly allowed Egan-Jones to receive its critical designation to become an official credit rating agency. Regulations at every level in virtually every company prevent mutual funds, banks, trust companies, insurance companies, and other financial institutions around the world from investing in a security that does not have the blessing of a company that has received the SEC's official designation as a ratings organization. It is only after the SEC has given a ratings organization its designation as an NRSRO, or nationally recognized statistical ratings organization, that a rating agency's ratings "really count."

In April 2012, the SEC announced that it was suing Egan-Jones and would try to take away the NRSRO designation that it had bestowed on it only a few years earlier. In an article called "SEC Sues the One Rating Firm Not on Wall Street's Take," *Bloomberg*'s William D. Cohan presciently observed that, in bringing this suit, "the Securities and Exchange Commission, it seems, has finally lost its mind."[3] Motivated apparently by "pure maliciousness," the SEC sued the small firm (20 employees). It has never sued any of the major credit rating agencies for their role in the collapse.

According to *Bloomberg*, the Egan-Jones SEC problems began on July 16, 2011, when Egan-Jones downgraded the U.S.'s sovereign debt by one notch, to AA+ from AAA, due to "the relatively high level of debt and the difficulty in significantly cutting spending" in the U.S.[4] This downgrade was significantly earlier than the subsequent downgrades of Moody's and Standard & Poor's. Two days after Egan-Jones's downgrade, the SEC's Office of Compliance Inspections and Examinations contacted the firm seeking information about its rating decision.

On October 12, 2011, which is extremely fast by SEC standards, Egan-Jones received a call from the SEC notifying the firm that it was about to receive what is known among securities lawyers as a Wells Notice, which is a formal letter notifying the target of an investigation that the SEC staff is going to recommend to the Commission that legal action be taken against the target, in this case, Egan-Jones. On April 19, 2012, leaks started emanating from the SEC that it had voted to start an "administrative law proceeding" against the firm. And six days later, the SEC staff filed its complaint, but only after news of the lawsuit first was leaked to the press a week earlier.[5]

The SEC's lawsuit against Egan-Jones was highly technical. It did not raise any issues about Egan-Jones's ability to rate companies or countries. It did not even quibble with, much less call into question, a single rating that Egan-Jones ever had given. Rather, the SEC claimed that in a supplement to its application for NRSRO status Egan-Jones had exaggerated the number of asset-backed securities and sovereign-debt issues that it had rated in order to conceal its lack of experience. Part of the dispute involved whether Egan-Jones met a technical SEC requirement that ratings be "disseminated publicly" in order to count. Of course, giving a rating provides a rating organization with experience whether or not it is disseminated.

Moreover, the Egan-Jones business model prevents Egan-Jones from disseminating its ratings publicly in the way the SEC seems to prefer. The traditional rating agencies are all paid by the firms that issue the securities. These rating agencies get paid the same amount regardless of how broadly they disseminate a company's ratings. These ratings often are published on the Internet and in public filings that the companies issuing the securities make with the SEC. In contrast, to avoid conflicts of interest with issuers, Egan-Jones—and only Egan-Jones among NRSROs—is not paid by the companies issuing the securities. It is paid by the customers who receive the ratings. Unlike the issuers, who want high ratings to make it easier for them to sell their securities at low cost, customers only want to know the facts, namely the actual quality of the securities they are considering buying. Because it uses a customer-paid business model rather than an issuer-paid business model, Egan-Jones, unlike the established rating agencies/NRSROs, cannot make money if it publishes its ratings. After all, no customer will buy something that it can get free because it already has been published! Thus, the SEC's lawsuit essentially told Egan-Jones that it had to go out of business, or change its business model if it wanted to keep its SEC license.

The SEC's campaign against Egan-Jones harmed the SEC's reputation more than Egan-Jones's reputation. As well-regarded journalist Jesse Eisinger observed, "Before the S.E.C. charges, Egan-Jones was best known for two things: having made some bold calls about shaky credit prospects and having a business model that was different than that of the big boys—Moody's Investors Service, Standard & Poor's and Fitch. Mr. Egan's outfit gets paid by the users of his ratings; the oligopoly gets paid by the issuers whose debt is going to be rated." Mr. Eisinger boldly announced to his readers that "this is your SEC, folks. It courageously assails tiny firms, and at the pace of a three-toed sloth. And when it goes after its prey, it's because it has found a box unchecked, rather than any kind of deep, systemic rot. Unfortunately, there's an even worse problem here. The action against Mr. Egan gives the appearance, perhaps inadvertently, that the agency is persecuting a longstanding critic of the rating agencies. That just solidifies the woeful ratings oligopoly we have today."[6]

Another troubling aspect of the lawsuit is that there were significant ambiguities in the regulations about how a prospective credit rating agency should count multiple securities issues and multiple "tranches" of securities issues that had to be analyzed separately by raters because they were sold at different times and with different sources of repayment of principal and interest. Still another disturbing aspect of the SEC's lawsuit was the fact that none of the incumbent ratings organizations had to file an application for an NRSRO designation by the SEC at the time they got their designations long, long ago. In other words, Standard & Poor's and Moody's never faced the same problems that Egan-Jones did because they never had to report to the SEC before they were established as credit rating agencies.

Let's Sue Them All and Let Investors Decide for Themselves Who the Bad Guys Are

Time and time again, the SEC has employed a litigation strategy that involves suing all industry participants. Of course, this is because all industry participants sometimes are involved in the same conduct. But in the Egan-Jones case, the SEC sued only one industry participant, and it happened to choose to sue the only competitor in the credit rating industry that threatened to make the business more competitive. The target of the SEC's litigation wrath also happened to be the only major competitor that was not a major source of employment for SEC alumni.

When the SEC chooses to sue an entire industry, its lawsuits are not likely to have any reputational impact, because such suits make it difficult for investors and other members of the general public to distinguish bad guys from good guys. In any case, such a distinction will not be made on the basis of who is sued and who is not. Of course, when all the companies in an industry are engaged in the same conduct, the SEC has little choice but to sue them all. For example, when virtually all the major banks in the world engage in manipulation of a key interest rate such as LIBOR (which is used to set the interest rates on floating rate loans and mortgages), it is not the SEC's fault. In such situations regulators have no basis to pick and choose among possible defendants. There are no good guys.

Industrywide wrongdoing happens more often than one might think. For example, in the largest price-fixing case in U.S. history, every single financial firm that quoted stock prices was involved in illegally fixing the prices of the securities they were trading with their customers. The financial firms that set prices for financial assets like stocks are called "market makers." They set prices by quoting a "bid price," which is the price at which they are willing to buy the securities in which they are making a market, and by simultaneously quoting an "offer price," which is the price at which they are willing to sell the same securities. Thus, if a market maker quotes a market for a particular stock of $99.50 bid and $99.75 offered, the market maker is willing to buy the stock for the bid price of $99.50 and to sell it for $99.75. The market maker's profit is the so-called "spread," between the bid price and the offer price, which in this case is the $0.25 on each security bought and sold. The wider the spread between the bid price and the offer price, the greater the profit for the market makers.

In 1994, two young financial economists at Vanderbilt, William Christie and Paul Schultz, published the results of some empirical research.[7] The study, which was reported by several national newspapers on May 26 and May 27, 1994, observed pricing patterns in the stock market that were unexplainable other than on the grounds that the firms quoting the prices were colluding. Studying the price data captured by the National Association of Securities Dealers Automated Quotation (NASDAQ) system, they noticed that the market makers appeared to avoid quoting certain prices. When Christie and Schultz did their study, stock prices for companies like Apple and Microsoft had to be quoted in multiples of the fraction one-eighth. This meant that a quotation of 100 and 1/8th bid and 100 and 1/4th offered was legal, but a quote of less than 1/8th, such as 1/16th, was not allowed. Of course, Wall Street companies quoting these prices did not object at all to this rule because they did not want narrow quotes of 1/16th. The wider quotes meant wider spreads and wider spreads are more profitable for the Wall Street market makers. Christie and Schultz's brilliant insight was their observation that if the market wasn't rigged, one should not expect to see any particular fractions in quoted prices more often than any others. As one scholar explained Christie and Schultz's research:

> Bid or ask quotes must be multiples of an eighth of a dollar.... Bid or ask quotes end in either even-eighths (0, 2/8, 4/8, 6/8) or odd-eighths (1/8, 3/8, 5/8, 7/8). Thus, the narrowest inside spread is one-eighth. For example, if the bid price is $25.50 and the ask price is $25.625, the spread is one-eighth of a dollar, or 12.5¢ per share. Christie and Schultz expected, if the market was competitive, that all fractions would be seen with roughly equal frequencies—as is the case on the New York Stock Exchange.

Yet, the scholar explained, Christie and Schultz found that "virtually no inside spreads on Apple Computer stock" were "as small as one-eighth. Indeed, virtually all bids were in even eighths (which ensures that no one-eighth spreads will occur)." Christie and Schultz expanded their research, looking at more stocks:

> When they looked at the 100 most actively traded stocks, they found that odd-eighth quotes were extremely rare for 70 of them, including such highly visible and actively traded stocks as Intel, Amgen, Microsoft, and Cisco Systems. Thus, Christie and Schultz concluded that the market makers had an understanding not to use odd-eighth quotes on these 70 stocks, a practice that ensured that their inside spread would not fall below two-eighths, 25¢, per trade.[8]

Detecting odd-eighth bids is easy because the market maker who posts such a bid is identified on the computer screens at every financial company.

After newspapers ran a story on their paper, lawyers filed a series of class action antitrust lawsuits against the major brokerage firms claiming that they had engaged in illegal price fixing. The SEC and the U.S. Department of Justice also began investigations. Of course, the defendants never acknowledged wrongdoing, but over $1 billion in fines and settlements was paid.

The SEC Has Priorities All Its Own

Often, however, the SEC targets an entire industry for the same sort of wrongdoing for its own reasons. For example, when SEC staffers develop a new theory or new rule or a new technical interpretation of an old rule, they often find that the conduct that has just become suspect is practiced across an entire industry. A good example of this is the SEC's confused enforcement efforts against late trading and market timing in mutual funds, which ultimately became yet another source of embarrassment for the Commission.

The SEC's embarrassment stemmed from the fact that Eliot Spitzer, then the Attorney General of New York, launched a number of very high-profile lawsuits against major mutual funds. These mutual funds were supposed to be regulated by the SEC. And Spitzer lost no opportunity to ridicule the SEC about how it had failed in its responsibility to protect the public. On October 29, 2003, for example, Spitzer harshly criticized the SEC division with responsibility for the mutual fund industry, famously asserting to the press that "heads should roll at the [SEC]," observing that "there is a whole division at the [SEC] that is supposed to be looking at mutual funds," and asking, "where have they been?"[9]

Most mutual funds are what are known as "open-end" funds, which means that the funds collect money from investors by selling them shares in the mutual fund. The mutual funds then invest this money for their clients in stocks and other financial assets. When the customers want their money back, the mutual funds "redeem" the shares that the investors have bought, paying them the value of their shares at the market price on the day that the investor redeems. Suppose, for example, that an investor buys a share in a mutual fund for $1.00; the mutual fund will buy $1.00 worth of securities with that investment. Then, if the investor wants to sell or redeem her shares a year later, if the securities have increased in value the investor will receive more than $1.00 in the redemption. If the shares have declined in value, the investor will receive only the lower value that the shares are worth on the day of the redemption. Of course, the fees that the mutual fund has to pay to its advisors and directors will reduce the amount of money that the investor ultimately receives.

The value of investors' shares in a mutual fund at any particular time is called the "per-share net asset value" of the mutual fund. The per-share net asset value is commonly referred to simply as the NAV, for "net asset value," of the mutual fund. Determining the NAV requires figuring out the value of all the assets of the mutual fund, such as cash and securities, subtracting costs such as fees, and then dividing that number by the number of shares that the mutual fund has outstanding. Generally, the fund's daily accrued costs are netted against the fund portfolio's value (including cash) to determine the fund's net asset value, which then is divided by the number of outstanding shares to arrive at the NAV.

One problem facing the mutual fund industry was "late trading," which, in its worst form, permits certain favored clients of mutual funds to buy or sell shares in the fund after the NAV has already been determined. This practice often is compared to letting people bet on horse races after the race is over.

Typically, mutual funds calculate their funds' NAVs sometime after 4:00 p.m. on every trading day, often using the 4:00 p.m. prices to value their funds' assets. Late trading allows customers to place trades late enough in the day to give them a big edge. Suppose, for example, that at 4:15 p.m. there is an announcement by the Federal Reserve that it is going to make a major reduction in the interest rates it charges for lending to banks. It is widely expected that this change will send stock prices sharply higher. If a customer can learn this information, and then place a trade, say at 4:20 p.m., but still get that day's price, which doesn't reflect the new information, then the favored customer can make a virtually riskless profit by selling at the higher price set the next day when the mutual fund's NAV finally adjusts to reflect the new information.

A lot of information, including corporate earnings reports, certain announcements about industry trends, merger and acquisition announcements, and interest rate changes, typically is announced after 4:00 p.m., meaning after the close of the markets on the East Coast of the United States. As a result, if a customer is allowed to participate in late trading, he "is permitted to capitalize on new information by turning back the clock and placing a trade as though it had been placed before learning the new information." This allows the investor to "sell the fund share at a profit."[10]

Eliot Spitzer investigated Bank of America and a large hedge fund called Canary Capital Partners, LLC, that bought mutual funds from Bank of America. The companies had entered into an agreement in which Bank of America agreed to provide access to Canary to engage in remote computer trading of its mutual funds after the NAVs for the funds had been determined—sometimes as late as 9:00 p.m.—in exchange for Canary agreeing to keep significant investments in various accounts that generated fees for the bank.

Other cases involved fraudulent conduct by mutual funds such as using time stamps that falsely indicated that buy and sell orders had been placed earlier than such orders really had been placed. Multiple orders might be placed during the day, and then broker-dealers allegedly would communicate with their customers late in the day, allowing the customers to cancel the unprofitable orders but to effectuate the profitable orders. The SEC was deeply embarrassed and discredited by these scandals. Avoiding any real reform, the SEC ultimately responded with still more complexity and ambiguity. The new rules required mutual funds and their advisors to develop Codes of Ethics and make complex new disclosures of their activities. The new disclosure rules related to the approval of Investment Advisory Contracts by Mutual Funds' boards of directors, rules regarding the selective disclosure of portfolio holdings, details of programs aimed at ensuring compliance with regulations, the corporate governance of mutual funds, and the people managing the portfolios of such funds. All of these new rules increased the demand for compliance personnel, creating new job openings for SEC alumni as well as the need for more SEC staffers to review the new disclosures. Thus, individual professionals within the SEC may have benefited from the scandals. Substantive rules that would have clarified or simplified the way NAVs actually were calculated were considered and rejected.

Given the low esteem in which the SEC is held, it certainly is no wonder that the enforcement actions by the SEC no longer send much of a signal to market participants about the target of the enforcement action. Besides the SEC's decayed reputation, the SEC's enforcement agenda is poorly designed to send any sort of reputational signal to the public. Often the SEC's charges against firms are highly technical. As in the case of the lawsuit against Egan-Jones, the SEC's cases sometimes appear politicized or motivated by the personal or institutional self-interest of staffers. There is rarely any admission of responsibility, much less of actual guilt, on the part of companies or individuals targeted by the SEC because parties are allowed to settle without accepting any blame whatsoever. Often every industry participant is implicated in the wrongdoing targeted by the SEC.

Still another reason the SEC's standard operating procedures prevent any sort of reputational signal from being associated with its actions is that the SEC purposely pursues a strategy of keeping its rules vague and in flux. An archetypal example of the SEC's strategy of intentional vagueness and calculated ambiguity is the Commission's decades-old policy and enforcement strategies concerning insider trading. In fact, the SEC has been waging an unusual, epic battle against the Supreme Court about how the laws against insider trading should be interpreted and enforced. This battle, which the SEC is losing badly, also has been highly damaging to the SEC's reputation.

The battle is a dispute over doctrine that pits the rather extreme views of the SEC against the carefully considered law of insider trading articulated by the Supreme Court in a number of landmark cases.[11] The basic problem is that, unlike the Supreme Court, the SEC does not draw a distinction between trading on the basis of legitimate albeit unorthodox research and illegal trading on the basis of improperly acquired proprietary information. Such a distinction between legitimate trading and illegitimate trading is necessary and in the public interest, because in the absence of such a distinction, trading on the basis of legitimate research and superior insight or skill is just as suspect as trading on the basis of information that has been wrongfully purloined by crooked insiders.

The SEC Versus the Supreme Court and the Department of Justice

The line in the sand between the SEC and the nation's highest court—as well as between the SEC and the United States Department of Justice—was drawn most vividly by the Supreme Court in 1983 in its decision against the SEC and in favor of an investment analyst named Raymond Dirks, whom the SEC had sued for insider trading. Using a combination of his own dogged research and a valuable tip from Ronald Secrist, a disgruntled insider, Raymond Dirks discovered a massive fraud inside a giant insurance company called Equity Funding Corporation of America. Equity Funding was running every sort of scam imaginable. It was reselling life insurance policies on people who did not even exist to other insurance companies. It was faking the deaths of the fabricated people whose fake insurance policies it had sold in order to collect the death benefits. Apparently hundreds, if not thousands, of people inside the company knew of the scam, which Equity Funding managed to have kept hidden by intimidating and threatening employees, and through the use of "doctored computer tapes."[12]

Justice Lewis Powell, speaking for the Court in the case, which was styled Dirks v. SEC, made clear that traders should be free to collect information and trade on it. The Court also made clear that the SEC's vague rules were inefficient and self-serving. In fact, the SEC's persecution of Dirks was so "out there" that another, more sensible government agency, the Department of Justice, wrote its own brief disagreeing with the SEC. The DOJ in its brief observed that "in the view of the United States, the Commission's order censuring [Raymond Dirks] cannot be reconciled with this Court's decision in [previous cases] and threatens to impair private initiative in uncovering violations of federal law."

The Justice Department brief, which reads in part like an unusually well-written detective novel, pointed out that

> Dirks is a securities analyst, "well-known for his investigative talents," who researched insurance company securities. In March 1973, Dirks applied those investigative talents to uncover a major fraud perpetrated by the officers of a publicly-owned insurance company.

> In two weeks of concerted effort, at times resembling something from detective fiction, Dirks investigated and confirmed rumors of massive fraud by the Equity Funding Corporation of America, an insurance holding company whose stock traded on the New York Stock Exchange. Largely thanks to Dirks, one of the most infamous frauds in recent memory was uncovered and exposed.

> Despite his efforts to uncover and expose the criminal scheme at Equity Funding, the Securities and Exchange Commission charged Dirks with [violations] of Section 10(b) of the Securities Exchange Act of 1934.

The Court went on to describe precisely how Dirks learned of the fraud:

> Dirks first learned of the fraud at Equity Funding from a former officer of the company, Ronald Secrist, who met with him for several hours on March 7, 1973. Secrist made a series of detailed but nearly incredible allegations about Equity Funding, including allegations that "the company had produced large numbers of spurious insurance policies to inflate its sales revenues" and that "its top officers had Mafia connections which they used to threaten the lives of employees who objected to the fabrications." Secrist urged Dirks to verify the existence of the fraud and then expose it. He expected Dirks to transmit evidence of the fraud to "his firm's customers" and "clients," thereby triggering large-volume securities sales that would lead to a full investigation.

The Department of Justice fully recognized that the strategy for exposing the fraud developed by Secrist and implemented by Dirks was to "jar the corporation" by wreaking havoc on the price of its stock:

"By jarring the stock, he would jar the corporation—this was my plan—he would jar the corporate officers and would also rattle the Wall Street financial community to the extent that someone would take action very quickly." Secrist believed that selling pressure would cause the price of Equity Funding stock to "drop close to zero very quickly," and thus "reveal the fraud to the world" and "prevent its continuation."

Significantly, the strategy of simply notifying the authorities or the press was considered and rejected by Dirks and Secrist:

During their initial meeting, Dirks sought and obtained Secrist's permission to convey evidence of the fraud to *The Wall Street Journal.* Secrist warned, however, that merely presenting the information to regulatory authorities, including the SEC, would be abortive. Secrist stated that employees who attempted to do this in the past had been "brushed aside with a comment that that's a ridiculous story"; those employees also found that the information was sometimes relayed back to Equity Funding and that "they were placed in personal jeopardy as a result of having gone there."

As early as March 12, 1973, Dirks also attempted to communicate his evidence to *The Wall Street Journal.* "Dirks expected that a highly respected publication like the [Journal] could be effective in helping him investigate the Secrist allegations and to expose the fraud if it proved to exist." Those efforts also were unavailing.

During the entire week that Dirks was in Los Angeles investigating Equity Funding, he was also in touch regularly with William Blundell, *The Wall Street Journal*'s Los Angeles bureau chief. Dirks kept Blundell up to date on the progress of the investigation and badgered him to write a story for the Journal on the allegations of fraud at Equity Funding. Blundell, however, was afraid that publishing such damaging rumors supported only by hearsay from former employees might be libelous, so he declined to write the story.

Dirks provided Blundell with "the substance of all he knew," including his "notes" and the "names" of all witnesses. Nevertheless, given the "scope of the fraud," Blundell doubted that it could have been "missed by an honest auditor" and discounted the entire allegation.

Increasing circulation of rumors about the fraud led Dirks to believe that it was "unlikely that Equity Funding stock would open for trading on Monday, March 26, because trading would be halted by the NYSE." This did not occur, however, and Dirks again spoke to William Blundell of *The Wall Street Journal* and urged him to publish a story exposing the fraud. Blundell refused to do so but stated that he intended to discuss the matter with the SEC's Los Angeles Regional Office. Blundell secured Dirks' permission to propose a meeting with the SEC that would include himself and two other key witnesses. Dirks then contacted the SEC and voluntarily presented all of his information at the SEC's regional office beginning on March 27 and continuing throughout the next three days.

Dirks's work in uncovering the Equity Funding fraud was not limited simply to listening to Ronald Secrist's stories about the company:

In addition to interviewing former employees of Equity Funding, Dirks also met with Equity Funding's present and former auditors in an attempt to spread word of the fraud and bring it to a halt. As the [Securities and Exchange] Commission explained:

"Dirks also learned that Equity Funding's auditors were about to release certified financial statements for the company on March 26. He immediately contacted them and apprised them of the fraud allegations, hoping that they would withhold release of their report and seek a halt in the trading of Equity Funding securities. Instead, the auditors merely reported Dirks' allegations to management."

❊ ❊ ❊

During the two-week period in which Dirks pursued his investigation and spread word of Secrist's charges, the price of Equity Funding stock fell precipitously from $26 per share to less than $15. This led the NYSE to halt trading in the stock on March 27. Shortly thereafter, Illinois and California insurance authorities impounded Equity Funding's records and uncovered evidence of the fraud. Only then did the SEC file a complaint against Equity Funding and only then did *The Wall Street Journal* publish "a front page story written by Blundell but based largely on information assembled by Dirks." Three days later, Equity Funding filed a petition (for bankruptcy).

While Dirks's investigative activities succeeded in revealing in a few days that "one of the darlings of Wall Street, a company that had managed to produce continued high earnings growth for a decade, was, instead, a gigantic fraud," government authorities with jurisdiction over Equity Funding did not move so quickly. As early as 1971, the SEC had received allegations of fraudulent accounting practices at Equity Funding. Moreover, on March 9, 1973, an official of the California Insurance Department informed the SEC's regional office in Los Angeles of Secrist's charges of fraud. The SEC's staff attorney "stated that similar allegations had been made about Equity Funding before by disgruntled employees." He nonetheless recommended "[sic] delaying any type of inspection of the Equity Funding operations until next year absent further corroboration. Equity Funding's Chairman—one of the principal architects of the fraud—testified that, prior to March 1973, he received no questions from auditors, state regulatory authorities, or federal regulatory authorities that suggested "they suspected there was a fraud at Equity Funding." When asked whether Dirks was "personally responsible for having uncovered the events at Equity Funding," he candidly stated: "I think Mr. Dirks is entitled to personal credit for that."

Following public revelation of the Equity Funding scandal, a federal grand jury in Los Angeles returned a 105 count indictment against 22 persons, including many of Equity Funding's officers and directors. [Guilty pleas or convictions were obtained on all 22. Chairman Stanley Goldblum received an 8-year prison sentence and a substantial fine.]

While *The Wall Street Journal*'s reporter, William Blundell, was "nominated for a Pulitzer Prize for his coverage of the Equity Funding scandal," Dirks was charged by the SEC with violating the antifraud provisions of the federal securities laws based on his selective revelation of information about Equity Funding prior to general public disclosure. Following an administrative hearing, the Commission found that Dirks had "tipped" nonpublic information concerning Equity Funding in violation of those provisions. It observed that "Dirks received the information from inside corporate sources."

According to the SEC, because Dirks had nonpublic information when he advised his clients to dump their Equity Funding shares, he was guilty of insider trading. The SEC's truly incredible view of the law of insider trading as applied to the Dirks case was that the information about this fraud should have been kept private. The SEC held this view because Dirks's sources had received the information they passed along to Dirks "during the course of their corporate duties, and that the company intended that it should be kept in confidence." So, even though the SEC fully acknowledged that Dirks was essential in exposing Equity Funding's "massive fraud...and that he reported the fraud allegations to Equity Funding's auditors and sought to have the information published in *The Wall Street Journal*," the SEC sued Dirks anyway.

In exonerating Dirks, the Supreme Court explained to the SEC how it should do its job. The Court pointed out that imposing a duty to abstain from trading in a stock "solely because a person knowingly receives material nonpublic information from an insider and trades on it could have an inhibiting influence on the role of market analysts, which the SEC itself recognizes is necessary to the preservation of a healthy market." Justice Powell, an expert in corporate and securities law before joining the bench, presciently added that it is "commonplace for analysts to ferret out and analyze information and this often is done by meeting with and questioning corporate officers and others who are insiders."

Before and after its decision in Dirks, the Supreme Court recognized that if a person acquires information in the course of legitimate business activities, such as research or mining sources appropriately, then he has a right to that information and should be able to trade without disclosing it. The SEC, on the other hand, espouses a socialist philosophy that valuable information belongs to the people—regardless of how it was obtained.

Of course, sometimes the SEC does go after the bad guys. The line between legitimate research and illegitimate insider trading is not always unclear. In the first criminal prosecution for insider trading in the 1970s, Vincent Chiarella was accused of stealing the identities of takeover targets from the disclosure documents he saw as an employee of Pandick Press, which was printing them for would-be acquirers. There is little doubt his actions were objectionable, though he made only $30,000 on his trades. The same holds true for disbarred attorney James O'Hagan, who also was sued by the SEC. O'Hagan, a partner in a big Minneapolis law firm, made $4.3 million trading in Pillsbury stock and stock options in the late 1980s after learning that his firm's client, London-based Grand-Metropolitan P.L.C., was planning a hostile takeover bid of Pillsbury. Mr. O'Hagan rightfully was convicted of stealing this information from his law firm's files and trading on it. The problem with the SEC's insider trading enforcement regime is that the SEC does not want to distinguish between good guys like Dirks and bad guys like Chiarella and O'Hagan. The SEC's incentives for keeping the rules vague and constantly shifting are clear. To navigate the perilous and uncharted realm of securities trading, one needs the help and the expertise of the soothsayers at the SEC.

Every day, thousands of hedge fund managers, private investors, mutual fund advisors, stock market analysts, and others compete fiercely, using various tactics to obtain new information about the companies they cover. These tactics range from analyzing public disclosures, which are increasingly useless as sources of information, to staking out the courtrooms in which the companies they follow are litigating. They cultivate friendships with employees and analyze everything about them, down to the makes and models of the cars in company parking lots.

This research is rarely glamorous. Rooting around in a company's discarded garbage in order to ferret out information is undignified. But often an SEC alumnus is needed to determine whether the trade is illegal. For decades, the SEC has kept the insider trading rules vague and undefined. This ambiguity increases the SEC's power and allows government lawyers to pick and choose among prosecution targets. Some, though by no means all, trading on the basis of informational advantage is and should be illegal. But the government should be compelled to provide clear guidance as to what constitutes illegal insider trading and what constitutes legitimate, albeit aggressive, research.

Regulation and reputation are closely connected. A thoughtful, well-considered regulatory strategy might, for example, use scarce enforcement resources in order to reinforce rather than to undermine the value of companies' investments in their own reputations for honesty and fair dealing with customers. Unfortunately, the opposite has occurred. The SEC's enforcement strategies over the past several decades have further undermined the value of investments made by financial firms in developing reputations for integrity. Now the SEC's enforcement agenda sends little if any discernible signal about the reputations of the firms targeted for litigation.

Perhaps an even more depressing consequence of the SEC's focus on highly technical securities law violations like front-running instead of on simple frauds like Ponzi schemes is that the SEC no longer does much, if anything, to protect the relatively small investors who are caught in simple frauds. Only the biggest, most sophisticated clients are victims of front-running schemes. The reason for this is simple. For front-running to be profitable for the financial firm that engages in it, the customer's order must be big enough to move the market. Nobody can make money trading ahead of a small customer order to buy or sell securities, because such orders do not change the prices of the securities being bought and sold. On the other hand, when a large institutional customer places an order to trade a significant block of securities, its order is likely to move the market at least temporarily due to its sheer size.

Large institutional clients are the only customers who worry about front-running. Front-running is not a risk to small, less sophisticated clients. Interestingly, the more sophisticated a client is, the greater the risk from front-running. This is because securities prices move most when a trade reveals information about the company whose shares are being traded that is not already reflected in the company's share prices. Insider trading is illegal, of course. Because the insiders with easy access to new information cannot legally trade, sophisticated traders are the only traders who are capable of doing the difficult research and analysis necessary to discover information about a company before it becomes reflected in a company's share price. It is this group of the most sophisticated investors that has the most to lose by front-running. This is the group that the SEC is protecting by focusing on complex issues like front-running instead of the basic sorts of frauds that snare small investors.

Likewise, as discussed in Chapter 2, "Thriving the New Way: With Little or No Reputation—The Goldman Sachs Story," the SEC's largest enforcement actions protect important institutions like the German bank Deutsche Industriebank AG, and the Royal Bank of Scotland N.V. The SEC's enforcement action earned nothing for small investors but garnered settlements of $150 million for Deutsche Industriebank and $100 million for the Royal Bank of Scotland (RBS). The SEC's lawsuit on behalf of these banks accused Goldman of allowing—and failing to disclose—the participation by one of the firm's large hedge fund clients, Paulson & Company, in selecting a portfolio of securities that Deutsche Industriebank and RBS were going to buy and that the favored Goldman customer was going to sell.[13] Again, there is a future for SEC officials who have experience and expertise in investigating and litigating these sorts of complex transactions. But litigating on behalf of the small investor does not appear to have a professional payoff for ambitious SEC lawyers. It is no wonder, then, that the SEC's reputation has suffered over the past few decades at least as much as, if not more than, the reputations of the big Wall Street banks that hire so many of its alumni.

In an interesting footnote to the Dirks case, which was discussed at length in this chapter, after he was fully acquitted by the Supreme Court, Dirks made the following observation about the enforcement officials at the New York Stock Exchange (NYSE), which had worked closely with the SEC in its case against him. He observed that the NYSE was "a venerated American institution which advertises the safety and security of investing in its listed companies." In his view, though, the NYSE "is an antique, costly and dangerous system perpetuated for the convenience of its members."[14] The same appears to hold true for the SEC itself. And this system has not served to maintain the reputation of either the SEC or the financial institutions it is supposed to safeguard and secure.

The SEC appears to have a mission. Unfortunately, its mission appears to be that of advancing its own agenda, including its own budget and power, along with the careers of its most highly placed executives. New SEC Commissioners focus more on trying to improve the Commission's status in Washington instead of trying to improve the Commission itself. One recent Commissioner even tried, unsuccessfully, to have the position of SEC Chairman raised to Cabinet-level status. Other Commissioners spend more time explaining the SEC's failings and in suing small firms and new entrants than they do on the important issues of the day. Worst of all, the SEC has played an active role in undermining the ability of firms to maintain their reputations and in destroying the incentives of firms to build reputations in the first place. Certainly, having a great reputation was never a way to impress the SEC because the SEC sues all market participants with equal fervor.

Endnotes

1. Jeffry Manns, "The Revenge of the Rating Agencies," *The New York Times*, August 19, 2011, available at http://www.nytimes.com/2011/08/10/opinion/the-revenge-of-the-rating-agencies.html.

2. Thomas Gorman, "Dodd Frank Impact on Credit Rating Agencies," LexisNexis Corporate and Securities Law Community, Nationally Recognized Statistical Rating Organizations, credit rating agencies, Dodd-Frank bill, SEC Office of Credit Ratings, August 24, 2010, www.lexisnexis.com/community/corpsec/blogs/corporateandsecuritieslawblog/archive/2010/08/24/dodd-frank-impact-on-credit-rating-agencies.aspx.

3. William Cohan, "SEC Sues the One Rating Firm Not on Wall Street's Take," *Bloomberg*, September 30, 2012, www.bloomberg.com/news/2012-09-30/sec-sues-the-one-rating-firm-not-on-wall-street-s-take.html.

4. Ibid.

5. Ibid.

6. Jesse Eisinger, "SEC Keeps Ratings Game Rigged," ProPublica, May 2, 2012, available at http://www.propublica.org/thetrade/item/sec-keeps-ratings-game-rigged (accessed January 21, 2013).

7. William Christie and Paul Schultz, "Why Do Nasdaq Market Makers Avoid Odd-Eighth Quotes?" *Journal of Finance* 49 (December 1994): 1813-40; see also William Christie and Paul Schultz, "Did Nasdaq Market Makers Implicitly Collude?" *Journal of Economic Perspectives* 9 (1995): 199-208.

8. Jeffrey M. Perloff, *Microeconomics: Theory and Applications with Calculus,* Ch. 14, "Economists Prevent Collusion," (Second Edition, Pearson 2012).

9.   Riva Atlas, "Spitzer Vows Legal Action Against Head of Fund Family," *The New York Times,* October 30, 2003, www.nytimes. com/2003/10/30/business/spitzer-vows-legal-action-against-head-of-fund-family.html.

10. Brian Carroll, "The Mutual Fund Trading Scandals: Implications for CPAs and Their Clients," *Journal of Accountancy* 198 (December 2004), www.journalofaccountancy.com/.

11. Jonathan Macey, "Deconstructing the Galleon Insider Trading Case," *The Wall Street Journal,* April 19, 2011, http://professional. wsj.com/article/SB10001424052748704529204576256754289698630. html?mg=reno-wsj.

12. Robert Cole, *New York Times,* April 15, 1973; Lee Seidler, Marc Epstein, and Frederick Andrews, *The Equity Funding Papers: The Anatomy of a Fraud* (1977).

13. See discussion of SEC v. Goldman Sachs & Co., and Fabrice Tourre, Complaint, Case No. 10-CV-3229 in Chapter 2.

14. This quotation is from the Brief of the United States as Amicus Curiae in Raymond L. Dirks v. SEC, Case No. 82-276, October Term 1982, http://www.justice.gov/osg/briefs/1982/sg820094.txt. The quoted text also can be found in Brian Trumbore, "Ray Dirks and the Equity Funding Scandal," *Stocks and News Archives*, www. buyandhold.com/bh/en/education/history/2004/ray_dirks.html.

12

Where We Are and Where We Are Headed: A Conclusion of Sorts

In the financial world, reputation no longer exists as a way to engender trust and, as a result, does little if anything to facilitate market interactions. Certain phenomena such as social discrimination using religion, ethnic, or cultural distinctions; social networks; self-help institutions; and regulation, at least in theory, can serve either as supplements or replacements to reputation as a source of trust. Regulation is, however, a dangerous replacement for reputation. The better a regulatory system in an economy is perceived to be, the less incentive exists for firms to invest in reputation, as investors will already be confident of the firms' actions due to the regulations. As for the other three substitutes for reputation, social discrimination is illegal, and rightfully so, and does not function particularly well in any case. Social networks that facilitate trust have been eroding in the United States over the past several decades and do not permit particularly large circles of trust in the best of circumstances. Other recently emergent institutions, such as dark pools or electronic communications networks (ECNs), allow traders to bypass financial intermediaries. Though effective regulation is a substitute for reputation, the current regulatory apparatus in the United States, led by the SEC, is not effective. The SEC focuses on measureable factors such as the raw number of cases it brings and the size of the fines it collects, even though this is not the best data with which to evaluate the conduct of the SEC. This regulatory model cannot take the place of reputational capital. Though the reputations of financial firms in the United States have decreased, and rebuilding them will be difficult, it must be done to ensure the continued vitality of U.S. financial institutions. There are some signs, particularly from the mega-bank Morgan Stanley, that the hard work of reputation rebuilding has begun.

Thus far, the point of this book has been that the traditional theory of reputation as it used to exist no longer exists in any recognizable form in the financial world. This chapter explores some of the implications of this observation and considers alternatives to reputation as a means of fostering and facilitating trust. In particular, this chapter examines (1) religious, ethnic, cultural, national, and other more or less endogenous forms of identification that might create particular zones of trust in which people can feel confident interacting; (2) social networks of the kind identified by thinkers like Robert Putnam and Frances Fukuyama; (3) various self-help remedies; and (4) regulation as a means for fostering trust and its byproduct, economic interaction in financial markets.

At least in theory, these four phenomena can serve either as supplements to reputation as a source of trust, or, where reputations are nonexistent or unreliable, as alternatives to reputation. Here I mainly analyze these phenomena as alternatives to reputation and not as supplements to reputation because the evidence of the decline in reputation means that substitutes must be found. Nevertheless, the interaction between these four phenomena and reputation is important. The relationship between reputation and regulation is particularly important. The first three phenomena—endogenous affiliations like nationality or ethnicity, social networks, and self-help—can reinforce reputation in serving as foundations for trust in economic relationships.

Regulation, which is the fourth and probably the most important trust-generating phenomenon, is not a complement to reputation as a source of trust. Rather, regulation is a substitute for reputation. This is because regulation causes a decline in companies' incentives to invest in their reputation. The more effective a regulatory scheme is considered to be, the lower will be companies' incentives to invest in reputation. Reputation plays a more important role in free market, laissez faire economies in which regulation is scant than in economies like those in the U.S. and Europe, in which regulation is considered comprehensive and, historically at least, more or less effective.

Reputation played a major role in the development of U.S. capital markets for a very long time. It is no exaggeration to point to the exceptional quality and quantity of reputational intermediaries in the U.S. as the decisive factor in the lengthy post–World War II domination of U.S. capital markets and U.S. reputational intermediaries. Certainly the decline and fall of reputational intermediaries is not the only explanation for the long, slow demise of U.S. capital markets. But it certainly is part of the story.

Deeply imbedded in the traditional economic theory of reputation is the highly plausible assumption that markets and economies cannot develop very far unless prospective market participants can find a way to trust each other. Investing in, developing, and maintaining reputations for honesty and integrity are how companies do this. It stands to reason, then, that if participants in financial markets stop trusting the companies and institutions they deal with, those financial markets will be significantly less efficient than they otherwise would be. People will be reluctant to deal with institutions they do not trust. When people do engage in transactions with institutions they do not trust, they will demand higher interest rates to compensate themselves for the risks associated with dealing with counterparties that they fear are likely to cheat them if they can.

In fact, a reasonable interpretation of the traditional theory of reputation is that reputation is so important to the operation of the financial markets that such markets could virtually disintegrate and perhaps even cease to operate in the absence of trust. For example, honest but unknown companies that wanted to raise capital by selling their securities used to be able to "rent" the reputations of powerful reputational intermediaries such as accounting firms, law firms, credit rating agencies, and even the investment banks that were underwriting their securities. Rational investors could be quite confident in the securities sold by a hitherto unknown company whose books were audited by one of the major accounting firms and whose representations to prospective investors had been vetted by a nationally known law firm, and whose actual securities were underwritten by highly reputed investment banks and rated by well-respected credit rating agencies.

Now the reputations of all of these former "reputational interme-diaries" are in tatters. It is pretty hard to find anybody who is willing to defend the integrity of institutions like credit rating agencies, account-ing firms, or investment banks. In a recent survey of various industries in terms of reputation, the only industry with a reputation worse than that of the financial services industry was tobacco.[1] Also, interestingly, U.S. financial services firms were at the bottom of the list of all firms worldwide when these firms were ranked by reputation.[2]

There are no financial services firms within the top 20 companies in the world in terms of reputation. Interestingly, the highest-ranked financial services firm in the world on the basis of reputation was China Merchants Bank, which is ranked 24th. The next financial insti-tution on the list was the Russian bank Sherbank, ranked 27th, fol-lowed by the State Bank of India, which ranked 29th. Unsurprisingly, well-known U.S. financial institutions including Bank of America, Citigroup, Goldman Sachs, JPMorgan Chase, and Morgan Stanley simply do not appear on the list. At first blush, the strong reputational showing by financial institutions in low-trust, lightly regulated devel-oping economies seems strange.

But these results make sense when we consider the relation-ship between reputation and regulation. Regulation and reputation interact in complex and interesting ways. First, and perhaps most important, reputation and regulation are substitutes for each other. Imagine—and admittedly this takes a healthy imagination—a highly regulated financial system in which regulation functions perfectly. In such an environment, firms would not have to invest in developing reputations for integrity. The value to financial institutions of invest-ing in reputation declines as a regulatory system increases in effec-tiveness, because the investing community is able to rely on the extant regulatory regime. This eliminates the need for firms to invest in and to develop reputation in order to give investors the confidence and trust required to motivate them to engage in financial transactions.

Taking this line of argument one more step, suppose that the opposite were the case, and that a particular economy existed in an environment in which the regulatory regime was highly ineffective, corrupt, inept, or simply nonexistent. In such an environment, com-panies would have to develop their own reputations in order to attract customers and survive. It is in this way that reputation and regulation are substitutes. The fact that regulation and reputation are substitutes is an aspect of the study of both regulation and reputation that heretofore has had important implications.

First, the substitutability of regulation and reputation explains, to a very large extent, the demise of the reputational intermediaries discussed in this book. The SEC has not always had its current reputation for ineptitude and for being captured by the companies it ostensibly regulates. Rather, from the 1950s through much of the 1990s, the SEC enjoyed a very strong reputation for integrity, competence, and professionalism. This reputation did not survive the determined assault of then New York Attorney General Eliot Spitzer, who blamed the SEC for several major financial scandals that occurred during that period. Perhaps most famously, Attorney General Spitzer proclaimed that "heads should roll" at the SEC. He notoriously charged, "There is a whole division at the [SEC] that is supposed to be looking at mutual funds. Where have they been?"[3] Exacerbating the corrosive effects of internecine bureaucratic infighting on the SEC's reputation was an apparently unending series of scandals and highly salient failures of oversight that gradually eroded the SEC's historic reputation as America's iconic administrative agency.

During the period when the SEC's prestige was ascendant, scholars and policymakers generally ignored the role of reputation in U.S. capital markets and instead identified strict U.S. laws and tough, efficient regulatory enforcement by the SEC as the explanations for the almost complete domination of U.S. capital markets in the decades after World War II. People gave U.S. regulation and firm but fair enforcement by the SEC much of the credit for the success of U.S. capital markets.

As more and more investors and traders came to trust and rely on U.S. regulation and U.S. regulatory enforcement for protection against sharp dealing and fraud, the returns to market participants from investing in their own reputations experienced a sharp decline. This is because investing in reputation makes little sense if investors are looking to regulation rather than to reputation to protect them from fraud. Investing in reputation is costly, which, in turn, means that any firm investing in reputation must charge higher prices than firms that have made no investments in reputation in order to recoup their prior investments in reputation. If rival firms with no investment in reputation can easily attract clients simply by locating themselves in jurisdictions like the U.S. that boast fabled regulatory regimes, then such firms will out-compete firms with significant investments in reputation because they can attract customers with lower prices. Such customers will not be concerned with these firms' lack of reputations because they trust and rely on the extant regulatory regime to protect them from the unscrupulous business practices of the firms with which they are doing business.

Perhaps it is only coincidence that firms' investments in reputation appear to have started their long, steady decline just as the SEC's reputation reached its apogee. Regardless, the fact remains that reputation and regulation are substitutes. And an unavoidable implication of this insight is that firms' incentives to invest in regulation inevitably will decline as market participants' confidence in the efficacy and integrity of regulation increases. This is because reputation and regulation, both of which serve the role of providing contracting parties with some reassurance that they won't be cheated or taken advantage of in the course of financial dealings, are substitutes for one another.

The theory of regulation and reputation has at least two empirical implications. First, as a general matter, to the extent that a particular industry, such as the financial services industry, is highly regulated, the individual firms in that industry will have fewer incentives to invest in reputational capital. Thus, we would expect, in general, firms in the financial services industry to have weaker reputations than firms in less regulated industries. Second, in a country like the United States, which has a vast and complete system of financial regulation and securities law as well as a highly vigorous enforcement regime for such laws, locally domiciled financial firms will be less willing to invest in developing their reputations.

To summarize the implications of the arguments made in this book, over the past 20 years or so, market participants have lost confidence both in the reputations of the various companies in the financial markets (accounting firms, credit rating agencies, investment banks, etc.), and in the regulatory regime that is supposed to protect investors from fraud and unscrupulous dealings by investment banks.

And now it seems that we are in quite a pickle, because if people do not feel that they can trust either the extant regulatory system or the companies in the financial services industry, then capital formation will become very difficult and expensive.

Of course, our current condition is by no means new. For long periods of history, various economies around the world lacked reputational intermediaries and managed to survive and even to grow. There are plenty of economies scattered around the Middle East and Africa that have never had functioning reputational intermediaries, though these economies are not thriving. But these past and present economies, as well as our own experience in the wake of the financial crisis of 2007–2008, provide important insights about what the U.S. financial markets will come to look like in the new, post-modern, post-reputation epoch. There are alternatives to financial markets based on a reputational model.

Max Weber and Statistical Discrimination

The economist Max Weber provides an excellent starting point for thinking about our post-reputation capital markets. In his classic work *The Protestant Ethic and the Spirit of Capitalism,* Weber articulated a theory for how markets could develop beyond the narrow confines of one's immediate family or clan (which Weber called one's sib). Weber identified the morality of puritanical Protestantism, especially Calvinism, with the success of entrepreneurship and capitalism. Weber's insight was that the Protestant religious admonition to treat all people—even strangers—in a morally acceptable way would dramatically expand the size and scope of markets. Religious ethic would expand the number of people with whom one could transact business by paving the way for cooperative economic activity to occur beyond one's immediate kinship group or clan.

In other words, if a particular group of people embracing a particular set of religious beliefs could be trusted to deal fairly with their counterparties, then such counterparties would find the people in that religious group to be an extremely attractive group of people with whom to do business. In this context, religious identity and affiliation would serve the same role as reputation, that is, as a mechanism for sending a credible signal of trustworthiness and integrity to potential clients and counterparties.

The use of general categories of groups (cultural, demographic, ethnic, religious, etc.) to determine trustworthiness might actually predate the use of reputation. In any event, discrimination for the purpose of determining reliability in trading, like the use of reputation, probably has been going on for as long as economic transactions have occurred. The use of general categories, also known as stereotypes, to sort out desirable from undesirable trading partners is called "statistical discrimination."[4] Statistical discrimination is the practice of hiring or sorting customers, suppliers, clients, or trading partners on the basis of statistical inferences about particular groups.

The economists' notion of statistical discrimination is that rational people might discriminate against a particular group even if they are not prejudiced against the particular group. Rather than discriminating on the basis of prejudice, people who engage in statistical discrimination discriminate because it is too difficult or expensive to obtain the information they need about people on an individualized basis. If, for example, a financial company is thinking about making a loan to, or engaging in a securities trade with, a particular individual and the financial company does not have complete or reliable information about that individual, they might find it profitable to make the decision about whether to engage in transactions with that person on the basis of stereotypes based on statistical inferences about the group rather than the individual.

If a bank or trading firm has a lot of information about one group, but lacks information about another group, the bank or trading firm might find it efficient to trade with the group about whom it has the most information. There are all sorts of examples of statistical discrimination. Employers often refuse to hire people with criminal records, even though not everybody with a criminal record will commit a crime in the future. Absent laws forbidding such discrimination, auto insurance companies will impose higher rates for teenage drivers, particularly for male teenage drivers, than for older drivers. Sometimes companies discriminate against married women or women who are pregnant or engaged to be married, on the grounds that they might not be sufficiently committed to the workforce. Such lack of commitment will lower the returns to an employer of hiring and training a new employee. The same sort of statistical discrimination might affect unmarried men.

Statistical discrimination is generally not effective in the realm of financial services. As the Madoff fiasco illustrated all too clearly, religious affiliation is a highly imperfect signal of trustworthiness. Religious affiliation is underinclusive, in the sense that many nonbelievers are trustworthy but left out of a trading circle based on religious affiliation. Also, centuries of experience demonstrate that religious affiliation also is unreliable because it is overinclusive as well as underinclusive. Many, many fraudsters demonstrate no reluctance whatsoever to cheat their own co-religionists or other members of their own race or culture.

Another failing of religious, ethnic, racial, or cultural affiliation is that it often (though not always) is very easy for fraudsters to fake these sorts of affiliations. In cases in which pretending to have actual membership in a particular religious, ethnic, racial, or cultural group is not possible, it still might be possible for unscrupulous financial professionals to dupe members of such groups into thinking that they have empathy or identity with the group. Perhaps the most significant modern problem with using religious, ethnic, cultural, or ethnic affiliation as a baseline for creating trading groups is that such practices are, as they should be, strictly illegal. Dealing only with members of particular, allegedly trustworthy groups necessarily requires excluding others. A host of federal and state laws—not to mention the U.S. Constitution itself—forbids discrimination on the basis of race, color, religion, sex, national origin, disability, genetic information, or age or on stereotypes or assumptions about the abilities, traits, or performance of individuals of a certain sex, race, age, religion, or ethnic group, or individuals with disabilities, or based on myths or assumptions about an individual.

To mention just one of many antidiscrimination rules, the Equal Credit Opportunity Act (ECOA) prohibits credit discrimination on the basis of race, color, religion, national origin, sex, marital status, age, or whether a person receives any form of public assistance. Creditors may not use this information in deciding whether to extend credit or when setting the terms of a loan or another type of credit. Counterparties in credit transactions are not even allowed to ask one's religion. Everyone who participates in the decision to grant credit or in setting the terms of that credit, including real estate brokers who arrange financing, must follow the provisions of the ECOA.[5] In light of the ineffectiveness of using ethnic or religious affiliations to create "zones of trust," these antidiscrimination rules make sense, as do the efforts of schools and governments to reduce the use of cultural, religious, and ethnic stereotypes.

A particular problem with using discrimination as a substitute for reputation in identifying trustworthy trading partners is that securities trading is inherently inclusive. Limited markets are inefficient markets. Similarly, even if it were morally permissible to engage in any sort of discrimination, which it is not, it is very costly—and in many contexts it is practically impossible—to engage in statistical discrimination in financial markets because one trades with institutions, not with individuals. Trading is generally anonymous in the sense that one places an order to trade with one's broker or directly over a market; the ultimate counterparty to the trade often is quite remote, because the counterparty deals with her own broker or with an anonymous trading facility and does not ever know the identity of the party with whom she is trading. The fact that the real buyers and sellers in securities transactions generally do not know each others' identities means that discrimination does not work very well in financial markets as a substitute for reputation.

Nevertheless, the sociologist Robert Putnam also has found evidence that supports the notion that people are more willing to trust others with whom they share common endogenous characteristics such as culture, religious affiliation, ethnicity, national identity, or creed. Putnam has found that as a community becomes more diverse, people tend to trust each other less.

Putnam's research is quite discouraging because it is inconsistent with the politically correct assumption that in social settings that are ethnically, religiously, and culturally diverse and tolerant, people slowly begin to interact with each other and will gradually learn to trust one another. Somewhat depressingly, Putnam finds instead that people do what he calls "hunkering down," which means that they simply come to decline to engage either with others of the same group or with members of different groups. This, in turn, leads to the demise of social networks and feelings of community.

Putnam's empirical findings are that as a society becomes more diverse, people begin to doubt the value of their own participation in civic affairs because they no longer believe that they have the ability to influence policy. For example, they don't vote or otherwise participate in government and they have lower rates of charitable giving and volunteer work. Diversity also is correlated with the loss of trust in government, politicians, and news organizations at the local level, and greater collective action problems, which manifest themselves in an unwillingness to cooperate voluntarily in efforts to clean up the environment or to conserve resources like energy or water.[6]

Social Capital

Over time the developed world has become both more secular and more ethnically diverse. It is not easy, or even possible, to lump people together by characteristics like religion, race, or ethnicity any more. Religion has come to play a smaller role in commercial life, particularly in the financial sector, where, despite their other problems, the large, dominant institutions are international and diverse. Within such firms, people often identify with their own institutions more than with any other group. For example, Goldman bankers and JP Morgan bankers might see their institutional affiliations as their most important affiliation. In other words, people might identify more closely with their firms than with other possible sources of identification, such as religion, ethnicity, or race. Alternatively, for many, national identification—for example, identification as U.S. citizens— is more important than historical or ethnic identification, although in many places such as post-War Germany, Japan, or Sweden it might not be possible to distinguish between people's national identity and their ethnic identity.

Increasingly, social scientists have focused on the concept of social capital and social networks as an alternative to reputation or ethnic identity as a mechanism for generating the trust necessary for economic transactions to exist. The basic idea is that trust can thrive and develop in social networks. Today we tend to think of social networks as websites like Facebook or applications like Twitter, in other words as dedicated websites or software applications that enable members, subscribers, or users to communicate with one another by sending messages or by posting comments, notices, or images that convey preferences, information, opinions, or data. More formalistically, social networks have been defined as "bounded systems" that allow people to create public or semipublic profiles within the systems. These profiles allow them to identify and contact others with whom they might share common views, traits, or interests, and to "view and traverse their list of connections and those made by others within the system."[7] Historically, however, the term *social network* was more broadly defined simply as a "network of social interactions and personal relationships."[8]

Here again the research of Robert Putnam is relevant. Putnam used social networks in an effort to explain long-standing, systemic differences in the economic and institutional performance in the high-performing north of Italy and in the low-performing south of the country.[9] Putnam's work is the source of the important idea that the existence of a variety of social organizations and (non-Internet-based) social networks is consistent with the development of trust, social norms, and networks. Unfortunately, it is not clear whether the causal chain starts with the existence of social organizations that lead to trust or whether the causal chain starts with the existence of trust, which then leads to the creation of social networks, or whether all of these things develop simultaneously. Putnam places great emphasis on "features of social life—networks, norms, and trust—that enable participants to act together more effectively to pursue shared objectives,"[10] as well as on the fact that successful social networks have great economic value because they "affect the productivity of individuals and groups."[11] Social networks generate norms of reciprocity and trustworthiness, and ultimately trust, all of which lead to the creation of "social capital" and, ultimately, to economic development and prosperity.

Like Putnam, the social philosopher Frances Fukuyama has also analyzed the relationship between various social networks and the concomitant development of trust. Consistent with the analysis in this book, Fukuyama's research indicates that societal trust in the United States, as well as in Japan and Germany, has been rapidly eroding in recent years. For Fukuyama, the information economy and other technological and scientific advances have led to the rise of individualism, the diminution of community, and a general decrease in the level of trust in society. Robert Putnam, working in a similar framework to Fukuyama, though focusing a bit more on "social networks" as the catalysts for trust, argued that such social networks were on the decline as people in places like the United States participated less in civic life.

In the famous book *Bowling Alone: The Collapse and Revival of American Community,* Putnam presented various forms of evidence that trust and social capital were on the decline. His primary measure of this decline was the decline of social organizations and networks like bowling leagues (hence the title of the book). Putnam pointed out, for example, that even though more and more people were bowling, fewer people were joining bowling leagues. Putnam found that levels of social engagement and participation in social networks (not including the Internet) were on the decline from historical levels.

Self-Help and New Institutions as Sources of Trust

Because there are significant gains to financial interaction, people in low-trust/low-reputation environments have strong incentives to develop technological substitutes that permit people to engage in financial transactions in an environment in which institutions like investment banks lack reputations for trustworthiness. Consistent with this hypothesis, some of the most important institutions in the field of finance can best be explained as mechanisms for facilitating transactions in low-trust environments.

Take, for example, the basic problems that significant investors have when they want to buy or sell large blocks of shares. The problems facing such investors are market impact and front-running. Market impact refers to the problem in which the buying or selling of large blocks of stock generally causes prices to move. If information leakage occurs and other market participants become aware that an institutional investor is about to place a large buy or sell order, prices rise or fall in advance of the order being completed. This, in turn, causes the price of the financial assets being bought or sold to rise or fall in value before the investor can execute the trade, thereby making the trade more expensive. This then not only lowers the returns directly associated with the trading, but also lowers the expected returns from engaging in research about the prices of financial assets. The problem of information leakage also raises the costs of engaging in financial transactions generally and raises the cost of capital by lowering people's incentives to invest in mutual funds, pension funds, and other institutions.

Front-running, a breach-of-trust problem discussed in a previous chapter, has the same effect as information leakage. In front-running, a customer is cheated when the investment banks or brokerages to whom a customer entrusts an order to buy or sell a financial instrument buys or sells for their own account before the customer's. Armed with the information content of the customer's order, an investment firm engaged in front-running can buy low before a customer's large buy order drives a security's price up, or sell high before a customer's large sell order drives a security's price down.

Large customers increasingly deal with their lack of trust about confidentiality of orders and front-running in various ways. For example, sophisticated investors with large orders frequently break up their trades into small blocks and place their buy or sell orders with several different brokers in an effort to mask the size of these orders. This strategy often is unsuccessful because information can be gleaned by the financial institutions executing trades not only on the basis of the size of an order, but also on the basis of the identity of the trader. When the company or individual placing even a small order is known to be a large block trader or is simply known to be a skilled, sophisticated, or gifted trader, then the company or individual subjects itself to leakage and front-running. And the risks of being cheated grow as the number of financial institutions with which one deals goes up.

So-called dark pools or black pools are trading platforms designed in large part to deal with information leakage and front-running. These have become increasingly prominent for large block traders.

Dark pools are simply forums on which financial institutions can trade away from stock exchanges and other venues that are open to the general public. Traders sometimes access dark pools directly, and they sometimes access them through crossing networks, or directly between market participants.

Dark pools are trading systems that do not publicly display orders in the way that exchanges do, but instead effectuate trades in other ways, such as by matching buyers and sellers at particular price points that are built into the institutional framework of the exchange. A common price point is the midpoint between the bid and the offered side. Alternatively, some dark pools execute orders only if a bid price is high enough to match the lowest offered price. Some analysts have estimated that as much as 15% of U.S. equity trading occurs on dark pools, with somewhat smaller percentages of trading in dark pools in European and Asian equities. Dark pools solve the trust problem described previously. Specifically, they serve the needs of traders who want to buy or sell large blocks of stock "without showing their hands to others." Dark pools avoid problems of information leakage and front-running "because neither the price nor the identity of the trading company is displayed."[12]

Electronic communications networks (ECNs) are another innovation designed to deal with the lack of trust that customers have in financial middlemen. ECNs deal with the lack of trust in broker-dealer firms the old-fashioned way: by eliminating them. ECNs, as the name implies, automatically match buy orders with sell orders when bid prices match offer prices. Traders who use ECNs, which include institutional investors and professional traders, trade directly with each other on an ECN.

Lack of trust might account for the decline of participation by individual investors and the rise of institutional investors in financial markets. Financial intermediaries routinely rip off even mid-size banks and sophisticated corporate treasury departments. Small, retail investors who are rational and who do not trust financial intermediaries to deal with them fairly will decline to participate in the marketplace unless they can find an intermediary like a mutual fund that does not have the capability to cheat them. One such option that many investors prefer is the index fund. An index fund is a mutual fund that is on autopilot: Managers do not actively manage them by trying to beat the market by picking stocks. Instead, mutual funds that are index funds are engineered to match the returns on a particular index, like the S&P 500 or one of many other market indexes representing a wide variety of asset classes.

Index funds are a good investment, particularly in comparison to the alternative, actively managed funds. Many research studies have found that mutual fund portfolios that hold index funds generally earn higher returns than those holding actively managed funds. One researcher found that "the evidence in favor of all index funds, all of the time, is irrefutable, overwhelming and important to all investors."[13]

Other strategies for surviving in the rather new low-trust financial environment in which we find ourselves include shunning low-trust securities like stocks in favor of high-trust securities like debt securities, which, unlike stock and other equity securities, give their owners the legal right to payment of specified amounts of principal and interest at contractually defined intervals. Debt securities with relatively short maturities will be particularly favored. Similarly, there will be fewer public companies. Private equity firms and hedge funds will own more of corporate America, because these big sophisticated investors, who generally own controlling blocks of shares and hold positions on the boards of directors of the companies they invest in, rely on their own resources and contacts, rather than on the resources of reputational intermediaries hired by others, to protect their investments.

In other words, a good strategy for navigating in a low-trust financial world is to remove oneself as far as possible from the necessity of relying on the advice of our ethically challenged panoply of financial intermediaries. Nobody is forced to pay attention to credit rating agencies, even if issuers are required to hire them. Likewise, investors are not required to rely on audited financial statements or fairness opinions from investment bankers or true sale opinions from law firms or any of the other panoply of reputation-based services provided by the reputational intermediaries discussed in this book. At this point, now that the emperors of the financial world have been revealed to have no clothes, we can only fault ourselves for persisting in relying on their advice.

Regulation: The New Secular Religion

Much of this book is taken up with explaining the corrosive effects of regulation on reputation. In a world in which the economic theory of reputation worked perfectly, there would be no need for regulation because unregulated nongovernmental reputational intermediaries such as accounting firms, credit rating agencies, law firms, and investment banks would protect unsophisticated investors. Similarly, in a world in which the taxpayer-funded regulations designed to protect investors worked perfectly, there would be no need to pay for reputational intermediaries. The relationship between regulation and reputation becomes particularly telling when one considers that whenever a particular subset of reputational intermediaries suffers a blow to its reputation or there is a major financial scandal, the response is always the same: more regulation. The failure of the corporate governance systems, particularly the breakdown of the reputational audit function traditionally supplied by the accounting firms, was the immediate catalyst for Sarbanes-Oxley, which imposed a phalanx of new regulations on accounting firms. The collapse of the credit rating agencies and the greed and recklessness of the nation's banks led to the financial crisis of 2007–2008 and sparked Dodd-Frank, which tried to deal with the dangers of reckless risk-taking financial institutions and the collapse of the credit rating function.

The collapse in the traditional reputational model preceded these draconian regulatory initiatives. But these new regulations do not appear to have improved the health of our capital markets. Consistent with the analysis here, studies about the lack of competitiveness of U.S. capital markets abounded well before the 2007–2008 financial crisis. In November 2006, a market-oriented blue-ribbon Committee on Capital Regulation led by R. Glenn Hubbard and John Thornton observed that America was losing its dominance of world securities markets and urged modest deregulation. Then, in early 2007, a study commissioned by New York Senator Charles Schumer (no friend of regulation) and New York City Mayor Michael Bloomberg surprisingly urged deregulation as well. And in March 2007, a panel commissioned by the U.S. Chamber of Commerce was the focus of a conference led by then Secretary of the Treasury Henry Paulson. The

Securities and Exchange Commission, the body that oversees and enforces these regulations, is now a vocal part of the problem, hunting for headlines as it pursues high-profile cases against U.S. firms, thereby muddying any reputational signal associated with the lawsuits brought by the SEC. The SEC is failing in its mission to protect capital markets, but succeeding in its mission of imposing a heavy regulatory burden on those companies whose misfortune it is to be publicly listed on a U.S. trading venue.

The SEC, as currently constituted, suffers from three serious maladies. Malady number one is that the metrics of success used to evaluate the SEC create very perverse incentives. This causes the SEC to fail, even when it thinks that it is succeeding. Malady number two is that the SEC has no clearly defined clientele. In other words, the SEC has no idea whom it should help. Malady number three stems from the fact that the SEC is run entirely by lawyers. The few economists there are marginalized. As a result, the SEC does not understand the economics or financial implications of the regulations it generates by the boxcar.

Turning to malady number one, the SEC's most perverse incentive is its incentive to promote the appearance that the capital markets are in crisis and to discourage (or prohibit) the development of market mechanisms that might fix the very problems that the SEC is tasked with solving.

As long as it generally is viewed that the SEC is needed in times of crisis, and that there are no superior substitutes for the particular sort of crisis intervention done by the SEC, then there will be a felt need for the Commission. Ironically, the more financial crises there are, the more the SEC can claim that it needs greater resources to manage such crises.

The SEC is largely evaluated on the basis of how well its Division of Enforcement performs. In the words of the SEC's own website, "first and foremost, the SEC is a law enforcement agency." As the economic sociologist William Bealing has observed, the activities of the Enforcement Division of the SEC are what "legitimize the Commission's existence and its federal budget allocation to Congress." Political scientists have observed that the SEC's enforcement agenda is designed to meet the interests of the relevant congressional leaders responsible for the SEC's funding.

The SEC satisfies its monitors in Congress, in academia, and in the press by focusing on factors that can be measured. In particular, the SEC focuses on two factors: (1) the raw number of cases that it brings and (2) the sheer size of the fines that it collects. The more cases that are brought and the greater the amount of fines collected during a particular time frame, the better the enforcement staff at the SEC is thought to perform. This has long been the case, but the problem worsened as a result of the political challenge that the SEC has faced from politically opportunistic state attorneys general, particularly Eliot Spitzer.

For example, when criticized for failing to respond to numerous tips from whistle-blowers and red flags in the case of Bernard Madoff's massive Ponzi scheme, the SEC noted in Congressional testimony that "comparing the period from late January to the present to the same period in 2008, Enforcement has: opened more investigations (1377 compared to 1290); issued more than twice as many formal orders of investigation (335 compared to 143); filed more than twice as many emergency temporary restraining orders (57 compared to 25); and filed more actions overall (458 compared to 359)." The SEC's 2008 Annual Report is similarly clear in its emphasis on such easily measurable criteria: "During 2008, the SEC completed the highest number of enforcement investigations ever, brought the highest number of insider trading cases in the agency's history, and brought a record number of enforcement actions against market manipulation...." The report also noted, "The SEC in 2008 also initiated the second-highest number of enforcement actions in Commission history."

During each of the past two years, the SEC set the record for the highest number of corporate penalty cases in agency history. For the second year in a row, the Commission returned more than $1 billion to harmed investors using our Fair Funds authority under the Sarbanes-Oxley Act. To support this record level of law-enforcement activity, more than one-third of the SEC staff now serves in the enforcement program, a higher percentage of the SEC's total resources than at any time in the past 20 years.

The SEC devoted more funds to enforcement in 2008 than at any time in agency history. In 2008, the number of enforcement personnel grew by 4%. The perverse incentives facing the SEC explain what *The New York Times* has described as the "long-standing criticism that the S.E.C. has largely failed to prosecute cases against corporate executives, opting for quick settlements in which companies themselves are penalized instead of their leaders." The SEC rationally has pursued a policy of opting for quick settlements because it is largely judged on the basis of the number of cases it wins. (The SEC needs fewer resources to sue companies than individuals because companies don't defend themselves as vigorously as individuals do.) Hence, the SEC's penchant for suing and settling with entire industry groups, such as mutual funds, begins to make sense when one understands the SEC's desire to register large numbers of cases brought and fines collected.

Likewise, the SEC in recent years has pursued policies of attempting to expand the contours of the law (which makes it easier for them to bring cases) and of keeping the law vague (i.e., refusing to define insider trading).

Finally, and most important, the SEC has pursued a policy that is consistent with its rational self-interest but clearly suboptimal from a societal perspective: Namely, it scrimps on doing investigations because thorough investigations are costly and time-consuming. The SEC gets better mileage by suing and settling without much, if any, investigating. It's no wonder that the SEC goes after high-profile industry players like Goldman Sachs, which are more willing to settle, rather than low-profile crooks like Madoff.

The number of enforcement actions and the size of the fines are not the best criteria by which to evaluate the conduct of the SEC, but they are data that are "available," in the social psychology and behavioral finance sense of the word. Something is "available" in this context when it can be easily recalled from memory or readily available sources. The availability heuristic is one of the most widely shared assumptions in decision making as well as in social judgment research. The focus by the SEC (and Congress and the public) on how many cases the SEC brings and on the size of the fines collected appears to represent the availability heuristic in action. And, as in other contexts, this reliance on availability leads to predictable biases.

Thus, the SEC's apparently odd behavior in recent years is not due solely or even primarily to corruption or incompetence. Rather, the SEC simply has been responding, more or less rationally, to the rather odd set of incentives that it faces from its overseers in Congress and from other important constituents.

To that effect, the SEC has strong incentives to promote the appearance that the capital markets are in crisis and to eschew the development of reputational competition that might solve the very problems that the SEC is tasked with solving.

Over the past decade, starting with the collapse of Enron in 2001, there have been unprecedented budget increases for the SEC staff. In 2003 and 2004, the SEC was the only federal agency to receive substantial budget increases. And notwithstanding the fact that the SEC's budget nearly tripled between 2000 and 2010, the Commission's current chair and senior staff have argued that its recent failures can be addressed by increasing the agency's funding.

The historical strength of U.S. capital markets and the massive financial infrastructure of the world's top accounting firms, investment banks, commercial banks, and law firms long were a testament to the power of corporate and institutional reputation to generate the trust necessary to create vibrant markets. As of this writing, the historical reputational model has been replaced with a highly inefficient, poorly incentivized, costly government-funded regulatory model. This switch has weakened and shriveled U.S. capital markets and reduced their competitiveness in the global economy.

A particularly powerful way to repair a firm's reputation is to change the way that employees are compensated. Economists say that people respond to incentives. Whatever the validity of this assertion might be for particular individuals, it seems particularly powerful when applied to the people who work on Wall Street.

In a sharp break with modern Wall Street practice, in January 2013, the investment bank Morgan Stanley halted the policy of paying immediate cash bonuses to highly paid employees. Early each year,

Wall Street firms like Morgan Stanley and Goldman Sachs for years paid out massive bonuses to traders, top salesman, and other employees at the top of the pay scale in amounts that reflected the banks' estimates of the value of the services provided in the previous year.

The problem with this compensation strategy was that it promoted short-term trading perspectives and excessive risk-taking. If a trade placed in November looked good in January, a trader could get a huge bonus in January even if the trade had fallen apart completely by April. Also, bonuses got to be so huge that traders, who often were millionaires many times over, had incentives to make very risky trades all year. If the trades turned out badly, the traders were still millionaires, but in the off-chance that the trades produced big returns, the traders would make tens and sometimes hundreds of millions of dollars.

From a reputational perspective, what was needed was some way to align the interests of traders and other highly paid employees with the interests of the firms in which they worked, as well as a compensation system that would be highly undesirable to those in the firm with short-term perspectives but highly desirable for employees with longer-term perspectives. In other words, the ideal compensation scheme is one that helps to nurture the reputation of the investment bank over the long term by incentivizing desirable employees to stay with the firm and incentivizing those with short-term perspectives to look elsewhere.

In January 2013, Morgan Stanley stopped paying all-cash bonuses to its highest-paid employees, that is, those who make more than $350,000. Instead of cash on the barrel in May, bonuses will be paid to Morgan Stanley employees in a combination of one-half cash and one-half Morgan Stanley stock in four installments over the long period between May 2013 and the end of 2015. A *Wall Street Journal* story about this new policy said that the policy "would hit the securities company's highest-paid traders and investment bankers in the wallet."[14]

A particularly good thing about Morgan Stanley's compensation arrangement is that it rewards those employees who can replicate their short-term performance over a longer period of time, thereby reducing excessive risk-taking. I think this will help the reputation of the firm. As I told *The Wall Street Journal* reporters who were covering Morgan Stanley's new compensation strategy, "This is huge. It's going to help Morgan Stanley's reputation. If I were a counterparty, I'd rather do business with them because of it. I can't believe it's taken so long."[15]

Rebuilding reputations is a lengthy and difficult process, but it must be done. The fact that there are some early signs of change at a major investment bank is a positive sign. The next step is for bureaucrats to begin to focus more on ways that their regulations can help or hinder the efforts that private companies make to improve their reputations. U.S. capital markets cannot withstand continued deterioration and neglect of the reputations of the firms that make up the markets. Regulation does not serve as a substitute for reputation in U.S. markets because of the ineffectiveness of the SEC. Yet the regulatory system is effective in diminishing the incentive to invest in reputation. As such, the first, giant step on the road to rebuilding the lost reputational capital in the financial world necessarily will be deregulation. Although deregulation will not single-handedly solve the problem of the decline of reputation, it will help to reestablish incentives for firms to invest in reputation. Without a renewed focus on reputation, the United States risks the loss of the vitality of its financial markets in a world already defined by increasing international competition. An increased investment is essential to help to stop this decline.

Endnotes

1. The Reputation Institute, 2009 Global Reputation Pulse: "The World's Most Reputable Companies," *Global Section* 2 (2009), 10.

2. Ibid.

3. Riva Atlas, "Spitzer Vows Legal Action Against Head of Fund Family," *New York Times,* October 30, 2003, www.nytimes.com/2003/10/30/business/spitzer-vows-legal-action-against-head-of-fund-family.html.

4. Kenneth Arrow, "The Theory of Discrimination," in *Discrimination in Labor Markets,* eds. O. Ashenfelter and A. Rees (Princeton, NJ: Princeton University Press, 1973); Edmund Phelps, "The Statistical

Theory of Racism and Sexism," *American Economic Review* 62 (1972): 659-661.

5. Federal Trade Commission, Facts for Consumers, http://www.ftc. gov/bcp/edu/pubs/consumer/credit/cre15.shtm, accessed January 12, 2013.

6. Robert Putnam, *"E Pluribus Unum:* Diversity and Community in the Twenty-first Century—The 2006 Johan Skytte Prize Lecture," *Scandinavian Political Studies* 30, no. 2 (2007): 137-174; Robert Putnam, "Social Capital Community Benchmark Survey, 2000," Roper Center for Public Opinion Research, 2007, www.ropercenter. uconn.edu/data_access/data/datasets/social_capital_community_ survey.html#.UDTTcnCUpME, accessed December 10, 2012.

7. danah boyd and Nicole Ellison, "Social Network Sites: Definition, History, and Scholarship," *Journal of Computer-Mediated Communication* 13 (2008): 210-230.

8. http://oxforddictionaries.com/definition/english/social%2Bnetwork.

9. Robert Putnam, *Making Democracy Work: Civic Traditions in Modern Italy* (Princeton: Princeton University Press, 1993).

10. Robert Putnam, "Tuning In, Tuning Out: The Strange Disappearance Of Social Capital in America," *Political Science and Politics* 28, no. 4 (1995): 664-683.

11. Robert Putnam, *Bowling Alone: the Collapse and Revival of American Community* (New York: Simon and Schuster, 2000), 18-19.

12. Reuters Financial Glossary, Dark Pools, http://glossary.reuters.com/ index.php?title=Dark_Pools&diff=9293&oldid=9292, accessed December 10, 2012.

13. Rick Ferri, "Index Fund Portfolios Reign Superior," *Forbes,* August 20, 2012, www.forbes.com/sites/rickferri/2012/08/20/index-fund-portfolios-reign-superior/.

14. Aaron Luchetti, "Bankers Get IOUs Instead of Bonus Cash," *The Wall Street Journal,* January16, 2013, http://professional.wsj.com/ article/BT-CO-20130115-708719.html?mg=reno64-wsj.

15. Ibid.

Index

Procter & Gamble v. Bankers Trust
case study, 74-80
*Bankers Trust Company's
obligations under the swap,
75-80*
*Procter & Gamble's obligations
under the swap, 75*
total return swaps, 65-66

T

TANs (tax anticipation notes), 67
tax anticipation notes (TANs), 67
Tele-Communications, Inc., 107
Thornton, John, 269
Time Warner, 107
Title Guarantee & Trust Company, 58
total return swaps, 65-66
Tourre, Fabrice, 47, 98
traditional theory of reputation, 7-9
alternatives to reputation
explained, 254-259
regulation, 269-275
*self-help and new institutions,
265-268*
social capital, 263-265
*statistical discrimination,
259-263*
failure of, 253-259. *See also* case
studies
financial industry, 14-17
flawed assumptions
cheaters never prosper, 89-90
*corporate and individual
reputations are joined, 83-89,
96-100*
*employees go down with the
ship, 90-96*
government regulation and, 9-14
reputation as an investment, 11
reputational industries, 124-125
warranties, 17-20

Trepp, Warren, 110
true sale opinions, 155-156
Turner Broadcasting, 107

U-V

underwriting, 16
U.S. Securities and Exchange
Commission (SEC). *See* SEC
(U.S. Securities and Exchange
Commission)
Vinson & Elkins, 156-158
Virchow Krause, 139

W-X-Y-Z

warranties, 17-20
Weber, Max, 259-263
Westchester County Trust
Company, 58
White, Larry, 173
Whitehead, John, 117
Wikipedia, 25
Winner's Curse, 23
Winnick, Gary, 110
zones of trust, 262

FINANCIAL TIMES

In an increasingly competitive world, it is quality
of thinking that gives an edge—an idea that opens new
doors, a technique that solves a problem, or an insight
that simply helps make sense of it all.

We work with leading authors in the various arenas
of business and finance to bring cutting-edge thinking
and best-learning practices to a global market.

It is our goal to create world-class print publications
and electronic products that give readers
knowledge and understanding that can then be
applied, whether studying or at work.

To find out more about our business
products, you can visit us at www.ftpress.com.